5/14/03

Dear Carol,

You're not my favorite because you throw moderately successful autograph parties for me. You're my favorite because you're an "up" bookstore manager. [See ENTHUSIASM.]

I also strongly suspect that I would like you a lot, even without your Waldenbooks apron on. Thanks for making this book feel at home in your store. I know you'll make it feel at home in your home.

One of the fringe benefits of writing this book was getting to meet you.

Love,

Rich

The DEVIL'S *New* DICTIONARY

compiled by
RICHARD IANNELLI

CITADEL PRESS   *Secaucus, N.J.*

To Ambrose Bierce

First Edition

Copyright © 1983 by Richard Iannelli

Published by Citadel Press
A division of Lyle Stuart Inc.
120 Enterprise Avenue, Secaucus, N.J. 07094
In Canada: Musson Book Company
A division of General Publishing Co. Limited
Don Mills, Ontario

Queries regarding rights and permissions should be
addressed to: Lyle Stuart Inc., 120 Enterprise Avenue,
Secaucus, N.J. 07094

Manufactured in the United States of America

Library of Congress Cataloging in Publication Data
Iannelli, Richard.
  The Devil's new dictionary.
  1. American wit and humor. I. Title.
PN6162.I26 1983 818'.5402 82-22059
ISBN 0-8065-0791-8

Preface

The thing I remember most about school is that English class was boring. Just once I would have loved to see an English teacher burst into the classroom, barely able to contain his excitement, and exclaim, "I've just heard the most wonderful metaphor!" Perhaps we all would have thought he was crazy, but then perhaps one crazy English teacher would have done the trick.

Unfortunately, nothing remotely resembling this occurred during my academic experience. Like the vast majority of my fellow schoolmates, I maintained the attitude that, since English class was dull, so too must the language be. It wasn't until I had left school and travelled around the country that I began to develop a fascination with the wonder of words. I came to realize that the only thing dull about the English language is the way most people teach it.

My interest first manifested itself to a noticeable degree while I was on tour as a singer/songwriter in the early 70's. I became enchanted with unusual figures of speech, especially those peculiar to a given locale. I began to wonder about the origins of some of them. For instance, what could possibly be the source of the expression "in a pig's eye"? And what is it supposed to mean? And why do we say that something is "bigger than a breadbox," as opposed to anything else?

This curiosity of mine extended also into the area of different words that are used in different places for the same thing. An example is the word "faucet" which is known as a "tap" in certain areas. I've also heard it called a "spigot." In Philadelphia, our "hero" sandwiches bear the name "hoagie." Elsewhere, they are labeled "submarines."

I was too busy writing and performing songs at the time to explore these avenues of interest in depth. For years, they served as nothing more—or less—than my hobby, although I did keep a notebook of curious words and expressions. Then one fateful day, I happened to be flipping through a Norton Anthology and chanced upon an excerpt from a book which I had not encountered in my travels (and certainly not in my schools).

The book was *The Devil's Dictionary* by Ambrose Bierce. Only twelve entries from it comprised the excerpt before me, but they were more than enough to whet my appetite. How could I have remained ignorant of this classic book's existence for 25 years? And why did only two bookstores in Philadelphia carry it? These questions have no adequate answers. They are two of the great mysteries of my early life.

When at last I had procured a copy of *The Devil's Dictionary,* I devoured it at one sitting. For a short time thereafter, I felt cerebrally sated. It was as though I had been set free in a verbal bakery shop, where I could stuff myself with as many goodies as my sweet tooth desired. The analogy, however, soon proved to be a disconcerting one. There was a catch. Once I left the shop, I could not go elsewhere when I became hungry again.

That no one had written a satirical dictionary of the English language in eighty years (at least not one that is still in print) came as a shock to me. Surely, others had read Bierce's masterpiece and been as captivated and inspired as I. Why had none of them embarked on a similar project? This was another great mystery of my early life. Under the circumstances, I was left with no other choice. If I wanted to read a modern satirical dictionary, I would have to write it myself.

At the outset of the work, I was still too much in awe of Ambrose Bierce to presume that anything I might produce would be worthy of standing alongside *The Devil's Dictionary.* I wrote initially, therefore, purely for my own amusement. However, as the composition progressed, I began to think of Bierce less as a literary hero and more as a colleague. The merits of our respective lexicons notwithstanding, we were, after all, in the same line of work.

I was as careful as possible to avoid what I perceived to be the major pitfall of my undertaking, which was to define a word employing an idea that was essentially the same as Bierce's. In this regard, I made a list of all the words defined in *The Devil's Dictionary.* Then I wrote my own definitions for these words and compared them with those of Bierce, eliminating the ones which derived from similar or identical notions. Naturally, I accept responsibility for a certain degree of unconscious influence. Some of the definitions in this book, despite my scrutiny, smack of Bierce. For these, I ask the reader's kind indulgence.

My prime objective (to borrow a sci-fi term) in creating the present text is simply to provide the reader with another way of looking at words. Since they are the principal means by which we communicate as a species, it behooves us to explore their meanings from as many perspectives as possible. There is a strong case to be made for the stance that many of our most fundamental problems stem from our inability to communicate with one another. The more we consider the words we use, the better we will be able to make use of them.

I also share with many others the concern for the future of the art of conversation. If music can be said to be the universal language, then I think it can also be said that language is the universal music. There is nothing more lyrical than a beautifully turned phrase. Consider Dylan Thomas reciting one of his poems. Is he not, in fact, singing?

I join in the effort to preseve the music of language. I applaud the movement to preserve conversation as an art form. If this book can aid, however nominally, in that preservation, if it can spur even one person's interest in the beauty and power of words, I will be satisfied.

Yet we stand on the verge of a new era. Already, computer games are learning to talk. Television screens are getting bigger. Cable stations are providing us with more choices of programming than most of us are prepared to make. I see nothing wrong with these technological changes, provided we do not lose sight of the basics, provided we do not, in our rush to become a part of the new communication boom, fail to retain our ability to communicate as individuals.

On a less profound but no less significant level, I also intend this book to be fun. I have endeavored to refrain from esoteric references that require of the reader a certain cultural or educational background in order to appreciate the humor. There is something here for everyone, since this is a book about our language, and our language is in the public domain.

Although I have directed *The Devil's Other Dictionary* to readers of all ages and all occupations, my fondest hope is that someday somewhere an English teacher will read this book and just one of the entries herein will excite him enough to go bursting into his classroom and say, "I've just read the most wonderful definition!"

Then I will be one happy writer.

Acknowledgments

I would like to express my gratitude, first and foremost, to my mother for managing to restrain herself from coming over here and cleaning the house while I worked on this book. I would also like to thank the following people who read portions of the manuscript in progress, offered criticism, and (most importantly) laughed in the right places: Brian Gallagher, Jonette Keefer, Howard Kairys and Susan Dressler. Liz Lewis bought me some food at a time when I had spent my last two bucks on a typewriter ribbon and Alice Dugas prepared me a home-cooked meal when I was subsisting mainly on scrapple and (overly) scrambled eggs. Special appreciation belongs to Mrs. Lucy Romano, librarian at the Whitman branch of the Philadelphia Public Library, for her patient and thorough assistance in my research work. Also, I would be remiss if I did not acknowledge Peter Tchaikovsky, Serge Prokofiev and Walter Piston, whose music accompanied the typing of this manuscript. It not only made the job more aesthetically pleasing, but it also served the practical function of blocking out the dogs barking in the alley.

Finally, I'd like to thank Allan J. Wilson, for his precise editing and astute observations. This is a much better book than it would have been without his input. I can't prove that, but you'll have to take my words for it.

RICHARD IANNELLI

The Devil's New Dictionary

ABACUS An ancient calculator so technologically inferior to its modern counterpart that it does not even require a battery.

ABBEY A place of religious seclusion where a life of constant prayer is rewarded by freedom from soap operas, supermarkets and parking meters.

ABDOMEN That part of the body responsible for converting processed food into processed tissue.

ABILITY Desire's partner in accomplishment.

A-BOMB An explosive mechanism designed to promote cultural cohesiveness by demonstrating that a flattened Japanese city is no different from a flattened city anywhere else.

ABOMINABLE Regarding a person who is so utterly loathsome and detestable that people just can't seem to get enough of him, as is evidenced by the growing number and increasing popularity of books about Adolf Hitler.

ABSENCE That which makes the heart grow fonder, usually of someone else. 2. The end result of an effective excuse.

ABSTAINER A person who denies himself one of life's pleasures and then proceeds to make everyone around him miserable by being pious about it.

ABSTRUSE Difficult to understand yet quite clear, in the sense that it is clearly difficult to understand; as, this definition is abstruse.

ABSURDITY Anything that makes sense to one's adversaries.

ABUSE To force the children to visit relatives.

ACCENT That which causes other people to talk funny.

ACCIDENT A collision between two vehicles which is caused by the other driver.

ACCOMPLICE Anybody whose boss is a crook.

ACCREDITED Officially endorsed by an official authority, which has been authorized by a certified sanctioning body, which has been sanctioned by an acknowledged validating board, with the complete and unremitting approval of God.

ACOLYTE An altar boy, whose acquaintance with the inner workings of religious ceremonies provides him with the benefit of a broader base for future disbelief.

ACQUAINTANCE Anyone whom seeing is not more important than your favorite television show.

ACROBAT A circus performer who catapults to the top of his profession, using a seesaw. 2. A circus performer who stands at the bottom of a pyramid and shoulders his responsibilities.

ACROPHOBIA Morbid fear resulting from the ancient superstition that falling to the ground from a great height brings bad luck.

ACTOR Someone whose job frequently alternates between memorizing lines at the theater and standing in lines at the unemployment office.

ACUPUNCTURE A medical practice, employing needles, which offers relief from pain but no backing out. Once the patient agrees to the treatment, he's stuck with it.

ADAGE A saying that has gained popularity by long use, such as "You can lead a horse to water, but you'd have a hell of a time getting him to do the dishes."

ADAM The first man, but by no means the last, to be driven from Paradise for listening to his wife.

ADDICT One who condemns himself without a fair trial and then proceeds to pay his own executioner for the poison with which he carries out the sentence.

ADDICTION The agony of perpetually dying without the comfort of being dead.

ADDITIVE An artificial ingredient that is added to a food or drink to give it a natural color and flavor, thus having an appealing effect upon the user's sight and taste, while thoroughly disregarding the user's digestive system, where the ingredient promptly returns to its purest state of artificiality, thus having an unappealing effect upon the user's vital internal organs.

ADDRESS The place where one receives one's bills. 2. The place where one receives one's trash mail. 3. The place where one receives one's damaged packages. 4. The place where one receives one's personal letters, along with more bills, more trash mail and more damaged packages.

ADJECTIVE A word, such as preposterous, used to describe a noun, such as definition; as, the adjective in this preposterous definition is preposterous.

ADJUSTED In harmony with one's own attitudes and opinions.

ADMINISTRATION The collective group of people in government who help to insure that each president, in his turn, is unpopular and ineffective.

ADMIRAL A high ranking naval officer who is either a fast runner, known as a fleet admiral, or someone who prefers to stand at the end of a line, known as a rear admiral.

ADMIRE To set the stage for future disillusionment.

ADO The response of a Southern bride and groom as they take their wedding vows.

ADOLESCENCE The period of life that begins with your believing that your parents know everything and ends with your believing that they know nothing.

ADONIS A beautiful youth who was loved by Aphrodite, but not, according to legend, for his mind.

ADULT Someone who has finally run out of other people to blame for mistakes and personal misfortunes, and assumes the responsibility for them. 2. A person who honors commitments already made before accepting new ones.

ADVENTURE   Walking alone down any city street after midnight.

ADVERSITY   A condition of affliction, which some people accept willingly because they say it builds their characters, while other people object to it, preferring to leave their characters exactly the way they are, unafflicted.

ADVERTISING   The business of giving the public the business.

ADVISE   To counsel someone and recommend a course of action, keeping in mind that you will probably not receive any credit if things go right and most likely to be blamed if things go wrong.

AEON   An indefinitely long period of time, such as that spent waiting for a bus.

AFFAIR   That which is occurring when Mr. and Mrs. John Smith check into a motel without baggage. 2. An undercover meeting under a cover.

AFFECTATION   A self-mockery in the form of dress, speech or behavior.

AFFECTED   Pretending to be what one is not, and to the extent that one succeeds in fooling another, it is to that extent that one succeeds in being a fool.

AFFLUENCE   An abundance of everything for the present, except the common sense to conserve for the future.

AFOUL   In collision, especially with a chicken or a duck.

AFRAID   Having reason to believe that the police have not pulled up in front of your house to change a tire.

AFTERMATH   The subject or subjects following arithmetic.

AGE   Merely the number of years that a person has been alive, and the least useful criterion for determining anything about that person's character.

AGENT   Someone who can appreciate the value of true talent, or at least 10 percent of the value of true talent. 2. A little bald guy who sits behind a big desk, smokes a cigar, and tells you that you need a gimmick.

AGGRAVATION A contagious disease which takes the form of any thing or any situation that gets on a person's nerves, causing the person to become aggravated. The peculiar quality of the disease is such that the aggravated person feels induced to aggravate one or more other people, usually a subordinate at work, a spouse or a child, thus spreading the disease. The aggravated subordinate, spouse or child feels similarly induced, and so on.

AGNOSTIC One who professes the profound doctrine that the unknowable cannot be known. 2. One who takes a firm position of indifference regarding the existence of God; a theological bystander.

AGORAPHOBIA The morbid fear of being in the midst of open spaces, which is an affliction that has been prevented from reaching epidemic proportions by the dedicated efforts of city planners and land developers, who make certain that public exposure to open spaces is kept well below dangerous levels.

AGREED Settled by common consent, or by one person who controls common consent.

AGRICULTURE The art of paying for expensive farming machinery.

AH An exclamation expressing pain or joy or, in the case of a masochist, both.

AIDA The title of Verdi's opera, which is the stirring drama of two young lovers who sacrifice everything, including food and air, so that they can settle down and raise a family in a crypt.

AIDE-DE-CAMP Someone who helps Boy Scouts pitch their tents.

AIMLESS Quite inept at sports such as archery, skeet shooting, etc.

AIN'T Contraction of are not, am not and is not, which is said by people that don't talk English good.

AIR   The invisible mixture of gases surrounding the earth, which is used to transport pollutants into the lungs. In some parts of the planet, it is used strictly for breathing.

AIRLINE   An air transportation company which, for no extra charge, will transport your luggage to a city three hundred miles away from your destination.

AIRPLANE   A craft which travels through the air at astounding heights and amazing speeds, offering its passengers not only faster trips but also a sparkling opportunity to reduce an incredible experience to the commonplace.

AIR POCKET   The pocket of someone who is completely broke.

AIRPORT   A place where the jet set mixes with the plane folk.

AISLE   An open passageway in a theater in which the audience rolls during the funniest parts of a comedy.

ALARMIST   A news anchorperson.

ALCHEMY   The medieval chemical science practiced by alchemists, who were dedicated to curing diseases, indefinitely prolonging life, and making big puffs of smoke appear wherever they pointed their fingers.

ALCOHOL   The active ingredient, not only in fermented and distilled liquors, but also in many social functions. 2. Liquid liver liquidation.

ALCOHOLIC   A person with the serious disease of alcoholism, or someone trying desperately to catch the disease.

ALGOPHOBIA   Morbid fear of pain, which can become so extreme that the person afflicted with this fear will refuse to be punched or kicked, even by members of his own family.

ALIBI   Any place where you were when the thing which you couldn't have done because you were elsewhere occurred. The most commonly used alibis are: working late at the office, by husbands; and reading alone at home, by murder suspects.

ALIEN   A creature from another planet or a person from another country, neither of whom is allowed to run for president.

ALIMONY   Money paid after a divorce from one party, usually the husband, to the other party, usually the wife, so that both of them will be able to maintain the life style which contributed to their divorce in the first place.

ALIVE   Having a sense of self-awareness and self-worth, things to do, people and animals to love, and goals to achieve. 2. Content to eat, sleep, breathe, make money and look after one's own interests; not dead yet.

ALLEGATION   A way of saying that a person is guilty until proven innocent.

ALLEGIANCE   Remaining loyal to one's country and following its laws, no matter how many of them are broken by the leaders of the government.

ALLIGATOR   An endangered species of handbag.

ALLITERATION   A series of similar sounding syllables situated sequentially in a sentence or stanza.

ALLOWANCE   A sum of money given by a parent to a child for performing household chores, for doing well in school, or for being.

ALLY   To join by an alliance, which is an agreement signed by two or more countries to declare formally their mutual hatred for two or more other countries.

ALPHABET   The letters which make up a language and which are used in words, soup, and baby blocks.

ALRIGHT   A popular form of all right, which is not as proper as the proper form of all right (all right) but which is nonetheless alright.

ALTRUIST   A person who is not afraid of ingratitude. 2. A person who feels best after making someone else feel better.

ALUMINUM   A light, malleable metal, pronounced "alunimum" by people who cannot say "aluminum."

AMBASSADOR   A presidential appointee, who is sent to a friendly country to attend parties, to a neutral country to enjoy a prolonged vacation, or to a hostile country to spy.

AMBITIOUS Possessing a keen appetite, as do all participants in rat races.

AMBROSIA The sole food of the gods.

AMBULANCE A vehicle with backward letters painted on it.

AMERICAN A person who enjoys the excesses of capitalism, including excessive pressure and excessive anxiety.

AMMUNITION Anything that one human body directs at another human body for the purpose of puncturing it, maiming it, or blowing it to smithereens. Under such circumstances, it is clear that the human mind does not come into play. 2. Words of attack or defense which, since there is an unlimited supply, tend to lose their effectiveness when used too often and in too large a quantity.

AMNESIA An affliction, usually caused by a deep shock, trauma or a bump on the head, which renders a person unable to remember who he is. Most people don't know who they are in the first place, and are therefore immune.

AMNESTY A general pardon, most commonly occurring after a war, by which a government sees fit to forgive a citizen who is guilty of having a conscience.

AMOEBA A tiny mass of protoplasm, so small that ten million of them could fit on a rug.

AMOROUS Inclined to be unsatisfied with a goodnight kiss.

AMPHION A son of Zeus, who built the great wall around the city of Thebes but forgot to leave a way to get in and out. He was not one of the brighter sons of Zeus.

AMULET A good luck charm which guards its wearer against evils, such as the evil of con artists selling good luck charms.

AMUSED Pleasingly diverted, while also often gathering fuel with which to ridicule the amuser at a later time.

ANALYST A shrink, so named because of what he does to the bankrolls of his patients.

ANARCHISM The theory that all government is evil and should be abolished, in favor of a society in which the people are so happy not to have to pay taxes that they gladly volunteer to patrol the streets at night preventing crime, to take turns collecting their neighbors' trash every week, and to spend Saturday morning filling in potholes and Sundays replacing broken streetlamps.

ANARCHIST One who advocates a society in which there are no laws and no supreme political power, or, in other words, a society which is run by trade unions and organized crime.

ANATOMY The branch of morphology treating of the various parts of the human body, which is studied not only by students of the science, but also by young children who sneak books on the subject into the back of the library and look at the pictures.

ANCESTOR One of the people to blame for present discontentment, physical disorder, or poverty.

ANDROMEDA An Ethiopian princess who was chained to a cliff and rescued by Perseus, who married her but later discovered that she enjoyed being chained, and also wearing rubber suits.

ANGEL In religion, one of the spiritual beings who fought against the rebellious army of Lucifer and who were the only combatants ever to be totally certain that God was on their side. 2. The daughter of a spoiled father.

ANGER A strong emotion of displeasure, sometimes unavoidable, but more often than not a person's own fault for not circumventing the antagonizer.

ANIMAL A living creature that is not a plant, the distinction being difficult to make in the case of creatures that spend large amounts of time watching commercial television.

ANNIVERSARY The day when a wife is reminded that her wedding gown is one size smaller than it was the year before.

ANNOINTED Smeared with oil, as a car mechanic.

ANSWER The solution of a problem, such as sending him to camp.

ANT An insect known for its sense of organization, meaning that it knows which things to throw away and which to keep.

ANTAGONIST Someone who has made the despicable mistake of wanting to win something as badly as you do.

ANTHROPOID Resembling man, such as an ape in a tweed suit.

ANTHROPOLOGY The science of human development and what happened along the way to make everyone so neurotic.

ANTHROPOMORPHISM The conception of God with human attributes, such as back pains and occasional irregularity.

ANTHROPOMORPHOSIS Metamorphosis into human form, as is the case when Las Vegas showgirls enter the dressing room after their act.

ANTHROPONOMY The science which treats of the relationship between human behavior and the way people act.

ANTHROPOPHAGY The eating of human flesh, usually fried in butter, with salt, pepper and just a hint of garlic.

ANTIBODY Anybody who's against any other body.

ANTIFREEZE A series of drinks intended to get an uncompromising woman into a compromising position.

ANYBODY A person who, with a million dollars, can grow up to be president.

APARTMENT The nearest thing to a home in a society of transients.

APATHETIC Not interested in a runaway lion until it's eating someone in the family.

APE A monkey most closely related to man, in the sense that it looks and acts like one of the in-laws.

APHORISM A short pithy sentence, such as "Let sleeping dogs lie, except under oath."

APHRODISIAC A certain type of food that arouses in people the desire to put off doing the dishes.

APOLLO The god of youth, beauty, light, poetry, music, oracles, healing, and specialization.

APOLLYON   The angel of the bottomless pit; hence, the mascot of people who can't stop eating.

APOLOGY   Merely words of regret for having caused some injury by word or deed, which are better left unsaid unless they are accompanied by a firm commitment not to repeat the injury.

APOTHEGM   A short and instructive saying, such as "You can't fool all the people all the time, but you can make a fortune fooling some of the people some of the time."

APPETITE   The desire to eat, which is spoiled by eating something that is desired.

APPLAUD   To clap your hands together, exactly as long as the person sitting next to you.

APPLE   The fruit that cost Adam and Eve paradise, immortality and the friendship of God—and it isn't even that much better than an orange.

APPOINTEE   A person who is related to the appointer or someone who has made a sizable campaign contribution.

APPREHENSIVE   Experienced in dealings with human beings.

APRIL   National Ulcer Month, the first half of which is spent worrying about making the income tax deadline and the second half worrying about being audited.

APRIL FOOL   Anyone who plays stupid jokes on people on the first day of April.

AQUARIUS   The Water Bearer, or the sign of the zodiac attributed to kids who don't make the team.

ARBORESCENT   Resembling a tree in appearance, structure, or ability to follow instructions.

ARCADE   A very noisy building filled with machines that test the user's skill at spending quarters.

ARCHAEOLOGIST   A scientist who really digs his work. 2. Someone who believes that all primitive people should have their heads examined.

ARCHAEOLOGY   The scientific study which seeks to explain why many ancient people chose to live in buried cities.

ARCHANGEL   The chief angel, or the one with the biggest headdress.

ARCHITECT   A person who creates modern stories based on traditional plots.

ARGUE   To take your fingers out of your ears long enough to put your foot in your mouth and then to take your foot out of your mouth long enough to put your fingers back in your ears and so on.

ARIES   The first sign of the zodiac, pictured as a ram, but it is unclear whether the Ram is a lineman or a running back.

ARISTOCRAT   A member of the ruling class which controls the power of the government; hence, any high ranking official of a large corporation.

ARITHMETIC   A subject taught in school which is known to promote division among the students.

ARMS   Any implements used in war, which are occasionally defensive but which are, for the most part, grossly offensive.

ARMY   A group of men for whom the joy of killing defenseless animals has faded. 2. Minds collectively forfeited to the mindlessness of war.

ARROGANCE   A sense of superiority, which everyone assumes to one degree or another, and it is often those who feel they have the least of it who manifest the most.

ARSENAL   A military storehouse maintained to insure that future generations will have the same opportunities to destroy themselves that their parents had.

ARSENIC   A substance which is used to turn any ordinary drink into a farewell toast.

ARSONIST   One who digs the graves of his victims with a match.

ART   Any application of knowledge and ingenuity whereby people rise above their animal nature and strive toward their humane nature.

ARTICHOKE A vegetable that is appropriately high-priced, because only people who can afford it know how to eat it.

ARTIFICIAL Truly fake.

ASGARD The abode of the gods, which is described in mythology as a place similar to Beverly Hills, but without as many swimming pools.

ASHAMED Found out.

ASPIRE To shoot for the stars, often without making sufficient preparations for coming back down to earth.

ASPIRIN Tablets used to relieve body aches, fever, and the pain associated with thinking.

ASSASSIN A poisonous snake, springing from the lowest place in the ground to strike an unsuspecting victim.

ASSIST To lend a helping hand, being careful not to end up giving an arm and a leg.

ASSUMPTION The act of taking for granted what a person meant without asking, which can lead to even more confusion and misunderstanding than if you had asked.

ASTARTE The Phoenician goddess of sexual love, who is pictured as having a big grin on her face.

ASTROLOGER One who studies the stars and sees that they predict great wealth for anyone who can figure out a way to market their secret influences upon human affairs.

ASTRONOMY The science of celestial bodies, making use of measurements and figures almost as incomprehensible to the average human being as the defense budget.

ASYLUM A place of protection from the violence and deception of sane people.

ATHANASIA Freedom from death, which is the same as slavery to life.

ATHEISM Denial in the existence of God, based upon the belief that no supreme being would allow such long lines at the checkout counter.

ATHEIST   One who believes only in gods that can be seen.

ATHLETE   A person with exceptional talent in sports, who is paid an enormous amount of money for providing the spectators with a vicarious sense of accomplishment.

ATLAS   A mythological Titan who was forced to support the heavens on his head and hands, which accounts for his terrible posture later in life.

ATONALITY   The characteristic of music approaching noise.

ATROCIOUS   Outrageously brutal, cruel, wicked, and repeatable.

ATTACK   To lack the courage to confront peacefully.

ATTEMPT   To succeed at making an effort.

ATTIC   A place for storing the past in boxes, to be relived by future explorers.

ATTITUDE   The beauty of falling snow or the pain of shoveling the sidewalk.

ATTORNEY   One who is trained in the law and who therefore is qualified to determine how much he may legally overcharge his clients for services rendered.

AUCTIONEER   A person who speaks very quickly but who evidently is hard of hearing, for he is constantly asking people questions like "Do I hear 250?" or "Do I hear 300?"

AUDIENCE   Entertainees.

AUGUST   National Pay the Piper month, when the credit card receipts from summer vacation arrive.

AUTHOR   A serious literary artist or, more loosely, any actor who feels like writing a book.

AUTOBIOGRAPHY   A book in which the author refutes the rumors that were spread about him in the past and creates new ones to be spread about him in the future.

AUTOMATIC   Self-acting, and therefore self-breaking.

AVARICE   The inordinate desire for wealth, which is not only the root of all evil, but also a large portion of the trunk and branches.

AZRAEL   The angel of death, who takes the soul from the body and, for a slight handling fee, gift wraps it for delivery into the hereafter.

BABBLE To talk meaninglessly about something or meaningfully about nothing.

BABY The greatest blessing in the world for an expectant couple and the greatest curse for a couple that wasn't expecting anything.

BABY SITTER Someone who gets paid to watch children when their grandmother is not available.

BACCALAUREATE The degree held by the vast majority of unemployed college graduates.

BACCHUS The Greek god of wine, represented as sleeping on a park bench with a newspaper over his face.

BACHELOR Someone who can appreciate the idea of marriage, from a distance. 2. Someone who hasn't found the wrong woman yet. 3. Any man who can stand his own cooking. 4. Someone who is searching for a woman just like his mother, and keeps finding women just like his Aunt Harriet.

BACK The part of a person's body that most people prefer to have toward them when they're talking about that person.

BACKSLIDE An extremely unorthodox approach to home plate.

BACKSTRETCH In the Middle Ages, an application of the rack.

BACON The missing ingredient in an LT sandwich.

BAD Not at all good, but better than worse and much better than worst, which, all things considered, is pretty fair.

BAG A woman who's forty trying desperately to look like she's thirty, who turns out looking like a woman who's fifty trying desperately to look like she's forty.

BAKERY A place that delights the nose and destroys the figure.

BALANCE The emblem of Justice, which is an instrument for weighing, having two metal pans of equal weight and a lawyer hiding underneath it with a magnet. 2. The one thing that can be lost and recovered without having to look for it.

BALD Unhampered by trips to the barber.

BALDERDASH A jumble of words which quite obviously makes no sense, as distinguished from an explanation by an insurance agent, which is less obvious.

BALL Something totally round, like a baseball, or almost round, like a cotton ball, or not very round, like a football, or not the least bit round, like a gala ball.

BALLET A type of dancing which must be meant for performances in front of people who are sleeping, for the dancers spend much of the time tiptoeing about the stage.

BALLISTICS The science which seeks to find the most effective use of artillery, so that the most people possible are blown to bits by the fewest possible projectiles.

BAN To forbid on the grounds that something is evil; as, to ban censorship.

BANALITY That which the mouth says when the brain is unoccupied.

BANJO An instrument that a person first picks out, then picks up, then picks away.

BANK A place where one keeps one's money in order to earn interest, so that by the time it is withdrawn it is worth almost as much as when it was deposited.

BANQUET An affair at which the participants have their mouths crammed with food, their eyes blinded with smoke, and their ears filled with speeches.

BANSHEE   According to Irish legend, a female spirit whose horrible wailing warned families of the imminent death of one of their members. These forecasts of doom always came true because, if at the end of a week of wailing no one had died, somebody in the family had to volunteer to die so that everyone else could get a decent night's sleep.

BAR   A social filling station in all societies that run on alcohol. 2. A good place to go if you've got any old ideas lying around that you'd like to throw away.

BARBARIAN   Someone who takes a Mozart sonata and arranges it for disco dancing.

BARBER   A person who makes no attempt whatsoever to hide the fact that he clips his customers.

BAREFACED   With uncovered face; nudefaced.

BAREFOOT   With uncovered feet; nudefoot.

BAREHEADED   With uncovered head; nudeheaded.

BARGAIN   Anything that still works a month after the warranty expires.

BARN   A farm building, hitting the broad side of which is considered by many to be a standard of marksmanship.

BARREL   A container for various liquids or monkeys.

BASEBALL   A game in which the object is to score as many runs as it takes to keep the typical fan watching on television from falling asleep.

BASHFUL   Naturally uneasy in unnatural surroundings and circumstances

BASKETBALL   A game played by giants, whose skill lies in the ability to take a large ball and insert it through a hoop with as much downward thrust as possible. The game may also be played by shorter people, who must direct the ball upward in order to score.

BATH   The act of sitting in a tub of water and sinking enemy ships.

BATTERY   A power cell that lasts between two weeks and two years, depending upon factors that defy rational analysis.

BATTLE A game of strategy in which the pieces are moved across the board in the direction of the opponent's pieces, in the course of which both the pieces and the board become saturated with blood and have to be discarded and replaced before another round can be played.

BAYONET A weapon preferred by soldiers who would rather take a stab at their work than give it their best shot.

BEACH One of the many places that can get on your nerves, but the only place that actually gets in your hair.

BEAR A large mammal whose reputation for being cute and friendly has been so firmly established, mostly through cartoons and stuffed toys, that people who are torn to shreds by one are usually greatly disappointed.

BEARD The hair on the face of a man who is extremely careful, and who therefore does not experience many close shaves.

BEAST One who does not allow his brain to interfere with his instincts.

BEAUTY That which is pleasant to the senses without being destructive to the spirit.

BEAVER An amphibious rodent that can never be accused of not giving a dam.

BED A piece of furniture designed for life's two most basic pleasures.

BEDBUG To bother someone who's trying to get some sleep.

BEE The one insect which has gained the respect and fear of humans, by behaving like them.

BEELZEBUB One of the most efficient and resourceful devils, whose chief responsibility is making sure that good deeds go unrewarded.

BEER A brew that is often used in drinking contests among males to prove that the winner's kidneys are as big as his mouth.

BEG To offer people the opportunity to feel sorrier for another than they feel for themselves.

BEGET   To procreate, Biblically.

BEGGAR   A public reminder of the unexplainable inequities in life.

BEGIN   To accomplish the hardest part of any activity.

BEHAVE   To act in accordance with socially accepted rules of conduct, even if in a given situation they make everyone boring, humorless and stuffy.

BELCH   To make a sound from the mouth which, when made in public, indicates that the person who made it has finished eating and is ready to pick his teeth.

BELIEF   Acceptance of something on faith, often assumed in childhood and used throughout life to shield oneself against confronting difficult moral and ethical questions.

BELLIGERENT   Eager to start wars, especially wars that other people have to fight.

BELLY   The part of the body that pays in aches the price of what the mouth intakes.

BELONGING   That which mutually possesses and is possessed by its owner.

BELOW   Under everything above, but above everything still further under everything above. 2. In Hades, commonly thought to be located about ten miles beneath the New York subway system.

BELT   A strip of leather used to uphold a person's pants or a parent's authority.

BENEDICT   A man who has been cured of bachelorhood after many years, only to discover that he has contracted marriage.

BENEFICIARY   One member of a married couple who, upon the death of the other, finally has enough money to take the trip they'd always planned.

BENEVOLENT   Deriving great self-satisfaction from promoting the prosperity of others, but finding that self-satisfaction has an extremely low rate of exchange in the market place.

BERSERK Having clenched fists, wide eyes, bulging veins, a foaming mouth, frazzled hair, inflated nostrils, and a diminished capacity for polite conversation.

BEST The highest possible degree of good, so much better, in fact, that it makes good almost seem bad by comparison and makes bad seem much worse than it normally seems, which is nothing compared to the way it makes worse seem.

BET To place a wager upon one's ability to withstand the temptation to place another wager.

BETRAY To stand behind someone, for the purpose of deciding exactly the right spot to stick the knife.

BETTER A higher degree of good, considerably worse than best, so much worse, in fact, that it does not make good almost seem bad by comparison and makes bad seem only a little bit worse than it normally seems.

BETTING The practice of trying to get a lot of money the easy way, and discovering after it's too late that someone else has found an easier way.

BEWARE To read between the lines of the small print; to be aware.

BIBLE A great book, except that no one laughs in it.

BIBLIOPOLE A dealer in rare and valuable books, as the one who sold the volume presently being read.

BIBLIOTICS The science of handwriting analysis, which is perfected by postal employees who are required to decipher seemingly illegible scribbling on the fronts of envelopes.

BIBLIST One who lives strictly according to the Bible and who therefore believes in overpopulation, enjoys a good war, and prays that God will destroy his enemies in as horrible a manner as possible.

BICEPHALOUS Having two heads, and an economy-size bottle of aspirin.

BICYCLE   The most essential material possession of childhood, because it is the mechanical extension of the primal human urge to run and, equally primal, it has wheels.

BIFARIOUS   Pointing two ways at once, as in the case of most politicians.

BIG   Large, but not as large as an elephant.

BIGGER   About as large as an elephant.

BIGGEST   Larger than an elephant, including one that eats a lot of fried food and smothers everything with tons of butter.

BIGOTRY   Proud ideas trapped in closed minds until they turn rancid.

BILINEAR   Pertaining to two lines, the second of which is kept in reserve in case she doesn't respond to the first.

BILL   A monthly greeting from the utility company designed to brighten the lives of those people who complain that they never get any mail.

BILLIARDS   A table game enjoyed by people who know how to take a cue.

BILLIONAIRE   A person whose wealth is outweighed only by his paranoia.

BIMANUAL   Requiring two hands, as in any job on a ship that cannot be done by one person.

BINET   An intelligence test administered to children to prove that children who are very nervous, upset, tired or fidgety when taking the test have no right to call themselves intelligent.

BINGO   A game played professionally by Catholics and on an amateur basis by members of other religions.

BIOGRAPHY   The private life of a person made public, and sometimes readable.

BIOLOGY   The science of dissecting frogs and discovering which kids in the class have weak stomachs.

BIPARTISAN Pertaining to two parties in government, one of which is out of power and has four years to undermine the progress of the other, so that it can gain the power and itself be undermined.

BIRD A feathered vertebrate with wings,
Free, aloft; no wonder it sings.

BIRTH The beginning of the end. 2. The first in a series of unsolicited and baffling experiences, culminating in death.

BIRTHDAY A day to be celebrated in youth, tolerated in middle age, and dedicated in old age.

BISECT To divide into two equal parts, so that there is no squabbling between the actors as to which one got more lines.

BISHOP A priest with ambition.

BIT The tiniest conceivable amount more than an iota, unless it is a little bit, which is the tiniest amount less than an iota.

BIZARRE Odd, as a man with blue hair, or as anyone who would associate with a man with blue hair, or as anyone who claims to have seen a man with blue hair, or as anyone who inhabits the same planet as a man with blue hair.

BLAB To slosh the tongue in the mouth, as though rinsing out a dirty sink with a rag.

BLACK Devoid of color; hence, pertaining to a sportscast that confines itself strictly to the action of the game.

BLACKBALL To join with others in ostracizing an individual or individuals, thus sanctioning a procedure which may be used, subsequently, against any of the ostracizers.

BLACKBOARD The principal ally of any class clown, for without it the teacher's back would never be turned.

BLACKMAIL A payment made to a parasite for the purpose of self-destruction, wherein the victim attempts to escape the past in exchange for being trapped in the present and hounded in the future.

BLAME To lay the fault for a mistake or a misunderstanding where it traditionally belongs, on someone else.

BLASPHEME   To call God a nasty name, such as fatso or meat-head. 2. To claim to be God, or at least to have spent a couple of weeks over the summer with Him.

BLATANT   Terribly unsuccessful at being coy.

BLEACH   A chemical substance used in the laundry which accidentally removes the floral print from the floral print sheets and pillow cases.

BLEED   To shed blood, usually against one's will, except in the rare cases of individuals who are obsessed with watching other people faint and who therefore cut themselves frequently for this reason. 2. To shave with a razor.

BLESS   To make something holy by pronouncing it holy, as though it would be any less holy if no one pronounced it.

BLIND   Unable to see with one's eyes. 2. Able to see only with one's eyes.

BLISSFUL   Irrationally happy and primed for deep depression.

BLIZZARD   The test papers of an entire class of students who haven't studied.

BLONDE   A woman with light-colored hair, sometimes also with light-colored roots.

BLOOD   The fluid which circulates through the body, having such distinct properties that all attempts to create an artificial substitute for it have been in vein.

BLOODSUCKER   Any member of one's family who is easily hustled in cards or pool.

BLUBBER   Endangered fat.

BLUE   The color that the sky and the sea have been for billions of years, although both of them are becoming progressively darkened with pollutants, and there is a great debate among scientists over which one will turn black first.

BLUFF   To pretend through your mannerisms that you are holding cards higher than the ones you are holding while your opponent pretends to be holding cards higher than the ones he is holding. Some players prefer restricted pretending, which means, for example, that a player holding a pair of queens cannot pretend that they are any higher than a pair of kings. Other players prefer unrestricted pretending.

BLURT   To set the mouth in first gear while the mind is still idling.

BOARDWALK   A long stretch of planking that runs parallel to a beach, where tourists get on rides that make them sick in the stomach, shoot water pistols at the mouths of plastic monkeys to win prizes, and buy salt water taffies that melt on the way home.

BOASTER   Anyone whose actions are not significant enough to speak for themselves.

BOAT   An open vessel used for traveling on water, clearly differing from a cruise ship in that there is no swimming pool or shuffleboard.

BODY   The physical substance of all living things, which come in an infinite variety of sizes, shapes and colors, but which nonetheless share in common one special trait that binds together even the largest elephant and the smallest insect: decay.

BOLD   Adopting a sexual attitude that saves all the time and energy wasted on ulterior motives.

BOMB   A device which, when dropped on a city, can destroy in a few seconds what it takes the inhabitants of the city years to destroy. 2. Unmistakable proof that the world is run by lunatics.

BOMBSIGHT   An instrument used for locating targets precisely from the air, thus helping to prevent perfectly good bombs from falling accidentally onto fields and hillsides, where they barely cause enough damage to make it worthwhile dropping them.

BOO   The battle cry of frustrated sports fans, who would give anything to be able to get out there on the field and show the players how to do it right.

BOOK   A universe between two covers. 2. A thing of rare beauty, which most people learn to fear and hate while in school.

BOOKWORM   A person who enjoys reading as deeply and passionately as other people enjoy having their brains eroded in front of the television set.

BOOZE   To attack one's senses with a merciless ingestion of intoxicating liquor, as though one were punishing a criminal.

BORE   A person who has everything to say about everything or nothing to say about anything.

BORROWER   Someone who takes the shirt off your back and returns it after it doesn't fit anymore.

BOSS   The person who is in charge of handling things wrong, whose employees are all experts who could fix everything in a jiffy if they had the chance.

BOTTLENECK   A place where a mass of cars and a mass of nerves meet and mutually overheat.

BOTTOM   The place where people start who were born with plastic spoons in their mouths.

BOUNCER   A person hired by a theater or a night club to take out the trash and make sure it doesn't come back in again.

BOURGEOIS   A member of the middle class, which is the part of society sandwiched between the upper class and the lower class and, although it is the most vital and substantive ingredient in the sandwich, it is also the one that gets covered over on both sides and squeezed.

BOW   An implement used as a weapon or, ironically, to make music.

BOWLING   A game for people who have the skill to make a strike and the time to spare.

BOXING   A sport in which the participants are paid to assault one another with the intent to do bodily harm, preferably to cause severe bleeding above the eyes.

BOY   Someone who covers everything he owns with dirt, except his mind.

BRAIN   An organ comprised of twisted tissue, which accounts for the kind of thoughts that often come from it.

BRAVERY Being unafraid of oneself. 2. One of the finest of human qualities, too often mistaken for savagery.

BREAD One of the basic foods, the white form of which is the least nutritious and therefore the most popular.

BREAKABLE In contact with a curious child.

BREAKFAST The meal which most people enjoy only on weekends and holidays, because on the other days they don't have the time to taste what they're eating.

BREATH A garlic lover's calling card.

BREEDING The careful process within certain families to insure that nothing tarnishes the silver spoon that is placed in the mouth of its new-born members.

BRIBE A payment from one skunk to another for the purpose of intensifying and broadening the range of their stink.

BRIDE A woman in a white gown with a noticeable lack of lines in her forehead.

BRIDEGROOM A man who has just exchanged half of his buddies for a wife.

BRINE Sea water, a saline solution said to drive people who drink it insane, which may account for some of the strange behavior at seashore resorts.

BRITISHER Someone who drinks tea all the time, even if he doesn't like it.

BROADCASTER A woman using a fishing rod.

BROAD-MINDED Willing to listen to all views on an issue, even the stupid ones voiced by the opposition.

BROILER A row house in the city in the summer.

BROTHEL A place where thin soup is served.

BROTHER A male child, who shares the same parents with the other male children in the family, and often the same clothes.

BUBBLE A globule of fantasies created by a person called a dreamer and burst by a pin called reality.

BUDGET   A mathematical system for living within your means and without most of the things you want.

BUFFALO   An animal most widely known in America for stopping bullets.

BULL   The participant in a bullfight that perennially comes in second.

BULLET   A ball of lead used as a substitute for reason, when there is a shortage. The advantage of using bullets over other substitutes is that there is an endless supply.

BUREAUCRAT   One who stands ready at the parapet to defend the bastion of incompetency against the assault of common sense.

BUS   A large vehicle for transporting late people, most of whom were on time before they started waiting at the bus stop.

BUSINESS   An enterprise designed to make money by selling a useful product, by offering a necessary service, or by false advertising.

BUTTERFLY   An insect with a pin sticking through it.

BYSTANDER   A person who innocently witnesses something, like a crime or an auto accident, and doesn't know how it happened and didn't see a thing.

CAB   A vehicle with a meter inside it, so that the passengers know just how far, and for how much, they are being taken.

CACOPHONY   The sound of music written by composers who are too busy being modern to bother with incidentals like themes or melodies.

CACTUS   A very popular plant to which people, if they're not careful, can become attached.

CADAVEROUS   Pertaining to a dead body or to the condition of someone after a couple of hours in front of the television set.

CADET   A serious-looking person with very shiny shoes.

CADMUS   A mythological prince who is said to have brought the alphabet from Phoenicia to Greece, thus making him one of the earliest known letter carriers.

CAFETERIA   A restaurant in which the food is not served but is instead encountered.

CAGE   An enclosure for confining birds so that they can relax and not waste all their energy flying.

CAJOLE   To seek votes in an election.

CAKE   A dessert which, contrary to popular belief, you can have and eat too, provided you're smart enough not to leave your lunch box out in the open where somebody can rifle it.

CALCULATOR   A compact, inexpensive math machine, which gives instant answers and which has helped tremendously in making basic arithmetic skills obsolete.

CALENDAR A chart for reminding you that your days, indeed, are numbered.

CALLOUS Having stepped on so many people that the skin has become hardened and they can no longer be felt. 2. Having been stepped on so often that the skin has formed a protective crust of hatred and resentment.

CALM Possessing nerves of steel, a totally unpressured lifestyle, or a doctor who prescribes heavy doses of tranquilizers.

CALORIE One of five thousand reasons not to have a second piece of strawberry shortcake.

CAMEL A large animal, usually of the desert, which people find easy to ride once they get over the hump.

CAMERA Something which tourists have hanging around their necks so that they can be identified by local swindlers and pickpockets.

CAMP A place where counselors quickly change their attitudes about having children. 2. A place where kids are sent to appreciate their mother's cooking.

CAMPAIGN A series of military operations in a war, similar to an election campaign but less vicious.

CANARY A little bird that sings, and if the district attorney likes what he hears, the little bird may be let out of the cage on parole.

CANDID See FRANK, but don't tell him who sent you.

CANDIDATE A person running for election, whose job is to make the old party rhetoric sound new and different and to make the old promises sound convincing and realistic.

CANDY Sugary stuff to eat, which is consumed regularly by children with a sweet tooth, usually decayed, and adults with a sweet tooth, usually false.

CANNED A type of taped laughter that was used at one time abundantly during television comedies to alert the people at home that something funny had just happened. It has since been replaced by the live studio audience and the teleprompter, which serve the exact same purpose.

CANNON A piece of artillery which fires large shells, killing a few people on the average or as many as a couple of dozen on a lucky shot.

CAPITALISM An economic system based upon a belief in the infinite power of money.

CAPITALIST Someone who staunchly defends the right to private property, so long as it isn't located where he wants to build a shopping mall. 2. Someone who will defend the free enterprise system against all threats, particularly ethical.

CAPITATION A tax which is levied upon a person for having a head, differing from a real estate tax in the sense that no assessment is made on the value of the property.

CAPITOL The building in which members of Congress gather to decide how many months it will take to get a week's work done.

CAPRICIOUS Apt to change suddenly, as from a dress to a pants suit.

CAPRICORN The sign of the horned goat, designating a person who will eat anything and is forever thinking about sex.

CAPSIZE The circumference of a baseball player's head.

CAPTAIN A military officer ranking below a major and above suspicion.

CAPTIVE The passive wife of a possessive husband.

CAPTURE To seize by force; as, they struggled for hours until finally she captured his fancy.

CAR An indispensable luxury, glorified and worshipped in all societies firmly committed to wasting energy.

CARD A greeting sent in the mail on various occasions, usually with a verse inside, designed to bring a smile to the average person and nausea to someone familiar with poetry.

CARDINAL A spiritual official, one step holier than an archbishop.

CARDIOLOGY The science of the heart, which is to say that it has a beat on other sciences.

CAREER The profession which a person chooses in adulthood as compensation for the dreams of his youth. 2. The profession which a person has always wanted and for which he is willing to strive, suffer and sacrifice, preferring the pain of perseverence to the agony of regret.

CAREFREE Free from care, or, in other words, living in a mansion on a remote island with plenty of food and friendly animals.

CAREFUL Taking the time to do something right, even though the guy down the street gets twice the business by doing it quickly. 2. Adept at not getting caught.

CARELESS Pertaining to people who like putting things together without reading instructions. 2. Neglecting to look both ways before doublecrossing.

CARICATURE A grotesque or ludicrous exaggeration, such as a woman wearing excessive amounts of eye shadow and rouge.

CARNIVAL A place with side shows for people who would rather spend money to see weird oddities of nature than stay at home and look in the mirror.

CAROL A joyful hymn, sung primarily at Christmas, which is the one time of the year when singing joyfully in public does not elicit strange looks from people.

CARPET A dog or cat that loves going for rides.

CARROT A vegetable which for years was mistakenly thought to improve eyesight, when what it actually does is dull the other senses.

CARTESIAN Pertaining to the philosopher Descartes, who thought, therefore he was. This is not to be confused with people who did not think, therefore they weren't, but it is to be confused with people who thought sometimes, therefore they may have been.

CARTOONIST An artist who is pleased when people laugh at his work, which sets him apart completely from any other type of artist.

CARVE To slice a turkey into portions so that it can be devoured readily, or to do likewise with a person's reputation.

CASH The means by which people without credit cards pay for things.

CASHIER The person in a store or restaurant who is always on the take. 2. A quick change artist.

CASINO A gambling house, where the old saying that there is a sucker born every minute is disproven. There are, in fact, several hundred of them.

CASSANDRA A princess of Troy, who was given the gift of prophecy by Apollo, but he later revoked it when he discovered that she was selling racing tips.

CASTLE What a man's home is, after he has completed his serfdom with the mortgage company.

CASUALTIES The term applied euphemistically by military authorities to the mangled and mutilated corpses of the victims of war.

CAT An animal which has the reputation of always landing on its feet no matter how it is dropped or from what height, although few cats seem anxious to confirm this.

CATEGORY A division into which people who refuse to be categorized are placed in order to distinguish them from people who do not refuse to be categorized.

CATERER The parent of a spoiled child.

CATGUT A tough cord used for strings of musical instruments and made from the intestines of sheep, which is awfully confusing for the sheep but a great relief to cats.

CATHAY China, as it was called before people realized that they were calling it the wrong thing.

CATTLE Herds of cows, bulls, steers, or people, all but the last of which are slaughtered regularly for food. Herds of people are slaughtered from time to time, but not for food.

CAUGHT Penitent.

CAUTIOUS Wearing pants with zippered pockets. 2. More frightened by potential danger than attracted by potential fun.

CAVALRY A military force on horseback, specially trained to arrive at a battle in the nick of time, just when all seemed hopeless and only a corny miracle could save the day.

CAVIAR The relish of the rich. It is prepared from the eggs of sturgeon and other fish that have made the social register.

CELEBRATE To observe a holiday, such as Christmas, by making every effort not to let the true meaning of the occasion interfere with a good time.

CELEBRATION Any excuse for getting drunk.

CELEBRITY A person whose picture appears on the covers of supermarket tabloids and who is misquoted at least twice a week. 2. Technically, anyone who appears as a panelist on a game show, even if this seems to be the only thing the person does.

CELIBATE A person who has taken a vow not to marry for reasons of religion or a person who has taken a vow not to marry for reasons of sanity.

CEMENT A substance used to make sidewalks, curbs and buildings, and to transport people who have the misfortune to find their feet encased in it to the bottom of a body of water.

CEMETERY A place which is dark and quite cramped, but at least you don't have to worry about the neighbors coming home at all hours of the morning and a guy knocking on the door every month to read your meter.

CENSOR A person who decides that viewing a naked body is immoral while viewing a clothed body riddled with bullets is perfectly fine, and whose powers are such that this view of morality is accepted as a standard for society.

CENT A unit of currency which, if dropped, is worth less than the energy it takes to pick it up.

CENTENARIAN A person who is too old to remember his own teeth.

CENTURY A period of one hundred income tax forms. 2. The amount of time it takes for a piece of junk to turn into an antique.

CERAMICS A class in which the students are taught to make articles of baked clay, which is not to be confused with home economics class, in which the students often make articles that taste like baked clay.

CEREAL Pertaining to sugar with some grain in it.

CEREMONY A formal act, usually symbolic, which is designed to look very impressive and meaningful, even if everyone, including the participants, has forgotten what it symbolizes.

CERES The goddess of vegetables, who is said to have had cauliflower ears, onion breath, and a pea brain.

CERTAIN Absolutely sure, or, if questioned, very sure, or, if challenged, pretty sure, or, if under oath, kind of sure.

CERTIFY To endorse authoritatively, having been authorized to endorse by a committee that endorses endorsers authoritatively, having been authorized to endorse endorsers by a committee that endorses endorser endorsers.

CHAIR A piece of furniture in which people sit, in order to take a load off their feet. It is used in most social settings, except at cocktail parties, where people stand, electing to keep a load on their feet, while they proceed to tie on another one.

CHALK A piece of soft white limestone, used by teachers to write on the blackboard and by students to throw at one another while the teacher is writing on the blackboard. It is also easily hidden.

CHALLENGE A prospect so inviting that the risk of failure only enhances it. 2. Another name for a pointless, foolhardy, and dangerous undertaking.

CHAMPAGNE A bubbly wine, drunk almost exclusively at weddings, which induces otherwise normal people to dance with their relatives.

CHAMPION A person who has too much class and integrity to compromise either in order to win first place.

CHANCE The principal governing factor in life. 2. The third party responsible for most people being born.

CHANGE   Any variation in the way things already are, which is resisted by many people because they fear it will make things worse or, more often, because they fear it will force them to grow.

CHANNEL   One of the digits on a television dial which corresponds to a particular station, so that the viewer can flip from one soap opera, game show or situation comedy to another, exercising what is laughingly known as a choice in programming.

CHAOS   A newsperson's paradise.

CHAPERONE   An older person who attends a dance for young people and tries to discourage them from doing at the dance what they're bound to do as soon as the dance is over.

CHARACTER   The thing that you are supposed to be building every time another part of your life is destroyed. 2. That which causes a person either to smile or look away when confronted with a mirror.

CHARGE   To pay for something with a plastic card, which makes shopping for unnecessary things seem essential and which makes going into debt simple and convenient.

CHARITY   A salve for the conscience of the well-disposed, whereby they provide a starving family of four enough to feed two.

CHARM   The ability to make other people forget for an instant that they are as boring as they think they are.

CHASTITY   The state or quality of being pure, which used to be considered a virtue but now is considered an embarrassment. 2. An ancient type of belt which, indirectly, kept the pants up.

CHAUFFEUR   The first of a group of pals to get his driver's license.

CHEAP   Less overpriced than usual.

CHEAT   To practice fraud at cards, particularly at solitaire, which is an extremely popular game because it affords the player unlimited opportunities for self-deception.

CHEEK   The fleshy wall on the left side of the face that gets slapped, provided the slapper is right handed; if the slapper is left handed, it is the right side.

CHEERLESS Overwhelmed with positive thinking; namely, thinking that everything is positively awful. 2. Too absorbed in one's own troubles to enjoy the troubles of other people.

CHEESE A dairy product that is used in sandwiches, in omelettes, and in taking pictures.

CHEESECAKE A dessert item which causes the mouth to water, the willpower to wilt, and the waistline to widen.

CHEF The person in a restaurant who is taking his sweet time preparing your meal while you are busy getting filled on bread.

CHEMISTRY The profession that has attracted most of the mad scientists in history, although many chemists today claim to be perfectly sane, pointing to physicists as the mad scientists of the future.

CHERRY A fruit which is closely related to the peach, although it is so much smaller that it would not be fair to pit one against the other.

CHERUB One of the angelic proletariat, created by God so that souls entering heaven will feel at home in the presence of a structured class system.

CHESS A game of strategy, which is similar to world war in that there are opposing armies and the object is to destroy the opponent's defenses, but different in that the winner does not pay the loser.

CHICKEN An animal whose major function on earth is to bring fathers and their children closer together through the commonly shared complaint of having it for dinner again.

CHILD Everyone who is not too old to discover new beauty in the world and to sense new wonder at the mysteries of life.

CHILDHOOD The time between being totally dependent upon your parents and being totally insecure on your own. 2. The next stage in life after the adorable stage. 3. The period of life when cruelty is administered for fun and not personal gain. 4. The only time in life when nothing hurts for more than an hour.

CHILI A pungent stew served at diners to truck drivers who have equipped their cabs with an ample supply of antacids.

CHINAMAN A Chinese sexist, who stubbornly refuses to refer to himself as a Chinaperson.

CHIP A small piece of cement broken off of a city sidewalk; hence, a chip off the old block.

CHIROMANCY The practice of palmistry, which involves looking into a person's hand and noting various lines, particularly the very prominent line of gullibility.

CHISEL To cut into wood, stone, metal, or someone else's pocket.

CHOCOLATE A kind of candy that is not as delicious as a toothache is painful, but close enough so that most people risk it.

CHOICE The act of choosing between two or more alternatives, which generally denotes that the alternatives are different, but this is not always the case, as studies of certain political elections reveal.

CHOKE To squeeze someone's neck so that air cannot pass through the windpipe, thus greatly curtailing the person's future plans.

CHOPSTICK Oneof two small sticks used to convey food from the plate to the lap.

CHOREOGRAPHY The art of making sure that, when a ballerina jumps, someone is there to catch her.

CHRISTMAS The day that separates the joy of buying gifts from the headache of paying the credit card company. 2. A day set aside to honor the birth of greed.

CHRONICLE An account of rumors surrounding historical events, with strict attention paid to the exact time when the rumors began, in order to assure historical accuracy.

CHURCH Any place where a person who believes in God is. 2. A building for those who feel more comfortable approaching God in a crowd.

CICADA   An insect which appears every seven years, takes one look at the economy, and promptly disappears for another seven years.

CIGAR   A small roll of tobacco leaf, which smells perfectly fine, as long as it isn't lit. 2. A tobacco product, chiefly used for chasing women out of a room.

CINNAMON   A powdered spice, also known as cimmanon.

CIRCLE   An extremely round square.

CIRCUMLOCUTORY   Pertaining to, relating to, referring to, alluding to, corresponding to, suggesting, implying, intimating, insinuating, or having in any way, shape, manner, form, or context to do with the use of many words when only a few are needed.

CIRCUS   A show at which animals demonstrate their backwardness and stupidity, by entertaining the very creatures who would exterminate them.

CITIZEN   Someone who pays taxes for the right to complain about what he doesn't get for his taxes.

CITY   Millions of people and millions of dogs, alternately barking. 2. A place where the sky is only as wide as a given street.

CIVILIZATION   An ongoing process which has not yet succeeded in feeding all of the people in the world but has succeeded in devising ways to kill them a dozen times over. 2. A system that defines backward countries as those that do not have the military might to destroy their neighbors. 3. The steady, relentless rise of the art of weaponry.

CLAIRVOYANCE   The extraordinary ability actually to see and hear the things that people in insane asylums only imagine they see and hear.

CLAM   An edible mollusk which some people eat directly from the shell in order to show off, by demonstrating that they are willing to put in their mouths an object which turns the stomachs of the more squeamish diners.

CLANDESTINE   Conducted with secrecy by professional sneaks, who are sometimes so sneaky that they manage to keep what they are doing absolutely secret from everyone, including themselves.

CLAPTRAP   A trick designed to gain applause, such as mentioning the name of any big city on a talk show.

CLARINET   A musical instrument most commonly found in high school bands and in the closets of people who once played in a high school band.

CLASS   That quality which distinguishes people who eat fried chicken with a knife and fork.

CLASSICAL   Pertaining to a type of music which has as its most characteristic feature the discernable absence of shouting.

CLAUSTROPHOBIA   The morbid dread of winding up in efficiency apartments for the rest of your life.

CLAVICHORD   A keyboard instrument which has completely gone out of popularity as the result of nobody knowing what it is.

CLEAN   Free from guilt, as a politician who does not take bribes, or free from filth, as a retired politician.

CLEAR   Regarding a high school trigonometry teacher's explanation of spherical triangles, assuming that he is addressing a roomful of nuclear physicists.

CLEMENCY   The disposition to be merciful to a criminal, evidently with the idea being that he, in turn, will be merciful to his next victim.

CLERK   A store employee who is trained in the art of remaining polite, despite the conviction among some members of the public that rudeness is a customer's prerogative.

CLEVER   Possessing a quickness of wit or intellect, which is frequently so quick that most people fail to follow it, and they therefore react the way people regularly do when they can't follow something, by calling the person a fool.

CLICHE   A trite phrase, but one that is never too trite to be used in a television commercial.

CLIFF   A high face of rock, such as that of a father whose teenage daughter gets home from a party at four o'clock in the morning.

CLIQUE   A small and exclusive group of people, whose peculiar odor prevents them from social contact with those outside the group.

CLOAK   A loose outer garment that is worn with a dagger.

CLOBBER   To pound or beat mercilessly, as opposed to the other ways there are to pound or beat, such as to pound or beat graciously.

CLOCK   The warden of all. 2. A face with twelve numbers on it and two hands that seem to spin.

CLOD   A person of great intellect, as compared with a turnip.

CLOISTER   A place where monks or nuns live lives of serenity and holiness away from the outside world, where the people who could use good examples are.

CLONE   An exact duplicate of a person, which will provide people of the future with the distinct advantage of being able to send their duplicates to the dentist.

CLOSET   A small room where people who are ashamed of the past keep their skeletons and people who are ashamed of the present keep themselves.

CLOTHES   The things which make the man and, considering the cost of a good suit, also break him.

CLOUD   A visible mass of fog suspended in the sky, every one of which, according to an old song, has a silver lining. The song makes no mention of the excessive tarnish noted by many people.

CLOWN   A circus performer who, through his appearance and behavior, succeeds in making most of the children in the audience laugh and some of the adults—those who don't identify too strongly with his act.

CLUMSY   Capable of performing the amazing feat of tripping four times over only three pieces of furniture.

COACH A person who contributes to crime in sports, by telling his players to hold up and to steal.

COAL A piece of glowing carbon or charred wood, generally considered the most anemic energy source, because it is usually found in beds.

COBWEB A network formed from the left-overs of a corn boil.

COCK The male of the common barnyard fowl whose responsibility it is to service all of the hens on the farm, and yet, amazingly, he still has enough energy left in the morning to crow.

COCKFIGHT An absurd contest which demonstrates that cocks are stupid enough to kill one another and men are stupid enough to bet on them.

COCOANUT Someone who is absolutely wild about hot chocolate.

COFFEE A drink which is extremely popular because it helps people to counteract the effects of their jobs. It keeps them awake.

COHABIT To share the same wardrobe with a nun.

COHEIR A joint heir, or someone who inherits the family stash.

COLD A condition in the body marked by a runny nose, a sore throat, congested sinuses, and a resurgence of the childhood desire for a lot of mothering.

COLLAR The part of a shirt or blouse which keeps the neck clean by thoroughly removing and retaining its dirt.

COLLEGE An institution where students go to earn marks, postponing their real education until after they graduate. 2. A place where the students learn to drink and smoke more than they ever did before, which is why it is known as higher education.

COLLUSION A secret agreement for a deceitful purpose, which is usually conducted between agents of the agreeing parties, but occasionally the agreeing parties themselves meet, and this is called a head-on collusion.

COLOGNE   A lotion which is applied to the face, frequently before a social engagement, so that its smell will clash with the smell of other people's faces.

COLONEL   A military officer who is only one rank away from smoking a big cigar.

COLOR   The mainstay of variety in the world, which human beings seem to enjoy and appreciate in all things, except skin.

COLOSSEUM   An ampitheater of ancient Rome where, through the miracle of advanced civilization, Romans who were not lucky enough to travel to distant battlefields could enjoy a similar display of gore and mutilation right in their own home town.

COMB   An instrument used by people who have a strict policy regarding the treatment of their hair and who really want to put some teeth into it.

COMBAT   Any kind of fighting, the degree of senselessness varying with the weapons and the number of participants involved.

COME   To go further away from the place of departure.

COMEDIAN   A person who intentionally evokes laughter from others, as opposed to someone with an impediment.

COMEDY   A play or a movie, which is supposed to be funny, even though the plot often includes one or more of the following elements: a man and a woman who hate each other, a husband who hates his wife or his wife's family, or vice versa, a character who hates everybody, large-scale deception, vicious arguments, and chases that injure innocent people and destroy their property. Ironically, there is always a happy ending.

COMIC   The section of a newspaper reserved primarily for those who do not appreciate the kind of humor frequently found on the front page.

COMMA   A period with a little hook sticking out of the bottom of it that is used to separate words phrases or clauses so that they don't run into each other as they do in this definition.

COMMANDANT   A small, crawling insect that is in charge of a colony.

COMMENCEMENT   The ceremonies at which graduates receive their diplomas. They are often emotional occasions, but never emotional enough, unfortunately, to render the people on the platform speechless.

COMMERCIAL   A radio or television ad, which can run from ten seconds to two minutes long, depending upon how merciful the advertiser is. 2. An exercise in fast-speed shouting. 3. A dramatized attempt to convince the average housewife that she is as utterly stupid as the woman on the screen.

COMMITTEE   A body of people appointed or elected to act upon a matter that requires improvement, although the funds needed to make the improvement are usually lacking because most of the money has gone to pay the salaries of all the people acting upon the matter.

COMMUNE   A society based on mutual ownership and the absence of competition, although there exists a very basic and ongoing competition, that of essential human selfishness versus desire for the common good.

COMMUNISM   A doctrine based upon the eventual formation of a classless society, which is sound in theory but which is untenable in practice, for the simple reason that no one is anywhere near the discovery of a cure for man's most ancient disease, greed, which is the cornerstone of class structure.

COMPASS   A device used by people who need direction but who don't feel they can go to their parents.

COMPASSION   The rare ability to lose oneself in the sufferings of another.

COMPATIBLE   Capable of living in harmony, provided that your partner agrees to take the melody.

COMPETE   To strive to win, without striving to humiliate. 2. To win at any cost, even at the cost of one's ethics. 3. To lose the enjoyment of the game to win the decision of it.

COMPLACENCY   A false sense of security which descends from the belief that the monkey on someone else's back has been trained to stay there.

COMPLACENT Unprepared for the sudden, jarring twists of fate which play an inescapably prominent role in life.

COMPLAIN To express dissatisfaction, usually not with a mind to correct the situation but only because it feels good. 2. To tell everybody under the sun what somebody said or did to you except the person who said or did it.

COMPLEXITY The state of being simple once you know how.

COMPLICATE To add your two cents to the solution of a problem when you have a penny's worth of knowledge on the subject.

COMPLIMENT To tell a woman that you think her hair looks nice so that she can tell you what a mess it is.

COMPOSER One who nourishes the ears with the most wholesome of audiodelicacies, music.

COMPROMISE To agree to something in such a tricky manner that both parties can go away thinking that the other is a sucker. 2. To send your principles on vacation while your base instincts go to work.

COMPUNCTION A feeling of uneasiness which arises whenever the mind is locked in a sleazy hotel room, plotting something underhanded, and the conscience is waiting outside under a streetlamp in a trench coat.

COMPUTER A machine with an astounding capacity for storing information and producing needed data in an instant. It can do the work of any number of people and has the added advantage of not being able to fake sickness.

CON To accept money from unsuspecting people in return for teaching them an invaluable lesson in trust.

CONCEITED Preferring one kind of company over all others, that being the company of a large mirror.

CONCENTRATION The act of clearing the mind of all distractions, such as the neighbor's dog barking, so that it can focus totally on a given subject, such as killing the neighbor's dog.

CONCERNED Anxious and worried and fearful that something dreadful has happened, which it has, to the psyche of the worrier.

CONCERTINA A small musical instrument, like an accordion, but not as Polish.

CONCERTMASTER A violinist who walks onto the stage just before the beginning of a concert as a test to see which members of the audience mistake him for the conductor and applaud.

CONCUBINE A woman who lives with a man, without the joy of a wedding in her past but without the fear of a divorce in her future.

CONCUPISCENT Ardently desirous and tired of cold showers.

CONDEMN To adjudge something, such as a building, to be unsafe for anyone other than a very poor person. 2. To pronounce to be different.

CONDENSE To take a writer's work and subject it to surgery, in which little pieces of a story's internal organs are removed, including, invariably, the heart.

CONDESCEND To act in a patronizing manner, as though the bestowing of one's ignorance upon one's social inferiors were a blessing.

CONDONATION Tacit forgiveness of an offense by treating the offender as if no offense had been committed, which is another way of telling him to make a habit of it.

CONDOR A very large vulture found in South America, where it is often seen flying over a country's capital, waiting for a coup.

CONDUCTOR The person who walks onto the stage just after the concertmaster, to the enthusiastic applause of the astute concert-goers and the hesitant applause of those who think it may be another trick. See CONCERTMASTER.

CONFABULATE To chat, which is a most innocent activity, although most people become extremely indignant if even the suggestion is made that they were confabulating with one of the neighbors.

CONFEDERATE A soldier whose uniform was grey soaked in red, as opposed to blue soaked in red.

58

CONFERENCE   A formal meeting at which views are exchanged and participants are made to feel that they are actually accomplishing something, when all it is is a lot of talk.

CONFESS   To acknowledge one's own guilt before somebody else acknowledges it. This is viewed as a courageous act by some people, while others contend that it takes far less courage to admit to a wrongdoing than it does to refrain from committing it in the first place.

CONFIDANT   A person who is entrusted with a friend's secrets, which are not only helpful in strengthening the relationship while it lasts but which are also always good for a laugh after the friendship dissolves.

CONFORM   To be like, and therefore to be liked, 2. To meet the standards set for a group and in so doing to spare the trouble of setting standards for oneself.

CONFOUND   To confuse in a manner similar to the definition which follows.

CONFUSE   To confound in a manner similar to the preceding definition.

CONGRATULATE   To express happiness in someone else's successful accomplishment, or, in the case of a marriage, to express hope that it will prove to be a successful accomplishment.

CONGRESS   The entire body of elected legislative officials, representing local and state corporations. 2. A bunch of politicians meeting in Washington, who maintain for themselves a lifestyle designed to insulate them as thoroughly as possible from the major problems they are ostensibly trying to solve.

CONJUGATE   To inflect a verb in one or more tenses, as was done in grade schools back in the days when teachers stressed grammar and students knew what a sentence is.

CONNIPTION   A fit of anger, hysteria, etc., although fits of etc. are rare.

CONNOISSEUR   A person who is specially qualified to state with authority that something stinks. This infers that people who like and enjoy it only do so because they don't known any better and that with time, effort, and proper training, they too could learn to hate it.

CONQUER To shoot first and make treaties later. 2. To demonstrate convincingly the practical purpose and effective application of advanced weapons. 3. To take the first step toward being conquered.

CONQUEST A fiancé, as viewed by a fiancée, or vice versa.

CONQUISTADOR A sixteenth-century Spanish murderer.

CONSCIENCE A sense of what is right and good, which many highly moral people exercise so strenuously on Sunday that they have to give it plenty of rest during the remainder of the week.

CONSECUTION A chain of reasoning, similar to, but not the same as, a rope of logic.

CONSECUTIVE Succeeding one another in a series. 2. Succeeding one another in a series. 3. Succeeding one another in a series.

CONSERVATION Protecting natural resources against unnatural elements, such as stupidity, carelessness and greed.

CONSERVATIONIST One who believes that, whereas the road of progress would be less wide were it not paved with destruction, it would be a lot more scenic. 2. A person who is not impressed by the idea of a synthetic butterfly.

CONSERVATIVE Disposed to leave existing institutions the way they are, with their good and bad aspects, provided that their bad aspects remain among the lower and middle classes where they belong. 2. Comfortable.

CONSPIRACY A plot for an evil purpose involving two or more persons, whose trust in and loyalty to one another are absolute, until one of them is caught.

CONSTIPATION A condition of the bowels which is as unpleasant to experience as a more graphic definition would be to read.

CONSTITUTION The written document which states the principles of government and in the name of which most large-scale unconstitutional acts have been perpetrated.

CONSTRICTOR A long and powerful snake that is so impressive it has a reputation for taking people's breath away.

CONSUMER A person who eats and uses things, as opposed to one who is locked in a box.

CONTAMINATE To build a chemical plant.

CONTEMPT A deep feeling of disgust and disapproval, which some people dislike as much as the cause of it, while others enjoy it immensely, constantly searching for new reasons to feel it, particularly in areas that are readily avoidable and none of their business.

CONTENT At peace with one's limitations; at rest on one's laurels; dreamless.

CONTESTANT A person on a game show who is subject to sudden guttural outbursts and spasmodic seizures.

CONTEXT The verbal field from which misquotes are plucked.

CONTINENT A land mass that is smaller than a hemisphere and larger than a bathysphere.

CONTINUE To keep going. 2. And going. 3. And going. 4. And going.

CONTORTIONIST A sideshow performer who can put his foot in his mouth and get paid for it.

CONTRABAND Anything that is smuggled into a country for the purpose of putting the children of crooked law enforcement officials through college.

CONTRACEPTIVE A device used to prevent the knitting of little booties.

CONTRADICT To forego the vast grey area of truth in search of the thin strips of black and white on the fringes.

CONTRAPUNTAL Absolutely against kicking the ball on fourth down.

CONTRIBUTION A tax deduction in sheep's clothing.

CONTROVERSIAL Relating to or of the nature of some person or some issue that places people in the unpleasant and bothersome position of having to form an opinion.

CONUNDRUM A fantastic kind of riddle, such as "What has three feet, eleven eyes, plays an electric guitar, and swims in the sewer?"

CONVENIENT Suited to reduce one's effort and thereby to increase one's dependence.

CONVENTION A body of delegates, members, or the like, periodically convened for a common purpose, carousing.

CONVERSATION Oral interchange between or among people, primarily reserved for those occasions when there is nothing good on television.

CONVICT A person serving a prison term, during which he is strongly encouraged to adjust to prison life and is rewarded for adjusting by having his sentence reduced, so that by the time he is ready to leave, he is so well adjusted to prison life that he is fully prepared for a return engagement.

CONVINCE To persuade by means of forceful argument, concrete proof, masterful con artistry or, if in a position of superiority, none of the above.

COO To make a sound like a pacifist.

COOK In traditional terms, to prepare food mostly by hand, using a knife, a pan, a spatula, etc. In modern terms, to pulverize food in a processor or to program it in a microwave oven.

COOL Warmer than an ice cube but colder than a serving of peach melba.

COON A contemptuous term for Negro, used by people whose vocabularies are as wanting as their morals.

COP A slang expression for policeman, which is commonly used when referring to one in the third person. However, when actually confronting a policeman on the street, particularly one who has just pulled your car over, most people find it advisable to address him as officer, sir, or your majesty.

COQUETTE A woman who does a great deal of flirting and thereby endeavors to attract the amorous attention of men, although there is some question as to whether those who fall for her flirting are actually men or just very large boys.

CORNER A collection point in the city for empty and half-full beer bottles.

CORNET A tame trumpet.

CORONER A public officer who examines a corpse that has been stabbed, shot, poisoned, run over, and hanged, and launches a thorough investigation to determine whether the person died from unnatural causes.

CORPORAL A noncommissioned officer who is below his sergeant but above his privates, which is an example of military humor.

CORPORATION A tax-sheltered entity dedicated to the proposition that making money is the only worthwhile undertaking in life.

CORRELATION One of twin cousins.

CORRESPONDENT A newsperson stationed in another country, who reports on foreign tragedies and thus comforts the populace back home by assuring them that people in other parts of the world are no better off than they are.

CORRIGIBLE Capable of being reformed, as long as the subject remains outside. Once he goes in the house, he becomes incorrigible and there is little hope.

CORROBORATIVE Tending to confirm; as, the bishop was corroborative.

CORRUPTION Moral cancer, which can be cured if it is diagnosed and treated in its early stages, but once it spreads through an entire individual or organization, all the doctored money in the world can't buy a remedy.

COSMETIC Any preparation which, applied sparingly, makes an attractive person look more attractive, or which, applied liberally, makes an unattractive person look ghastly.

COSMOPOLITAN Equally at home in any country, or equally away from home.

COSMOS The universe conceived as an orderly and harmonious system, due primarily to the lack of government intervention.

COST The amount paid for something, as opposed to what it's really worth.

COTTON A soft, downy substance used in the manufacture of clothing, the Civil War, thread, etc.

COUCH A piece of furniture on which motion picture transactions are finalized. 2. A sofa in a psychiatrist's office on which a patient's body rests while his sub-conscious goes to work.

COUGH To accompany a performing musician from the third row of the balcony, usually out of tempo.

COUNSELOR Someone who is paid to give advice, as opposed to a mother-in-law, who gives it for nothing.

COUNTERATTACK An assault upon a druggist or a clerk who is standing behind the cash register.

COUNTRY A nation, comprised of cities, suburbs and rural areas, which is separated from other nations by natural and man-made boundaries, but united with them in the sense that their governments are all essentially in the same business and only pretend to be different from one another.

COURAGE That quality which enables one to meet opposition and search for a way to live with it. It should not be confused with that quality which enables one to meet opposition and search for a way to destroy it.

COURTESY Being calm and friendly to other people, even when they absolutely insist that you be rude.

COUSIN In childhood, a kid who comes over with his parents to visit and uses your toys. In adulthood, a vaguely recognizable character seen at weddings dancing with his mother.

COW An animal which produces a drink that babies and small children consume in large quantities, until they are old enough to discover that it is non-carbonated and therefore unacceptable.

COWARD Someone who is not afraid to look danger right in the back. 2. A person who weakens under the temptation to use violence in place of reason.

COY Shrinking away with shyness, usually calculated shyness.

CRADLE A small bed, once used for the ignominious practice of torturing babies. According to an old lullaby, a baby was placed in a cradle on a treetop so that when the wind blew the cradle would rock, which caused the bough to break and the cradle to fall, resulting in serious, or even fatal, injury to the baby.

CRAM To stuff the brain with information until it begins to ache, so that learning is clearly associated with pain, the only remedy for which comes after the test is completed, when the painful information can be, and is, forgotten.

CRANIOLOGY The science of the cranium, which has advanced beyond other sciences, mainly because it had a head start.

CRAPPIE A North American fresh-water fish, which gets its name because it tastes terrible.

CRAPS A game of dice, which requires great skill, namely the skill to keep coming up with more money.

CRAYFISH Ghetto lobster.

CRAYON A coloring stick, used mainly by children for drawing on paper or for redecorating an entire house.

CRAZY Insane; too sane; perfectly sane.

CREATE To use one's mind as the computer of one's own ideas, and not merely as a mimeograph machine for the ideas of others. 2. To make anything from something else, with the injection of an idea.

CREATIONISM The theory that man did not evolve but was created by God exactly as he is, in the image of an advanced ape.

CREMATION The act of burning a corpse, and along with it any delusions about the person's continuing physical presence.

CRIBBAGE A game of cards, the chief object of which is to try to find somebody else who wants to play.

CRICKET A game played exclusively by the British, because they are the only ones who seem to have the slightest idea what's going on.

CRIME An act that is against the law and that doesn't pay, unless it is political graft, which is immensely profitable. Not only does the politician make money while in office but, even if he is caught, he returns after a short time in prison to make more money giving lectures and selling books. Other crimes that pay, although usually not as well, are successful robberies and extortions.

CRISIS A crucial situation, the handling of which is the only truly valid test of human strength and weakness.

CRITIC A writer who, on a regular basis, reminds readers of the pitiable fact that most people have to be told what they like. 2. Someone who protects the public from making the awful mistake of liking something that is without merit.

CRITICIZE To keep staring at a field of daisies long enough to spot a weed. 2. To do unto others as you would wish them to do unto others. 3. To pay someone the ultimate compliment of giving him your honest opinion of something he has done, especially when he is being deluged with, or deluded by, false flattery.

CROWN A headpiece worn by a member of royalty to confine the growth of his head and to keep it from becoming too big for his own good. In the past, whenever a royal head did swell in its crown, there was often difficulty removing it, which was a necessary procedure before removing the head.

CRUEL Disposed to cause pain to others, usually with little more than moderate success. It is only when one causes pain to oneself that true cruelty is realized.

CRUMB The portion of the meal traditionally reserved for the hungriest at the table.

CRUSADE A war fought with blessed weapons and sanctified rationalizations.

CRY To weep, either as an expression of sorrow or as part of a scheme.

CRYOGENY The science of freezing people with diseases, so that they can be defrosted and revived when a cure is found, even if that is well into the future, after their families and friends are dead and they are completely disoriented and their money has been drained keeping themselves frozen and they have no jobs and no visible means of paying for further treatment.

CUBIST An artist who uses geometric shapes in his paintings, considering algebraic and trigonometric shapes too radical.

CUISINE Food that sounds fancy and is priced accordingly, although it is important to note that the way a food sounds and the way it tastes are two entirely different things.

CULTIST One who is devoted to a religious sect based upon spiritual goals, such as the spiritual goal of raising money for its spiritual leader, so that he can maintain his mansion, staff his yacht, service his private jet, and see to other spiritual matters.

CULTURE The refinement of taste acquired by paying as much attention to what is cheap and faddish as to what is invaluable and timeless, so that the distinction is continually fresh in the mind and so that those things which are rare and beautiful are cherished all the more.

CUPID The Roman god of love, who flew around shooting arrows at people, possibly as a warning.

CURE A method of treating a disease, which may take years of scientific research to develop, frequently as many years as it took to develop whatever it is that causes the disease.

CURIOSITY A rare disease in cats, commonly thought to be fatal, although there is not a single documented case which proves that it does, in fact, kill the cat.

CURSED Having too little or too much of anything material. 2. Once blessed.

CUSTOMER A person who in the past was always right, but that was before the Shopkeeper Liberation Movement.

CUTE Dainty and adorable and, if spoiled, malicious.

CYNIC   Someone who has discovered that the only way he can be comfortable with his totally self-centered attitude is to convince himself that all people are equally self-centered. This is grossly inaccurate, for actually only three-quarters of all people are totally self-centered.

DABBLE To work at something, but not with enough time or effort to become proficient at it; as, to dabble in suicide.

DACHSHUND A small hound dog that is not very outgoing, preferring instead to keep a low profile.

DACTYLOLOGY The art of communication by signs made with the fingers, common among motorists who are displeased with one another's driving performance.

DAD The result of that process combining the complexities of fatherhood with the simplicity of a child's love.

DAGAN The Babylonian god of the earth, who was responsible for all things that happened on land but who would have nothing to do with occurrences at sea. This caused great confusion among fishermen, who caught their fish at sea but sold them on land and were therefore not sure if they owed their allegiance to the earth god or the sea god. Such religious turmoil eventually led to the downfall of the Babylonian empire.

DAGGER A short weapon which is specially suited for stabbing people at close range, because it can be concealed until the moment of attack. Another advantage of this weapon is that, when the victim is stabbed in the back, there is often no protrusion whatsoever in the front, thus permitting the victim to appear at his wake in the same suit in which he was stabbed.

DAIRY A place where butter is converted from milk into a luxury item.

DAMN A socially acceptable curse word and one of the few that is allowed to be said on television. The others are "gosh" and "golly."

DAMNATION An entire country that is surrounded by water barriers.

DAMNED Doomed to eternally unbearable punishment, such as being forced to watch an endless series of detergent commercials.

DAMON A Sicilian, who became known for his great bravery by offering his life in return for that of his friend, Pythias, who was condemned to die. The king, however, decided that Damon's life was not worth as much, and he agreed to the deal only after Damon had thrown in the lives of his neighbor, Marcello, and his two pet sheep.

DAMSEL A maiden who pretends to be in distress so that her knight in shining armor can pretend to save her and the two of them can pretend to live happily ever after.

DANCE To move one's feet in such a way as to avoid crushing one's partner's feet.

DANDY One who is dressed to kill, or if not to kill, at least to make very sick.

DANGER The middle name of secret agents, undercover police, and people who ride subways at night. 2. Exposure to human beings, generally speaking.

DANGEROUS Blonde, beautiful, and under sixteen.

DANK Requiring a fresh diaper.

DAPHNE A mythological nymph, who was pursued by Apollo but escaped by transforming herself into a laurel tree. Unfortunately, however, before she could transform herself back into a nymph, a woodsman chopped her down and used her for firewood.

DAREDEVIL Someone who has a sense of adventure, a sense of boldness, a sense of daring—every kind of sense except common sense.

DARK Suitably lit for a mugging.

DARLING   A term of endearment that is whispered softly into the ear of a man who is about to be hustled. 2. Any little child who comes into your home and leaves without breaking anything or throwing up on the carpet.

DARTS   A game which is learned very quickly, particularly by clumsy people, who are usually the first ones to get the point.

DASHBOARD   The part of a car that most people use in place of a seatbelt to restrain their bodies during a collision. It is very effective in keeping the torso from following the head through the windshield.

DASTARD   The very lowest type of coward, who sneakingly performs malicious deeds and who is considered unfit for the company of respectable cowards.

DATE   A social engagement between a man and a woman, during which the man pretends not to be overly eager to turn the occasion into a sexual encounter and the woman pretends to have other things on her mind.

DAUGHTER   A female member of a family, who has her mother's mouth, her father's eyes, and her brother's teeth marks on her arm.

DAWDLE   To work for the government.

DAY   A division of life, which seems very short to those who are enjoying themselves and very long to those who are not, thus seemingly expanding the lives of unhappy people, which is something that happy people wish they could do, and proving that there is justice in the world, after all. 2. The same as night, except that the sleeping is done with the eyes open. 3. The period of time in which Rome wasn't built.

DEAD   Unable to put off anything else until tomorrow. 2. Free at last from the doctor's instructions.

DEAF   Incapable of hearing anything. 2. Capable of hearing only what one wants to hear.

DEATH   The ultimate certainty of life, as well as the ultimate uncertainty.

DEBATE To argue both sides of an issue, in an effort to completely bewilder the minds of those who have not formed an opinion yet and to firmly close the minds of those who have.

DEBAUCHERY Sincere and extended effort to contract a social disease.

DEBT A type of enslavement that most people enter at a young age and in which they remain for the greater part of their lives, slowly cutting through their shackles with monthly installments.

DEBTOR One who, indirectly, works for the bank.

DEBUNK To burn history books.

DEBUTANTE Someone making her entrance into society, evidently having lived in a cave for the earlier part of her life.

DECADE The length of time it takes to buy three cars and to pay for two of them. 2. A group of years, such as the 70's, which fabricates its identity by resurrecting another group of years, such as the 50's. 3. A period of 120 electric bills.

DECADENCE A serious retrogression in arts or letters, marked by widespread crazes of nostalgia and the deification of dead rock stars.

DECALCOMANIA An excessive and uncontrollable desire for decals, especially the ones that come with model car kits.

DECAPITATE To employ the most extreme method of relieving a migraine.

DECARBONATE To fill a cup of soda with so much ice that it loses its fizz and tastes just like a soda from a fast food restaurant.

DECATHLON An Olympic contest, generally considered to be the most demanding, because the winner not only has to compete in ten events but he also has to make at least as many commercials when the Olympics are over.

DECEDENT A legally dead person, as opposed to an illegally dead person, such as one who died while going through a stop sign.

DECEIVE   To cheat or mislead another person or persons and, in so doing, to establish a foundation for mistrusting everyone, because of their possible likeness to oneself.

DECEMBER   National Splurge Month, when people are given new wallets for Christmas but don't have anything to put in them.

DECENCY   The belief that any personal gain which entails the undermining of another human being carries with it too great a corresponding personal loss. 2. The attitude that doing something right is its own reward, no matter how much one is taught that it must also be profitable. 3. Treating other people as co-workers struggling toward a common goal rather than as obstacles blocking the way to individual success.

DECENTRALIZE   To broaden the base of bureaucratic inefficiency.

DECISIVE   Possessing the ability to make decisions, which is an ability that is shared by many people who have to decide what others will do but by few who have to decide what they themselves will do.

DECLARANT   One who makes declarations, especially cake declarations for weddings and birthdays.

DECLINE   To turn down an invitation politely, as though you really would have wanted to go if you could.

DECLINOMETER   An instrument to measure the credibility of a person's excuse not to attend a social function.

DECODE   To translate a teen-ager's slang into English. 2. To take the big words that researchers and technicians invent to make what they're doing sound important and reduce them into language that can be understood.

DECOMPOSE   To destroy music that one has just written.

DECOY   Anything intended to lead into a trap or snare. Commonly, perfume.

DECREPIT   Worn out and broken down, as the average car is by the time it's paid for.

DECRESCENDO   An obsolete musical term, indicating a diminishing in volume, which was used in a time when music was not consistently ear-splitting.

DECRY   To discredit publicly, resulting often in the offended party filing a slander suit, which may lead to the decrier filing a counter suit, so that the initial incident becomes lost in a maze of legal drivel which drags on for months and the only people who really benefit from the situation, as usual, are the lawyers.

DEDICATE   To devote to sacred uses, such as playing bingo.

DEDUCTION   The process of taking known or assumed information, exposing it to the mental faculties, and drawing a conclusion from it. In political legislation, the process has been expedited by the exclusion of its second phase.

DEED   That which is accomplished by closing your mouth and opening your tool box. 2. Something for idlers to criticize.

DEEP   Extending between 46 and 981 feet below the surface of the ground or water.

DEEPER   Extending between 981 and 3,762 feet below the surface of the ground or water.

DEEPEST   Extending between 3,762 and 8,513 feet below the surface of the ground or water. Anything below that doesn't count.

DEER   An animal which is too beautiful for words, and so it is shot.

DEFACED   Made as ugly as the person or persons who destroyed it.

DEFEATISM   The attitude that, just because your football team is losing 42 to 0 with a minute left to play, there is no chance they can pull out the game.

DEFECTION   The desertion of writers and ballet dancers from one country to another, the reason they give being artistic freedom, although the money isn't bad, either.

DEFECTIVE   Designed to keep repairmen in business. 2. Recalled to the factory for adjustment, seldom before somebody has been killed or seriously injured.

DEFENCE   The British spelling of defense, which they perpetuate only to be obstinate.

DEFENDANT   Someone who is on trial, either because he committed a crime or because no one more suspicious could be located. 2. A person who is as innocent or as guilty as his lawyer is skillful.

DEFICIENT   Lacking some necessary element, as in a humorous definition that lacks humor.

DEFICIT   The normal operating status of a city, state or federal budget which is controlled by government officials who have an extraordinary knack for stretching a dollar into three quarters.

DEFILE   To remove all of the records from an office.

DEFINITION   The meaning or meanings of a word, set forth in clear and precise language, so that even the most confusing words are understandable and consequently no longer confusing, except to people who are confused by clear and precise language, which people are very difficult to define clearly and precisely because they are so confused, and therefore confusing, that they cannot be made understandable, and therefore understood, at least not in the same sense that the words which confuse them can be.

DEFLATED   Having exhausted one's supply of tall tales, fishing stories, or party jokes.

DEFOLIATE   To strip of leaves, which is what a drill sergeant may decide to do as a punishment if his men are particularly uncooperative.

DEFOREST   To make way for the natural beauty of concrete.

DEFROST   To get her away from the bar and onto the dance floor.

DEGENERATE   One who smokes and drinks beer at fifteen when his father did not do these things until he was sixteen.

DEHORN   To satisfy completely someone's sexual desires.

DEIANIRA   The wife of Hercules, who had a terrible time in the kitchen because he kept bringing home dead lions and bulls that he had killed and expecting her to clean them.

DEIFY To enroll among the gods. In ancient times, application forms were available at all Greek and Roman post offices, but this practice was discontinued after they realized that they had too many gods and not enough temples.

DEITY One of the gods or goddesses, all of whom are immortal, which is a shame because many of them would give anything for a big funeral.

DELATE To inform against someone who has committed an offense, such as the offense of informing against someone.

DELEGATION A group of people at a political convention who are so drunk that they need a sign to remind them what state they're from.

DELICATESSEN A store which specializes in cold sandwiches, cold beer, and warm people.

DELICIOUS Good enough to be compared with your mother's left-overs.

DELILAH The woman who got Samson to cut his hair. She is the patroness of all mothers with teen-age sons.

DELIRIUM A state of mental disturbance, characterized by confusion, disordered speech, hallucinations, and a growing conviction that you may have had one too many.

DELIVERY A free service for devotees of warm pizza.

DELUSION State of confusing fantasy with reality, common in people with vivid imaginations, as opposed to people with little or no imagination, who have nothing to confuse with reality except reality itself.

DEMAGOGUE Someone who takes advantage of social discontent by leading an opposition movement, so that he can gain political power and thereby create his own brand of social discontent.

DEMAND To lay aside courtesy in order to demonstrate authority. 2. To yell and scream and curse and refuse to budge until you get what's coming to you, having gotten nowhere by repeatedly asking politely.

DEMENTED   More insane than the average hotel employee but less insane than the guy who does the local TV weather report.

DEMENTIA   A condition of deteriorated mentality, marked by an irrational willingness to pay an outrageous fee to a psychiatrist.

DEMIGOD   A semidivine being, who differs from a divine being in the sense that he can only make half of a rock so heavy that he himself can't lift it.

DEMIJOHN   Half of a bathroom.

DEMILITARIZE   To come to their collective senses.

DEMIMONDE   Women of doubtful reputation, which is to say that no one is really sure if they are truly wicked or if they only appear to be wicked. There is no doubt, however, about the wickedness of those who sit in judgment of them.

DEMOCRACY   Government in which the people have the power to select those who control them.

DEMONIAC   One supposedly possessed by an evil spirit, although the evil spirit is just as likely to be found in the one doing the supposing.

DEMONOLOGY   The study of demons, which requires constant vigilance because they could turn up practically anywhere, including the supermarket or the laundromat. Even when they are located, research is greatly hampered by the fact that the vast majority of them stubbornly refuse to be interviewed.

DEMONSTRATION   A free concert where they sell buttons.

DEMURE   Grave; serious; mysteriously blinded to the essential absurdity of life.

DENDRIFORM   Resembling a tree, or a basketball player, in structure.

DENOUEMENT   The final resolution of a plot, which occurs in the average paperback novel at the point when the reader says to himself, "And I blew $3.50 for *this?*"

DENT A minor setback on the road to mastering parallel parking. 2. A term used by a wife to describe to her husband the amount of damage done to the car when she plowed it into a fire plug.

DENTIST A person who is justified in charging very high fees because he is expected to perform two jobs at the same time. His patients pay him not only to treat their teeth but also to frighten them.

DEODORANT A substance which protects people against offensive body odors but which also forces them to accept the fact that others are avoiding them strictly because of their personalities.

DEPARTMENT A division of government headed by a Cabinet member, which is established to keep specialized paper shufflers shuffling specialized papers and to maintain strict control of misappropriations.

DEPLORABLE Wretched enough to be pitied but not wretched enough to be corrected; as, the living conditions in that part of the city are deplorable.

DEPOLARIZE To rid an area of all Arctic bears.

DEPRESSION State or condition of dejection brought on by the sustained belief that things are as bad as they appear to be or that life is as meaningless as everyone tries to pretend it isn't.

DERANGED Left with nothing on which to cook. 2. Driven insane, by having nothing on which to cook.

DERMATOLOGY The science of blackheads.

DESENSITIZE To render an audience so numb to the hypnotizing effects of television that, compared with what they see on the screen, what they see on the street becomes a second-rate version of reality.

DESIRABLE Having good looks, a well-developed body, an interesting mind, an exceptional talent, or, if none of these, money.

DESPAIR To think that all is lost and that there will be no tomorrow. 2. To forget what happened the last time you thought that all was lost and that there would be no tomorrow.

DESSERT   The part of the meal that comes at the end and ends up in the middle.

DESTINY   That phenomenon which explains why the rich get richer and the poor get poorer.

DESTROY   To help insure that the world does not become hopelessly overrun with beautiful things.

DESTRUCTIONIST   Someone who feels a great surge of pleasure and power from destroying, the way a child will step on an insect.

DETECTIVE   A person regularly depicted in movies and on television, who is trained to search for clues and to solve mysteries, especially the mystery of why there always seems to be a beautiful woman involved in every murder and why she is always irresistably attracted to the detective.

DETENTION   A form of punishment in most high schools, which involves sitting in a room after class and developing an extra-curricular activity, that being a deep-seated hatred for everything that education represents.

DETESTABLE   Interesting and attractive enough to arouse intense antipathy.

DETRACTION   The act of sliding around and not being able to get a firm grip on the road.

DEUCE   A playing card which suffers from severe temper tantrums. Some card players go so far as to say, unconditionally, that deuces are wild.

DEUS VULT   The rallying cry of the First Crusade, meaning God wills it, which assumes, of course, that God was in the mood at the time for wholesale killing, raping, and plundering.

DEVIL   An evil spirit, whose chief job is to provide religious people with a feeling of smugness about their beliefs. 2. An evil spirit, who is wise enough to recognize that, as long as the good remain complacent, evil will take care of itself. 3. The chief soul recruiter and procurator of Hell, who will occasionally make special arrangements to buy a soul outright, but who generally prefers the lay away plan.

DEVOUT More concerned with divine service, which is performed out of the spotlight, than in splendid displays of religious fervor, which serve no one except the displayer.

DEXTERITY Quickness in using one's hands; as, she began to regret the dinner when she realized his dexterity.

DIABOLISM Demonic possession or, in cases when the Devil is not planning to stay very long, demonic leasing.

DIACRITIC Part of the motto of theater and movie reviewers: "To live a critic is to diacritic."

DIAGNOSTICIAN One who is an expert at guessing what's wrong with people.

DIAMOND A girl's best friend, often replacing the person who gave it to her.

DIAPER The one container which is useful only when it's empty.

DIAPHANOUS Pertaining to a fine, delicate material from which traps are made, commonly in the form of nightgowns.

DIARY A first-person soap opera; self-gossip.

DICE Small cubes with numbers on them, which are used both in games played by small children and in games played by adults with the common sense of small children.

DICTATION That which a secretary writes down when summoned to her boss's office, which usually includes everything he says, except for the things he says after he gets up and locks the door.

DICTIONARY A book in which words or terms are arranged alphabetically and defined; as, the dictionary I am presently reading is absolutely fascinating and enjoyable.

DIDACTICS The art of teaching, as distinguished from the art of cramming information into the heads of students.

DIE To end life as one had begun it, alone and with nothing certain. 2. To enter into a heavenly delight or a grave disappointment.

DIEHARD Someone who drowns in a vat of cement.

DIFFERENT   Threatening.

DIG   To understand something in a way that it is assumed an insurance salesman could never understand it.

DIGESTION   The process of breaking down food chemically and distributing all harmful ingredients to the places in the body where they can do the most damage.

DIGNIFIED   Marked by holding one's head very high, often higher than the sum of one's qualities.

DIGNITARY   One in a position of high rank and honor, as in the church, where humility and abstaining from desires for prestige and power are viewed as virtues.

DIGRESS   To speak or write in the manner of a politician answering a question.

DILEMMA   A situation which involves choosing between equally unpleasant alternatives, such as staying up all night with a toothache hoping it will go away by itself or picking up the telephone and calling the dentist.

DIMMER   A device used to lower a light's brightness and a woman's resistance.

DIMWIT   A person who keeps two sets of keys, so that there is always a set locked inside the house in case the other set gets locked inside the car.

DINER   A restaurant where you can order pancakes at three o'clock in the afternoon and a hamburger at three o'clock in the morning. 2. A hungry insomniac's greatest blessing.

DINNER   The meal with vegetables in it.

DINOSAUR   Any of a group of prehistoric reptiles that somehow managed, without man's help, to become extinct.

DIP   A substance in a bowl, which hosts and hostesses at parties are forever encouraging their guests to try, often with great pride and enthusiasm, as though mixing a packet of dried onion soup with some sour cream were a crowning achievement.

DIPLOMA   A document of completion from an educational institution which is sometimes hung on the wall, particularly by graduates who have found a job and can afford a frame.

DIPLOMAT   One who is skilled in the art of international double talk.

DIPTEROUS   Having two wings, such as a bird, a fly, or a small hospital.

DIRECTOR   A person with the amazing ability to take a movie with a five million dollar budget and, through the magic of cinematography, turn it into a movie with a ten million dollar budget.

DIRT   A boy's make-up.

DIS   The Roman god of the underworld, who is represented as smoking a big cigar, wearing a striped suit with wide lapels, and packing a .38.

DISAPPOINTED   Having set unrealistic expectations and gotten realistic results. 2. Having set realistic expectations and gotten realistic results.

DISARM   To take hold of someone's hand and twist it clockwise forcefully and continuously until the entire limb snaps off just below the shoulder blade.

DISASTER   A sudden and terrible calamity, such as a plane crash, a hurricane or an earthquake, designed by God for a twofold purpose: to encourage people to buy insurance and to provide the major networks with an opening news story.

DISBAR   To expel an attorney from the bar, usually after he tries to pick a fight with one of the regulars.

DISBELIEVE   Not to believe someone else's story, often because it sounds too much like one of your own.

DISCIPLE   A follower of some individual or school of thought, who tends to believe more in what he is told than he does in his own brain.

DISCONTENT   Dissatisfied with the way things are and prone to be dissatisfied no matter how things get.

DISCOUNT   A reduction in the price of a produce or service, sometimes so drastic that the thing ends up actually costing what it is worth.

DISCOURTEOUS   Making people feel at home, provided that their home is a zoo. 2. Behaving toward others in a manner that mirrors one's incivility toward oneself.

DISCURSIVE   Passing rapidly from one subject to another, which is the only way that most royalty find they can meet everybody at a party.

DISCUSS   To examine by argument, for the purpose of making someone with a differing viewpoint acknowledge and understand why he is wrong or, if he continues to hold the same viewpoint after a reasonable period of argument, to prove that he is obviously stupid and close-minded.

DISENCHANTMENT   The act of growing up and exchanging one's imagination for a firm grip on reality.

DISFIGURE   To eat an entire box of chocolates at one sitting.

DISGRACEFUL   Shameful and dishonorable enough to provide lively conversation at the next cocktail party.

DISGUISE   That which conceals and which is employed as a social necessity to insure that nobody ever makes the costly mistake of really knowing, or being known by, anybody else.

DISHONEST   Disposed to lie, cheat, steal, sell used cars, etc.

DISINHERITANCE   The exclusion of an heir from inheritance, which can really be a nasty trick, especially if the heir put a great deal of effort into showing emotion at the funeral.

DISLOYAL   Skilled in the amazing technique of smiling in the face while stabbing in the back.

DISOBEY   To risk a punishment by refusing to do what you are told in favor of what you want to do, assuming that what you want to do does not provide a punishment in and of itself.

DISPARAGER   One who brings reproach or discredit upon others, but who demonstrates that there are no hard feelings by attending the same church as they every Sunday.

DISPOSABLE   Designed to be thrown on the sidewalk or tossed from the window of a moving car.

DISPOSE   To turn one's head away from a camera.

DISQUALIFIED   Prevented from taking part in a sporting event, often for a silly reason; as, he was disqualified from the diving competition because he refused to jump in the water.

DISSATISFACTION   The inevitably unhappy result of expecting anything in reality ever to match anything in one's imagining.

DISSIDENT   One who disagrees, particularly with the way his teeth were fixed.

DISSOLVE   To break up an assembly or organization, either with a joke or a little skit.

DISSONANCE   Torturous tones; the musical rack; Mozart played backwards and upside down.

DISTANCE   That which forces friends and lovers of limited means into the position of having to write letters, a task so dreaded and requiring such monumental effort and sacrifice that most relationships do not survive it.

DISTICH   A rhyming couplet, simply put,
Distinguished by its metered foot.

DISTINCTIVE   Regarding one's own taste, as opposed to the tastes of one's neighbors.

DISTRUSTFUL   Suspicious and doubtful of others, based upon having been cheated, lied to and betrayed, usually by the age of three.

DITHEISM   The belief in two supreme gods who share everything equally, including bathroom facilities. 2. The belief in one supreme god and one almost supreme god, who share everything equally, except that the supreme god always gets to use the bathroom first.

DITTO   A symbol used to avoid the following: A symbol used to avoid the following: A symbol used to avoid the following: etc.

DIVE The act of plunging into water or falling onto canvas; as, Sonny took a dive (onto canvas) so that Big Al and his boys wouldn't tie chains around him and plunge him (into water).

DIVERSITY Two institutions of higher education put together.

DIVORCE The legal termination of a marriage that was made in limbo. 2. The complicated procedure of deciding who gets the color television set. 3. The death of love and the birth of resentment.

DIXIE That section of the United States where people are slow on their feet but quick on the drawl.

DO To stop talking about it.

DOCILE Readily trained or, if cheaper, trucked.

DOCTOR A person licensed to practice golf.

DOCUMENTARY A type of television program most noted for its high informational content and its small audience.

DOG A hairy, tail-wagging reception committee. 2. The only member of the family who will drop everything and come running to the door the moment he hears your voice.

DOGMA A system of tenets set down by a church for the convenience of its members, so that they will know exactly what to believe and how to believe it, without any bothersome questions.

DOLLAR A prophetically grim portrait of George Washington.

DOLPHIN A large marine mammal which at one time emerged onto land but which returned to the sea, having determined that any living environment that depends on mass transit systems is no place for intelligent creatures.

DOMINANT Pertaining to a person who is inherently insecure and who therefore seeks to maintain a strong self-image by exercising authority over someone who is either physically or emotionally incapable of challenging that authority.

DOMINATE To use one's power and influence to control others rather than to uplift them.

DOOMSDAY The day at the end of the world when all men will be judged, and it is believed that even corporate lawyers won't be able to intercede.

DOOR The heavily bolted barrier at the front or back of a house which keeps the crime out and the paranoia in.

DORMITORY The building on a college campus for live-in students, on every floor of which the student with the most putrid musical taste gets to play his radio the loudest.

DOUBLE A drink with twice the potential of getting her back to your apartment.

DOWAGER A woman whose good fortune began when her husband's ended.

DOZEN A contraction, in some states, of does not; as, he dozen come around here much anymore.

DRAFT A system of selection for military service, with exemptions designed to guarantee that the sons of the men who start wars will not have to fight in them.

DRAGON One of the legendary monsters thought by some to have survived on a steady diet of onions, garlic and chili peppers. It's no wonder they breathed fire.

DRESS A garment worn by women when their jeans are in the washer and their suits are all at the cleaners.

DRILL A tool that is used to put guests to sleep; as, to bore with a drill. 2. An exercise in military marching, intended to teach soldiers the difference between their left shoulders and their right shoulders. 3. A baboon of western Africa that can be trained for small parts in movies; hence, a drill bit.

DRIVE-IN An inexpensive outdoor motel featuring movies.

DROP A quantity of liquid large enough for an ant to drown in but too small for it to go boating.

DROWSE To attend a recital by your cousin who, according to your aunt, is a child prodigy if there ever was one.

DRUG One of innumerable chemical substances created to counteract the effects of being alive.

DRUM An instrument that makes music or a headache, depending upon who's playing it.

DRUNKARD A person who eventually ends up behind bars, having spent too much time inside them.

DUB To change the voices of the actors in a foreign movie so that they sound like they come from a foreign planet.

DUBIOUS Pertaining to the attitudes of two people conducting a transaction, each suspecting the other person to be as dishonest as he suspects himself to be.

DULL Applying to the people at a party, especially those who go home complaining about what a dull party it was. 2. Boring, but only as boring as people allow it to be.

DUMMY A wooden puppet that only speaks when spoken through.

DUST A finely powdered substance, used by many bachelors as a protective coating for furniture.

DWARF A person who is as small in size as a person who makes fun of him is in intelligence.

DYNAMOMETER A device for measuring the power of a mother.

EAGER   Spirited, keenly desirous, and usually pursuing someone else's job.

EAR   The organ of hearing, which in some people is directly connected to the mouth, so that what is heard from one person is repeated immediately to another person, without benefit of passing through the brain.

EARTH   The only planet in the universe known to support life. 2. The only planet in the universe known to support death.

EARTHQUAKE   A violent movement along the earth's surface, which cannot be blamed on celestial influences, for it is purely the earth's own fault.

EAST   Proceeding toward the direction in which the sun rises, although if one continues to proceed in this direction for a long enough distance, one will arrive at a point to the west of one's origin, a fact which remains one of the world's oldest mysteries.

EASTER   An annual holiday to celebrate the resurrection of candy manufacturers.

EASY   Difficult to appreciate. 2. Providing one with a false sense of accomplishment. 3. Long on immediate gratification but short on lasting pleasure.

EATING   An activity which provides enjoyment and satisfaction to those people in the world who do not happen to be starving and mere sustenance to those who do.

ECCENTRIC   Strange, but not as strange as normal.

ECHO AAA repititionrepetitionrepetition ofofof soundsound-sound.

ECLIPSE The phenomenon which occurs when the moon blocks the sun from the earth, called solar, or the earth blocks the sun from the moon, called lunar. Of the two, solar eclipses are more popular because they are the ones that cause blindness.

ECOLOGY Nature versus everybody.

ECONOMIST One who speaks with complete authority about the absolute uncertainty of the economy.

ECTOPLASM Any of a variety of gimmicks used by mediums to mystify and rob a gullible client.

EDEN The garden where Adam and Eve lived until they started having kids and decided that they needed a place with a yard.

EDUCATION An ongoing process of discovery and rediscovery, questioning and more questioning. 2. Searching for answers to questions, not having them given to you.

EERIE Weird and frightening, like the sound of laughter in a bank.

EFFEMINATE Pertaining to a male who is unwilling or unable to compete with other males in drinking, gambling, or abusing women. 2. Unafraid of softness and repulsed by brutality.

EFFORT A vigorous attempt to accomplish something, which is in itself an accomplishment that even failure cannot negate.

EGG Something which is laid by a hen that is producing or by a comedian that is not. 2. Something which a kid throws at a bus window when a tomato is unavailable. 3. Something that breaks and runs all over the box of macaroni on the way home from the supermarket.

EGO The self of a person, in its most basic, confusing and unknowable sense, as distinguished from the self of another person, in its most basic, confusing and unknowable sense.

EGOCENTRIC Placing oneself at the center of all things, where there is a vast emptiness and silence, as in the eye of a hurricane.

EGOISM   Selfishness in its purest state, without a trace of the common flaws found in everyday selfishness, such as concern or sentimentality.

EGOTIST   An overwhelmingly great and terrific person, who absolutely dreads going to parties where he is forced to spend hours on end entertaining and delighting an assortment of boring and cumbersome people by telling them how great and terrific he is.

EIGHT   The age when children start becoming awkward, a condition which generally corrects itself by the time they are forty.

EKATERINOSLAV   The former name of Dnepropetrovsk, which was changed because Dnepropetrovsk is easier to pronounce than Ekaterinoslav.

ELBOWROOM   That space which the person sitting next to you in a movie theater seems intent upon depriving you of.

ELDERBERRY   The berry with seniority.

ELECTION   A process involving two or more candidates, each of whom spends enormous amounts of money on a campaign in which each promises to cut expenses if elected. 2. Choosing the person least likely to be indicted by a Grand Jury.

ELECTRICIAN   A man who spares you the danger of getting shocked, until he sends you his bill.

ELECTRON   An extremely small particle, so tiny that an average-size person could sit on six billion of them and barely know it.

ELEMENTARY   The lowest school of formal education, where students are taught the basic skills that will enable most of them to make it through high school without being able to read or write properly.

ELEPHANT   A huge animal known to be frightened of rodents, especially those carrying high-powered rifles.

ELEVATOR   A mechanical device that can transport people within seconds from the first floor of a building to the twentieth floor, while leaving their stomachs at the nineteenth.

ELEVEN   The first number not used in a countdown.

ELF An imaginary being that is said to resemble a very small person wearing mountaineer's clothing, although most of the world's foremost authorities on imaginary beings are kept too sedated to give a precise description.

ELLIPSIS The omission of a . . . or words from a sentence.

ELM The name of a street with typical, wholesome families living on it.

ELOCUTION The art of putting an assemblage of people to sleep with style.

ELOPEMENT The act of getting married without plunging the bride's father into debt.

ELSE The unknown and tacitly ominous option presented to children by their parents; as, finish your vegetables or else.

ELYSIUM The paradise of Greek mythology, where the blessed persons go after death and get to spend eternity with the dozen or so other blessed persons.

EMANCIPATION The process of transposing people from slaves' quarters to slums.

EMBALM To pump a dead body full of drugs or chemicals so that it will take longer to rot, a thought which is a great comfort to the bereaved, as well as to the embalmer.

EMBEZZLER A person who believes strongly in justice, and it is certainly only just that his boss should have to pay the price for hiring a thief.

EMBRYO A baby fetus.

EMBRYOGENY The scientific study of embryos and the causes of their immature behavior.

EMCEE Another way of saying M. C., meaning master of ceremonies, for people who have trouble pronouncing M. C.

EMERALD A very precious gem of a deep-green color, roughly the same color as it causes people who see someone wearing one to become.

EMERGENCY   An urgent incident which provides the people involved with the rare opportunity to discover what they really believe in, what they really cherish, and who they really are.

EMETIC   Inducing vomit, as a medicinal substance or the dialogue on most television shows.

EMIGRANT   One who leaves his native country to go to a country where he hopes there aren't any natives.

EMOTIONS   Deep inner feelings, which men are taught to repress and women to exploit.

EMPATHY   A perceptive understanding of what another person is feeling, or what one thinks another person is feeling, or what one thinks another person may be feeling, or what one thinks another person thinks he may be feeling, etc.

EMPHATIC   *STRONGLY EXPRESSIVE!!!*

EMPLOYEE   An overworked and underpaid person, who works for an overpaid and unappreciative boss.

EMPLOYER   An overworked and unappreciated person, who has overpaid and underworked people working for him.

EMPTY   Completely full of nothing so that nothing more can possibly fit inside, except for something.

EMULATE   To look up to someone with the hope of someday being able to look down on him. 2. To look up to someone with the hope of someday being able, not having, to look up or down.

ENCHANTRESS   A woman who can cast a spell over a man's mind and, if he's not careful, over his bank account.

ENCORE   A song or instrumental which follows a well-received performance, as a means whereby the performer may reward the audience for its impeccable taste.

ENCYCLOPEDIA   A series of thick, heavy books which contribute greatly to the education of students and to the medical research of hernias, specifically the kind suffered by salesmen lugging thick, heavy books from door to door.

END The part of an hour movie that comes sixty minutes into it. 2. A football player who hits the bottle regularly; hence, a tight end.

ENDING The beginning of something else.

ENDOGAMY Marriage strictly within one's tribe or social class, a practice among certain primitive peoples, such as bankers.

ENDORSEMENT The recommendation of a product by a celebrity, who believes so much in the quality of the product that he refuses to accept more than a hundred thousand dollars for recommending it.

ENDURANCE The act of overcoming by undergoing.

ENEMY One who prefers the simplicity of hatred to the complexity of understanding.

ENGINE In scientific terms, the part of a car that makes the wheels go around.

ENIGMA Something that is puzzling, either in the sense that it does not make any sense or in the sense that it does not seem to make any sense, either in the sense that it will seem to make sense if one seems to understand or in the sense that it will actually make sense if one actually understands; as, this definition is an enigma.

ENIGMATIC At least as puzzling as the above definition and three times as puzzling as this definition; as, there is something enigmatic about both of these definitions, but whatever it is is an enigma.

ENJOY To experience pleasure, particularly the kind that will not cause regret or require an apology at a later time.

ENLIVEN To get things going, especially at a party, banquet or other occasion, thereby running the risk of becoming what is known in social circles as a fun person, a title which carries with it the responsibility for getting things going at future parties, banquets or other occasions.

ENMITY A feeling of ill-will, based upon the fear that the people of a "hostile" country are as wicked, ruthless and untrustworthy as they have been told the people of one's own country are.

ENORMOUS Texan.

ENOUGH One more than the doctor says you should have and one less than you want.

ENSNARE To capture in a drum.

ENTERPRISING Showing a bold and adventurous spirit, as when you are embarking on a project. 2. Showing a ruthless and undermining determination, as when someone else is embarking on a similar project.

ENTERTAIN To amuse people in a way that diverts them from their problems, from which they would not require diverting if they spent more time being amusing themselves and less time worrying about their problems.

ENTHUSIASM An inspired attitude, which is a primary ingredient in getting a difficult task accomplished and which acts as a buffer against the realistic point of view.

ENTOMOLOGY The science of insects, which seeks to explain why they stubbornly insist upon surviving when the overwhelming evidence indicates that they are nothing but pests with no socially redeeming qualities, other than the fact that some people find amusement in pulling their legs off.

ENUNCIATE To speak in such a way as to be misunderstood clearly.

ENVY The cornerstone of the free enterprise system. 2. The thing that turns an innocent desire into a compulsive need.

EOS The Greek goddess of dawn, who was the only immortal who never got to sleep in. She is best known as the patroness of insomniacs and milkmen.

EPAULET A comical-looking shoulder ornament, originally designed to be worn by clowns in the circus, but adapted for use on military uniforms, evidently as a practical joke of some sort.

EPIC A poem with a hero in it or, if not a hero, at least a corned beef sandwich.

EPICURE A remedy for heroic poetry.

EPIDEMIC An unarrested spread of something, such as ignorance.

EPIGRAM A one-bite feast for the mind.

EPITAPH Words inscribed on a tombstone, such as those at the famous grave site of Lucius Pitt: "What God has joined together let no man put asunder, and so I will not rest in peace until my wife is six feet under."

EPIZOOTIC Pertaining to something that is harmful to many animals at the same time, as a duck hunter with a machine gun.

EQUALITY A condition which, among humans, is equally as undesirable as the extreme of its opposite.

EQUATOR An imaginary line encircling an imaginary planet in an imaginary solar system in an imaginary universe.

EQUESTRIAN Pertaining to burgers served in fast-food restaurants.

EQUIVOCAL Having two or more meanings; ideal for use in a political speech.

EQUIVOQUE An ambiguous term, such as Calvin Coolidge's second.

ERADICATOR Someone whose religious or political beliefs dictate that a group of people must be destroyed, presumably in order to make the world a better place to live in.

EREBUS The place of dark foreboding through which the dead pass on their way to Hades. It is said to resemble the hallway leading to the dentist's chair.

EROGENOUS Pertaining to various zones on the human body which are either highly responsive to sexual stimulation, known as torrid zones, moderately responsive to sexual stimulation, known as temperate zones, or not responsive at all to sexual stimulation, known as frigid zones.

EROS The Greek god of love, not as popular as Cupid, except among makers of crossword puzzles.

ERROR A blunder, which every person makes, because to err is human, but which few people forgive, because to forgive is divine.

ERUDITE Possessing a great deal of knowledge from many books, often so much knowledge that there is little room left for wisdom.

ESCAPISM Any attempt (through movies, music, etc.) to protect the mind from becoming hopelessly addicted to reality.

ESCHATOLOGY The branch of theology dealing with death and the various concepts of heaven, such as the concept that heaven is the freedom from theological speculation.

ESKIMO A frozen Indian.

ESPERANTO An artificial language, ideal for use at cocktail parties or other occasions where people talk artificially.

ESPIONAGE The practice of wearing a trench coat inconspicuously.

ESSAY A literary work of an analytical nature, the purpose of which is entirely dependent upon the writer. Some writers attempt to entertain and arouse their readers, as well as to inform and edify them, while other writers steadfastly maintain a single purpose, to help their readers to develop a deep and abiding lack of interest in the subject.

ESTABLISHMENT All of the people in a society who forego the responsibility of establishing their own values and adopt those established by others. This includes people whose idea of being anti-establishment is reading underground newspapers and attending a protest rally once a month.

ESTIMATE What a simple repair job is going to cost before the unforeseen complications.

ESTOVERS Necessaries allowed by law, as heat to a tenant, alimony to a wife, excessive fees to a lawyer, etc.

ETERNITY Twice the amount of time it takes for a commencement speech to end.

ETHICS Moral principles, which are observed by most people and given special attention by public officials, who must be particularly careful when violating them, due to the fact that they generally cannot be twisted as easily as the law.

ETHNIC   A type of joke with a peculiar quality, in that the nastier it is to one group of people the funnier it is to another.

ETIQUETTE   The observance of proper rules of decorum, such as removing one's shoes before placing one's feet on one's coffee table.

EUCLID   An ancient Greek mathmatician, whose principles of geometry are as useful today in confusing the average high school student as they were in 300 B. C.

EULOGY   An apology made to an unappreciated good person who has died or a pack of lies about a bad one.

EUPHEMISM   The substitution of an inoffensive word for an offensive one, such as "victory" for "bloodbath."

EUPHORIA   A joyous sense of well-being, considered by many people to be a sure sign that someone is on drugs.

EUTHANASIA   The act of depriving a person with an incurable disease of the God-given right to die slowly and painfully.

EVE   The wife of Adam, who was the first woman ever to take up with a lying snake, but hardly the last.

EVENING   The part of the day that serves as an armistice, between the time when the average person gets out of work and the time the average mugger, rapist or murderer begins. In the city particularly, the hours of the armistice are strictly observed, and there is ample opportunity to desert the streets.

EVERGREEN   Chronically envious.

EVERYBODY   Nobody, et al.

EVIL   Wicked enough to justify wholesale vindictiveness on the part of the morally upstanding.

EVOCATOR   One who summons forth the spirit of a dead relative and the cash of a living one.

EWE   A female sheep, commonly found in the mountains, in the meadows, and in the weekly crossword puzzle.

EXAGGERATE   To give a feature-length version of a short-subject truth.

EXAMINATION   A test given in school to determine if the student has satisfactorily limited his exploration of a subject to the expectations of the teacher.

EXCHANGE   To rectify a gift given by a well-meaning but tasteless friend or relative.

EXCLUSIVE   A type of club, restaurant or other organization designed to protect the general public against contracting the highly contagious disease of its patrons, snobbishness.

EXCUSE   The attempt to explain oneself out of an uncomfortable situation, which doesn't help to correct the situation but which helps tremendously to broaden one's imagination.

EXECUTOR   A kind of game show host, who informs the contestants of their winnings after a burial.

EXERCISE   Some form of physical exertion to keep the body in shape, such as getting up and changing the channel.

EXHAUSTION   The result of physical exertion, such as getting up and changing the channel, which is relieved by sitting in a chair or on a couch for two to three hours, snacking intermittently.

EXHIBITIONIST   A person who is willing to show for nothing what people pay money to see in the movies.

EXIST   To be, or in the case of certain movie stars, to have been.

EX LIBRIS   A Latin phrase placed inside of a book, meaning "A curse upon anyone who borrows this book and does not return it to," followed by the owner's name.

EXOGAMY   Marriage outside of the same clan, a custom which exists in most civilized societies to discourage young men from trying to marry their fathers.

EXORCISE   To expel an evil spirit by a complicated religious ceremony or simply by kicking him out of the house when he turns eighteen.

EXOTERIC   Suitable for the general public, as a movie made before 1960.

EXPENSIVE   Pertaining to the cost of anything that isn't drastically reduced.

EXPERT   Someone who has a wide view of a narrow landscape. 2. Anyone who is lucky enough to find himself in a room filled with people who know absolutely nothing about a subject of which he knows a little.

EXPLOIT   To give people a sense of purpose and direction by using them in a pragmatic way, as one uses toilet paper.

EXPLORER   One who sees an answer behind every question and a question behind every answer.

EXPORT   A product which is sent to another country, where it magically assumes a quality and distinction that it did not have when it was manufactured. The magic lies, it is believed, in a mystical word that is printed on the product's label. The word is "imported."

EXPOUND   A unit of weight that had been sixteen ounces at one time.

EXTEMPORARY   Now permanent.

EXTINCT   Of or pertaining to the sensibility in certain men regarding their fellow creatures, particularly the ones that stand in the way of progress or from which a profit can be made.

EXTORTION   The practice among public officials of supplementing their meager incomes by dipping into the public funds, which is just as well, they reason, because otherwise the money might get wasted on things like schools, parks, or street repairs.

EXTRAVAGANT   Excessively displaying outer trappings to mask the lack of inner substance.

EXTREMIST   One who ascribes to the philosophy that the whole world should just surrender to insanity once and for all and be done with it.

EXTROVERT A person who is concerned primarily with the external world, having determined that people who spend a lot of time dealing internally run the risk of discovering things about themselves.

EYE An organ of speech, which can aid the mouth when there are no words to say or betray it when there are.

FABLE A story intended to illustrate some fundamental truth, which may be hidden, as in the one about The Two Politicians who always smiled and shook hands when they had their pictures taken together. The truth is they hated each other's guts.

FACE The part of the head that contains the prominent features, including eyes, nose, acne, mascara, mouth, forehead, dentures, contact lenses, wrinkles and jowls. 2. The part of the body designed to contort in accordance with the emotions, and when those contortions are stifled, the result is a contortion elsewhere in the body.

FACSIMILE An exact copy. 2. An exact copy.

FACT A bit of information that was misconceived by A, who told it to B, who wrote it in a letter to C, whose letters were subsequently uncovered by an historian.

FACTORY A building where people who have not yet been replaced by machines are encouraged to prove that they are just as good as machines.

FACTOTUM A person employed to perform a variety of tasks; as, she liked being his secretary but she did not want to be his factotum.

FAD A craze, marked by a period of extreme enthusiasm, followed by extreme indifference, as in electing a president.

FAGGOT A bundle of twigs, sometimes mistakenly thought to have deviant sexual tendencies.

FAIL To succeed at attempting.

FAILURE An opportunity to do something better. 2. One who succumbs to the negative opinions of others and whose greatest failing lies in not recognizing that those who have the most criticism and discouragement to offer are frequently those who have the least of anything else.

FAIR In keeping with one's personal view of what is right and wrong. Anything else is a gross miscarriage of justice.

FAIR AND SQUARE A blond from Nebraska.

FAIRY A small supernatural being, common to Central Park.

FAITH Belief, particularly in one's ability to place one's trust where it will not be abused.

FAITHFUL True in allegiance to God, country, spouse, and above all, one's home team.

FALL To get a chance to strengthen the muscles (and the qualities) needed to pick oneself back up again.

FALSETTO The singing voice of a man who is a closet soprano.

FAME The price which celebrities must pay to the public in return for the huge sums of money they receive, even the hugest of which cannot purchase them their privacy.

FAMILY That select group with whom most people spend their early years, from whom most people cannot wait to depart after adolescence, and without whom most people feel quite alone.

FAMINE A condition which affects countries not afflicted by the plague of overeating.

FAMOUS Possessing an illegible autograph.

FANATIC A person who sacrifices his common sense at the altar of zeal.

FANGS Long sharp teeth used to seize prey, visible and conspicuous on most predators but concealed and figurative on man.

FANTASTIC Imaginary; unreal; as, that was a fantastic campaign speech.

FAR   At or to any distance which one is too lazy to travel, whether it be ten feet or ten miles.

FARCE   A foolish show, often featuring ridiculous behavior, the mockery of something important, and a sham masquerading as a meaningful development; a national political convention.

FARFETCHED   Thrown a great distance and retrieved by a dog.

FARM   A tract of land where crops are grown, as a wheat farm, where animals are raised, as a chicken farm, or where comedians are trained, as a funny farm.

FARMER   The person in the dell.

FASCINATING   Regarding anything which is said by a person who has something to a person who wants a part of that something; as, the young starlet found the fat producer's dull, vulgar, monotonous conversation absolutely fascinating.

FASCISM   People by the government, for the government and of the government.

FASHION   An arbitrary and generally ridiculous standard for the way people should dress, appealing to those who require the most superficial nourishment to feed their egos and serving as an outrageous justification for throwing away perfectly good clothing.

FASHIONABLE   Displaying a marked lack of personal taste but a large measure of the taste of some designer.

FAT   Involved in a love affair with food, which does for the body what a love affair with a miscreant does for the soul.

FATE   That which is destined and which those who try to escape sooner or later meet face to face in a dark corner called inevitability.

FATHER   A man who has replaced most of the money in his wallet with pictures of his kids. 2. A person who earns the respect and obedience of the other members of the family, by virtue of holding the car keys.

FATHER-IN-LAW   A figure who has been grossly neglected by comedians, presumably because he stubbornly refuses to be meddlesome.

FAULT Someone else's responsibility for that which goes wrong.

FAWN A young deer, sometimes characterized by a bullet hole through the head.

FEAR A cheap excuse for hating people one doesn't understand.

FEARLESS Foolishly free from fear.

FEAST An elaborate meal, usually eaten during the afternoon of a holiday, and usually regretted during the evening of a holiday and during the morning following a holiday.

FEAT A courageous deed, such as a mother's unzipping her son's gym bag.

FEBRUARY The month in which resolutions are revised and edited.

FEE The average lawyer's protection against contact with accused or accusing paupers.

FEMALE A woman or a girl, depending upon which classification will better serve her cause at the time.

FEMINIST One who believes in the equality of the sexes, in men and women taking turns picking each other up for dates, in women getting out and fixing flat tires, and in separate checks.

FENCE A barrier that defines the borders of one's property and the trust in one's neighbors.

FENDER The part of a car used to indicate whether or not a parking space is big enough.

FERRIFEROUS Iron-bearing; as, she must have been planning to press his shirts, for she was ferriferous.

FERRIS The wheel invented by G. Ferris, not to be confused with those invented by P. Wagon and H. Cart.

FERTILE Requiring abstinence or a birth control pill or else.

FETISHISM Erotic fixation on a part of the body that is not normally considered erotic, such as the eyelids, causing the fetishist to become physically aroused whenever anyone blinks.

FETUS An adult embryo.

FEW Several more than a couple and several less than some, give or take one or two.

FIANCE One who is committed, and ought to be. 2. A person who is engaged to be marred.

FIB A type of harmless falsehood playfully known as a little white lie, which is a very distant cousin of a pernicious variety known as the big black lie, and although the latter seldom comes to visit, when it does it stays.

FICTION Imaginary literature, such as novels, short stories, and much of history textbooks.

FIDDLE A violin that is played with a bow and a stomp.

FIELD A piece of open ground, suitable for pasture, condominiums, an office building, a shopping mall or a parking lot, all but the first of which signifying progress.

FIEND A person who is hopelessly addicted to stupid people; hence, a dope fiend.

FIERCE Inspiring terror and the kind of respect that a child with a whip inspires in a dog.

FIFTEEN The age of transition from the handle bar to the steering wheel, one of the foremost rites of passage in life.

FIGHT A difference of opinion that is loud enough to be heard by the neighbors two doors down. 2. A discussion which includes the throwing of hard objects, such as ashtrays, flatware, framed pictures or fists, in the general direction of another person.

FIGURE The human body, as observed by an art student or the War Department.

FILIBUSTER The act of speaking merely to consume time, perfected by United States Congressmen and practiced diligently by most of their constituents.

FILLING The part of a sweet tooth that is inserted after excavation, causing the recipient to reflect upon the age-old maxim, "Candy is delicious, but the dentist's drill is vicious."

FILTHY Dirty enough to make a mother sick and even a father to take notice.

FINANCE The science of applying modern technology to the ancient practice of squandering other people's money.

FINE A punishment designed to keep rich criminals out of jail and to make certain that people who commit offenses that they can't afford serve their just time.

FINGER One of five bony appendages of hands, including the index finger, the ring finger, the pinkie, the thumb, and the signal finger, so called because of its wide use in non-verbal communication.

FINISH Like the end of a European movie.

FINK According to underworld terminology, someone who informs to the police, usually for immunity and protection. This means that he is free from prosecution and that he will receive police protection for a month or for the rest of his life, whichever comes first.

FIRE One of the five elements that make up the world. The others are air, earth, water, and plastic.

FIRECRACKER A saltine covered with chili sauce.

FIRM A group of lawyers or other predatory creatures whose nature is to form packs; as, a wolves' firm.

FISH To draw one's meal or one's livelihood from the water, respecting in the process the delicate balance of nature. 2. To rape the water for profit or pleasure, respecting nothing.

FIST A closed hand attached to a closed mind.

FIT Prepared; ready; as, fit to be tied.

FIVE The last year of a child's unbridled imagination, before it is harnessed by formal education.

FLAGELLATION The act of being flogged, and loving it.

FLAMINGO A metal lawnbird.

FLANK The side of an animal or of an army, either of which is prepared to be butchered.

FLASHLIGHT A portable electric light, usually containing two or more dead batteries.

FLASK A container used for drinking liquor sneakily.

FLATTERY Praise that is so excessive that even the recipient will only believe half of it, which is half more than anyone else believes.

FLAUNT To attempt to inspire envy and to succeed in inspiring disgust.

FLAUTIST An affected flutist.

FLAVORING The artificial ingredient in grape soda that makes it taste exactly like grape lollipops and grape gelatin and grape popsicles and grape jelly beans and everything else that's grape, except grapes.

FLAW Something that is cleerly rong.

FLESH The soft parts of the body only, and no bones about it.

FLETCHERISM The practice of chewing food thoroughly, named after Horace Fletcher (1849–1919), who believed that swallowing pork chops, potatoes and other foods whole can lead to serious health problems.

FLOAT To remain on the surface of water, preferably with face up.

FLOPHOUSE A theater that consistently presents terrible plays.

FLORIST One who mortally injures flowers and arranges them in bouquets so that people can buy them to throw them away two days later or give them to somebody else to throw away two days later.

FLOWER One of nature's most exquisite things of beauty, which few people take the time to appreciate fully while they are alive and yet which, peculiarly, most people have surrounding their coffins and placed upon their graves after they are dead, when they can no longer see or smell them.

FLUNK   To have studied in front of the television set. 2. To have read the wrong book by mistake. 3. To have cheated from someone who knew even less than you did.

FLUSH   A swirl and ejection of water from the toilet of a king or queen; hence, a royal flush.

FLUTE   An instrument that requires frequent alternations of two tones a degree apart, which is difficult to do but once this is mastered it is an absolute trill.

FLY   A winged insect which seems to have two favorite pastimes: crawling along the rim of a glass filled with lemonade and landing on a hot dog bun just as mustard is about to be applied.

FOE   A clearly defined enemy, who openly appears hostile and hateful, as distinguished from the more dangerous kind of enemy, who appears friendly and congenial.

FOGY   A person who is behind the times, as opposed to a person who is behind the daily news.

FONDUE   A type of meal shared by dips.

FOOD   Any link on the endless natural chain, wherein the eater becomes the eaten. The only exception to the rule is civilized man, who selfishly refuses to become a part of the cycle by shutting up the bodies of his dead in tombs, denying both the earth and other links the vital nutrients human bodies have to offer.

FOOL   Someone who trusts everybody. 2. Someone who trusts nobody. 3. Someone who only trusts people with big smiles and warm handshakes.

FOOT   The part of the body that people use when they're doing something just for kicks.

FOOTBALL   A field game played with an ellipsoidal ball and two teams, one of which attempts to advance the ball across the field while the other attempts to stop the advance by surrounding the player carrying the ball and ramming him in the knees and back as hard as possible, causing pain and, with practice, serious injury.

FORBID To force a confrontation between a person's natural fear of reprisal and his natural curiosity.

FOREFATHER Someone who lived fourscore and seven years before the Gettysburg Address.

FOREGROUND A golf course.

FOREHAND A reverse backhand.

FOREHEAD The part of a parent's face with a line for each child.

FOREIGNER A person who thinks, talks and acts strangely, the same as one's next-door neighbor.

FORESIGHTEDNESS An eye affliction characterized by the ability to see what is ahead so clearly that one tends to miss what is right under one's nose.

FOREST Any place where large numbers of trees grow until progress arrives. 2. A wooded area, where the animals who live in trees are protected from the ones who live in concrete.

FORETELL To speak of things that will happen in the future, using a mysterious occult power, so mysterious, in fact, that it is literally hundreds of times more mysterious than it is accurate.

FOREVER Until someone or something better comes along.

FORGET To be unable to remember, often conveniently.

FORGIVE To accept an apology on three conditions: that it be an admission of guilt, an expression of regret for having committed an offense, and a statement of resolution not to repeat the offense. 2. To accept an apology without conditions, thereby priming oneself to become the victim of future offenses by the forgiven.

FORLORN Deserted; forsaken; wretched; bereft; unlikely to get up on a table and do a jig.

FORMALDEHYDE A chemical substance used to preserve corpses so that they won't appear too dead. It is also used as a disinfectant to keep them from catching any germs that may be lingering underground.

FORMATIVE   Pertaining to the years when the body is going through the process of growth, while the mind, on the other hand, is going through the process of school.

FORMULA   The recipe for a liquid that is fed to infants by their mothers, who place themselves in great danger, for there are countless secret agents who would stop at nothing to get their hands on it.

FORT   Any structure of any material built by children, usually in their neighborhood park, where they can go and hide from the outside world until they are old enough to internalize their defenses.

FORTITUDE   Patient courage under affliction, as that demonstrated by any adult who gets together with the family over the holidays without complaining.

FOSSIL   The traces of an animal found imbedded in a rock after thousands of years, indicating that the animal must have had a very strong personality to have left so lasting an impression.

FOUR   The child's age when parents who have spent three years teaching him to talk begin to have second thoughts.

FOURTEEN   The age when most girls learn the fine art of over-doing make-up.

FOX   An animal with such a notable reputation for cleverness that it has earned its way into the highest ranks of society, where it is afforded the esteemed honor of being hunted and killed by upper class barbarian socialites.

FOXHOLE   A ready-made grave for an unlucky soldier.

FRACAS   A barroom sporting event, which can be played in singles, doubles, or teams. The object is to shut the mouth(s) of the opposition, and the only requirements are that the participants be sufficiently inebriated and that they pick an utterly stupid topic upon which to disagree.

FRAGILE   A word that is stamped on packages, meaning DROP WITH CARE.

FRANKFURTER   A candid and open beef sausage.

FRATERNITY   A group of college students associated for their common interests in partying and drinking beer.

FREAK   A whimsical creature, native to San Francisco and New York, although occasionally one is discovered desperately trying to escape from Cleveland.

FRECKLES   Tiny spots on the skin, considered adorable on little girls until they reach the age of thirteen, when the spots suddenly seem to grow large and grotesque and every effort is made to conceal them cosmetically, causing the girls endless agony and embarrassment and casting shame on the side of the family whose genes were responsible for them.

FREE   Costing nothing and frequently worth less. 2. Pertaining to the best things in life, with the exception of food, clothing, shelter, utilities, education, theater tickets, automobiles, appliances, vacations, a new suit, and a decent burial.

FREEDOM   State of being at peace with oneself, regardless of external shackles. 2. The ability to move around at will within the confines of one's social or financial station. 3. The common right of all people in a free society to say whatever and as much as they like, provided that their verbosity remains a substitute for action.

FREETHINKER   One who holds the opinion that each person is endowed with an individual mind in order to engage in individual thinking. This is not only a minority opinion, but it is also considered heretical in many religious circles.

FREYA   The Norse goddess of love, who is said to have spent a great deal of time among the dwarfs. She is, consequently, also considered the goddess of kinkiness.

FRICASSEE   Nothing but stew with a French air; stew that is enjoyed heartily by people who hate stew that is called stew.

FRIDAY   The second longest day of the week, preceding the two shortest.

FRIEND   One whose opinion of you does not change once you've left the room. 2. One who is as anxious to hear the good news as the bad. 3. One who has the sensitivity to be there when you need him and the sense to stay away when you need to be alone.

FRIENDLESS Too honest. 2. Hopelessly devoted to a possessive spouse.

FRIGGA The mythological goddess of the sky, who was thought to be a little daffy by the other immortals because she always had her head in the clouds.

FROG One of the least prudent of all animals, so regarded because it is forever leaping to conclusions.

FRONT The back of the back.

FROWN To punish one's face, as well as everybody who has to look at it, for something that more than likely concerns neither.

FROZEN Pertaining to a kind of pizza that is extremely economical, in that it is specially made to taste remarkably like its container, so that the pizza itself and the picture on the box may be eaten together, thus doubling the number of servings.

FRUGAL Regarding a person who is prudently economical, as opposed to a person who gives you something inexpensive for your birthday.

FRUSTRATION The feeling that springs from the realization that the only way to get to the other side, where the grass is always greener, is to take a job mowing lawns.

FUEL A heat-producing substance with the amazing quality of being in a state of depletion just prior to a sharp price rise and then suddenly being in ample supply again.

FUGLEMAN A highly drilled soldier who is placed in the front ranks of a military company to serve as an example of how to take a bullet in the stomach without making a big fuss.

FUN The pleasure that results from letting one's imagination out to play. 2. That part of life which is relinquished by people who think that growing up means abandoning childhood.

FUNERAL The ritual that marks a human being's passage from a vastly unknown life to a totally unknown one. 2. A sad occasion in every respect, except that one gets to go through red lights on the way to the cemetery.

FURRIER   One who deals in the retail end of the animal extinction business.

FUTURE   The present in transit. 2. The time that belongs to the young, who don't have the slightest idea what to do with it until they are old enough to pass it on to the next generation of young, who don't have the slightest idea, either.

GAB   The one gift that is better neither to give nor to receive.

GABRIEL   An archangel of very low aptitude, used mostly as a messenger.

GADZOOKS   A mild oath, closest to Gadswoons (meaning unknown) in meaning and Godsbodikins (origin unknown) in origin.

GAG   To experience a TV dinner for the first time, especially if accustomed to eating food. 2. To perform a community service on a local gossip.

GAGMAN   One of an illustrious group of men whose invaluable contributions to Western Civilization include the immortal pie in the face, the unforgettable slip on the banana peel, and the ever-popular slap on the head with a rubber chicken.

GALAHAD   A knight of the Round Table, who was said to be the most chaste of all the knights, but the fact was that he simply didn't know how.

GALAXY   An enormous prison of stars floating in a vast penal colony called the universe, which is surrounded by countless rows of barbed wire fence and a sea of mine fields bordered by a wall three million miles thick, on the other side of which is another prison.

GALLOWS   A murderer's hangout.

GALOSH   An overshoe worn in wet weather that gets its name from the sound that is made when the wearer steps in a puddle.

GAMBADO   A spring of a horse; an autumn of a cow.

GAMBLER   One who plays the fool with his money in order to win more money and the chance to play the bigger fool.

GAMBRINUS   A mythical king and reputedly the inventor of beer, although there is no documentation of this because none of the people who were present at the time could remember anything the next morning.

GAME   A contest, physical or mental, which generally starts out as fun but ends up with a winner and a loser.

GANGSTER   Someone with a marked proclivity toward shooting people in restaurants while they are eating; also, one of the people thus shot.

GAP   The invisible barrier between generations, separating the idealism of youth from the conformism of middle age. Conversely, it also serves as a cementing agent for the irrationality and obstinacy of both.

GARAGE   A shop where cars with sore throats suddenly develop pneumonia.

GARDEN   A plot of ground where fruits, flowers, vegetables, and peace are cultivated.

GARETH   A knight of the Round Table, who only got chosen because he happened to be King Arthur's nephew, proving that there were political patronage jobs even in Camelot.

GARLIC   An herb used in preparing foods and bad breath.

GARNISH   To waste food, such as lettuce or parsley, by putting it under or on the side of a meal for the purpose of making it prettier and more expensive.

GASOLINE   A volatile liquid that powers cars, trucks, and Arab nations.

GASTRONOME   A connoisseur of good eating, who has a broad range of knowledge on the subject, from which vegetables go best with a peanut butter sandwich to the proper wine for hot dogs and beans.

GATLING   A type of gun, named after its inventor, which was a great blessing to those responsible for waging battles, because it could kill dozens of men simultaneously, making the process more convenient and less time-consuming.

GAUCHO   A Spanish cowboy noted for horsemanship and light-hearted torturing.

GAWAIN   Another nephew of King Arthur and knight of the Round Table, proving that there was actually an excess of political patronage jobs in Camelot.

GAY   A homosexual, particularly one who has brought his sexual activities out of the closet, where it was difficult to breathe and there was not much room to move around.

GAZELLE   A small antelope that is characterized by its graceful movements and lustrous eyes, except after it has been shot, when its grace and luster are reduced discernably.

GEEZER   An old person who is considered strange, especially by the neighborhood kids, who themselves are considered strange by their older brothers and sisters, who in turn are considered strange by their parents, who are considered strange by everyone.

GEISHA   A Japanese dancing girl, whose routines are limited somewhat by the fact that her dress prevents her from moving her feet more than a couple of inches in any direction.

GEM   Any stone used in the manufacturing and distribution of status.

GEMINI   The sign of the twins, Castor and Pollux, who are said to be so outraged at the unauthorized use of their likeness on posters, medallions and key chains that they plan to sue the companies that make them.

GENDARME   Le cop.

GENEALOGY   A history of the descent of a family, or the story of how they came to live in the basement.

GENERAL   A military officer who smokes fat cigars, wears a bunch of medals, and grunts a lot. 2. A man versed in the strategy of slaughter.

GENERATION   Any people born during the same period of time, who, as a group, reject the values of their parents and who, as a group, ultimately adopt those same values by the time their own children are old enough to reject.

GENESIS The Bible's account of creation, in which every detail is given of the way God made the world, but there is no mention of a warranty.

GENETHLIAC Pertaining to birthdays and their profound effect upon the aging process.

GENIUS One who is both blessed and cursed with an enormous talent.

GENOCIDE Systematic mass murder for political reasons, for racial reasons, or for sheer entertainment.

GENTLEMAN A man who does not have to defeat other men and slap women in the face to win their respect. 2. A man who is gentle not only in public, but in private.

GENUINE Sincere; authentic; as, this is a genuine fraud.

GEOLOGY The science of old rocks.

GEOPHAGY The practice of eating clay, usually sauteed with mushrooms and accompanied by a fresh green salad.

GEOPOLITICIAN An expert in international, as well as domestic, duplicity.

GEORGIC Relating to rural affairs, which are essentially the same as urban affairs, except that many of them take place in the back of a barn.

GERIATRICS The area of medicine dealing with the prevention and eventual cure of old age, one of the leading killers of senior citizens.

GERM One of billions of nasty little microbes that have nothing better to do than spread diseases and cause infection, with a kind of rampant ferocity that is absolutely without justification. There is not a trace of scientific evidence to suggest that anybody ever did anything so terrible to them to provoke such vengeful behavior.

GERONTOLOGY The science of senility, which seeks to find techniques to help people remember where they put their teeth.

GERYON   A mythological king who owned a great many cattle, all of which were carried away by Hercules, who was blessed by the gods and therefore entitled to be a thief.

GESTURE   A motion of the face or body intended among adults to express an idea or a passion and among children to express an idea or a need to use the bathroom.

GHASTLY   Horribly attractive; shocking enough to sell newspapers; as gruesome as a television police show.

GHETTO   An inner city pleasure resort for roaches.

GHOST   The spirit of a particularly stupid deceased person, who has chosen to return.

GIANT   A huge mythical manlike being known to inhabit mountain regions, forests, and basketball courts.

GIFT   A type of horse into whose mouth people are advised not to look. 2. Anything given, usually within the specific price bracket of something previously received.

GIGANTOMACHY   The great war between the Olympians and the Giants, which took place in the distant past, when the Giants were still in New York.

GIGGLE   To titter nervously, especially in a classroom when someone has made a strange noise.

GIGOLO   A sexual self-exploiter.

GIMMICK   A device used to promote a great talent, that being the talent to entertain the public without exposing it to substance. 2. Anything that sells a product, while sparing the consumer any unnecessary considerations, such as those regarding the product's quality.

GIN   A liquor that's distilled from grain which, when consumed, distills the brain.

GIRAFFE   An animal which, throughout history, has continued to grow taller thanks to its necks of kin.

GIRDLE   An undergarment designed to force a woman's stomach into the area normally occupied by her lungs, thus compelling her to take short, shallow breaths and to speak less. It is an article much beloved of husbands.

GIRL A female who has yet to discover the wiles of womanhood.

GIVE To receive the joy of gratitude. 2. To accept the risk of rejection. 3. To justify taking something later.

GLACIER A huge body of ice, enough to supply all of the cocktail parties in every state in the Union for a year, or all of the ones in Washington, D. C., for three weeks.

GLADIATOR A combatant of ancient Rome, similar to today's prize fighter, except that he did not receive a million dollars per contest and, if he lost, he had the consideration to die.

GLAMOROUS Having the benefits of an active publicity department and the liabilities of an uncertain identity. 2. Young and beautiful and under contract not to age.

GLASS A container for liquids designed to shatter when thrown into a fireplace, thereby adding a note of drama and intensity to a person's histrionics that is noticeably missing when a plastic cup is thrown.

GLASSHOUSE A building for growing plants or for people who shouldn't throw stones.

GLEE The kind of unrestricted joy that children display when they're playing or that old people display when they're watching children playing or that people between childhood and old age display when they're drunk.

GLIMMER That portion of hope that remains after numerous defeats and setbacks; it is as tiny or as vast as the faith of the person who is hoping.

GLOAT To make the world a happier place by deriving happiness from the misfortunes of others, thus giving them the opportunity to be equally happy when something terrible happens to you.

GLOSSOLOGY An obsolete term for the science of linguistics, studied by obsolete linguists.

GLOVE A handy article of attire; a finger clinger; a knuckle nestler.

GLUTTON Someone who eats the last piece of cake, which you wanted to eat.

GNARL A knot in wood, of the kind only an experienced boy scout can make.

GNOSTICISM A pre-Christian movement, based upon the doctrine that true freedom comes through knowledge. In modern times, it has been narrowed specifically to the knowledge of how to make a buck.

GOD The Supreme Being, concerning whom there are literally thousands of authorities but not one truly reliable source.

GODIVA One of the first bareback (and barefront) riders of England.

GOLD A girl's second best friend.

GOLDFISH An aquatic mutt.

GOLF A game comprised of hitting a ball into sand and then trying to hit it back out again. A variation of the game involves hitting the ball into a clump of trees.

GOLIATH A Philistine giant who got stoned only once and died as a result.

GOMORRAH An ancient city filled with wicked people desperately in need of redemption, which was utterly destroyed by an all-merciful God.

GOOD Not at all bad, but worse than better and much worse than best, which, all things considered, is only a little above fair.

GOODWILL A kindly feeling among people reserved for the Christmas season.

GOON A person with the intelligence of a piece of lawn furniture, used in a labor dispute to make negotiators appear competent and reasonable by contrast.

GORDIAN An incredibly complicated knot which was tied by Gordius, in accordance with an ancient oracle stating that whoever untied the knot would be master of Asia. It was cut in two by the sword of Alexander the Great, who declared himself master of

Asia, claiming that he would have been able to untie it except that he bit his nails.

GORILLA The largest of the apes and the closest evolutionary link to the middle linebacker.

GOSSIP Someone who tells you everything you didn't want to know but were afraid to ask.

GOVERNMENT A vast network dedicated to wasting tons of paper and misappropriating public funds.

GOWN A dress worn by a woman on formal occasions, such as a wedding, a graduation, or, if deceased, a wake.

GRACE A prayer of thanksgiving which is said before a meal, particularly in countries where there is something to eat.

GRADE A rating system for certain kinds of food, which is very peculiar in that it seems to consist only of grade A. The search for a dozen grade B eggs or a quart of grade C milk is still under way.

GRADUATION A ceremony at which the departing students are given the hardest test of all, the test of whether or not they can stay awake through the commencement speeches.

GRAFFITI Frustration's signature on the walls of buildings and subway platforms.

GRAFT The swift undercurrent of political business which threatens those who dive too low for coins.

GRAMMAR The science treating of the classes of words and their functions, popular during the days when word skills were stressed in school.

GRANDFATHER A man who enjoys playing with his grandchildren and allowing them to climb on his back, which, of course, explains why they descend from him.

GRAPE A fruit that is used in making derelicts.

GRAPHOLOGIST Someone who analyzes a person's handwriting in order to determine, for the proper fee, that he is intelligent and creative.

GRASS The stuff that is always greener on the other side, although the person who lives there is often too busy to notice.

GRATEFUL Aware that no one has to do anything for anybody and therefore thankful when someone does. 2. Expressing appreciation for past favors in anticipation of future ones.

GRATITUDE The one gift that everyone can use, that is appropriate for any occasion, and that has a value that enriches both the giver and the receiver.

GRAVITY That force which pulls all bodies to the earth, with the exception of certain movie actors.

GRAY The natural color of hair that has not been dyed to its previous natural color.

GREASE The specialty of the house in any diner where the cook wears an undershirt and the waitresses chew gum.

GREEDY Obsessed with having more of everything, except prudence.

GREEGREE A variation of grigri, which is a variation of grugru, which is a tree commonly known for its variations.

GREENHOUSE A place where inexperienced people are kept.

GRENADE A small, hand-thrown bomb that is good for killing several people who are spread apart or, under ideal conditions, as many as a dozen of them who are crouched together in a confined area.

GREYHOUND A dog with a bus painted on its side.

GRIN The thing you do with your mouth just before you bear it.

GRIPE To complain, most frequently to a fellow complainer, with the sound and effect of a broken record. 2. To exercise the mouth in pointing out a problem but not the backbone in doing something about it.

GROCER A dealer in food who is always very busy, mostly rushing around his store raising prices.

GROUCH A person whose morose moodiness makes him a pleasure to have around; namely, around twenty or more miles away.

122

GROUPER   Any of numerous fishes that resemble the sea bass, although some of them also resemble the sea baritone.

GROW   To keep wondering why, even after you know how.

GROWN-UP   Run-down.

GRUDGE   Something that a person can hold and still have both hands free to make into fists.

GUARANTEE   A promise from a manufacturer that a product will not break until shortly after a specified period of free repair or replacement.

GUEST   A visitor in front of whom members of the household do not walk around in their underwear. 2. Any person who is not welcome into one's home until the beds are made, the toilet is scrubbed, and the children's toys are put away.

GUILT   A feeling implanted and nourished from birth, primarily by mothers and religions, designed to make people feel bad about doing practically anything they find enjoyable.

GUITAR   An instrument with an unparalleled reputation of being easy to play, and for the large number of people who play it poorly, it is.

GUM   The tissue which surrounds the teeth. 2. The sugary chewing material that destroys the tissue which surrounds the teeth.

GUN   A device used to inflict injury, death, and shame upon creatures who call themselves civilized. 2. The single greatest proof of man's "superiority over the animals."

GURU   A venerable teacher of India in India, who seeks the road to truth; a not-so-venerable teacher of India in the United States, who seeks the road to a million dollars.

GUY   A male gal.

GYPSY   A moth that plays the tambourine.

HADES A gloomy subterranean realm, commonly thought to be located approximately ten miles below the New York subway system, although certain religious cults believe that it *is* the New York subway system.

HAG An old woman who calls the police just because some kids knocked on her door and ran away; a witch.

HALF-MOON Opening the buckle of one's pants and lowering them midway down the buttocks.

HALLOWEEN The night of the year most noted for a mysterious storm which sweeps across the country, leaving vast accumulations of candy wrappers on streets and sidewalks. 2. A day set aside for washing soap off your car's windshield.

HALLS Places decked with boughs of holly, for reasons which no one knows.

HALLUCINATE To see something that really isn't there, such as genuine concern in the face of a politician.

HALO A circle of light, surrounding the head of a saint or someone who is extremely high.

HAM An actor who specializes in playing a fool, regardless of the nature of the character he is portraying.

HAMMER A tool used to inflict severe pain in the thumb and index finger. It can also be dropped on the foot.

HAMMOCK A kind of hanging bed, commonly suspended between two trees, which is used primarily by suburbanites when suffering the extreme exhaustion that accompanies the contemplation of mowing the lawn.

HAMSTER   A rodent residing in a plastic apartment complex.

HAND   The part of the body second only to the mouth in making trouble for its owner.

HANDEL BAR   A tavern featuring oratorios and water music.

HANDLE BAR   A place where CBers socialize.

HAPPY   Possessing a weak memory.

HARDEN   To add difficult questions to an exam. 2. To add rocks.

HARDSHIP   An oppressive or discomforting condition meant to be borne without complaint by somebody else.

HARK   To listen to the herald angels sing.

HAS-BEEN   Someone who lives in a scrapbook. 2. An ex-celebrity. 3. A person who made the unhappy plunge from craving privacy to getting it.

HATE   To feel an intense aversion toward, as in the case of certain vegetables. 2. To dislike exceedingly, as in the case of people who invite you to dinner and serve certain vegetables.

HATRED   A social disease which emotionally cripples both the hater and the hated.

HAUNTED   Plagued by the ghost of one's iniquitous deeds.

HEAD   The part of the body that success swells, thus providing extra room for the brain to stretch, leaving gaping holes which can be filled with cement, thereby sealing the person's attitude for life.

HEARING   The auditory sense, which serves as the link between what the sayer says and what the hearer thinks the sayer says.

HEART   The organ which pumps blood through the system and, as though that weren't enough, also acts as the center of love, courage, and moral spirit. The fact that the spleen does not share at least some of this responsibility is a clear example of biological inequity.

HEARTACHE Sorrow, frequently resulting from the disillusioning discovery that the object of one's love interest has turned out to be an ordinary human being.

HEARTBURN The revenge of the stomach against the excesses of the appetite.

HEATHENS People who worship outdated gods.

HEAVEN The place where the good finally conquer the evil and savor their punishment for eternity. 2. The place where those who shunned materialism in life walk streets paved with gold.

HEAVY Weighing too much for you to lift. 2. Perfectly suited to the lifting capacity of your spouse or fellow worker.

HEDONICS The study which treats of the relationship between duty and pleasure, as in the case of certain top executives and their personal secretaries.

HEDONISM The doctrine that pleasure is the sole good in life and, accordingly, that nobody should have to do the dishes or vacuum.

HEEDFUL Taking heed, long enough to gain the upper hand.

HEGIRA The flight of Mohammed from Mecca in 622 A. D., considered a miracle in light of the fact that there were no airports or landing fields anywhere in the area at the time.

HEIGHT An eminence, such as a hill, a mountain, or an archbishop.

HEIGHTEN To elevate or to make high without altering the mind.

HEINOUS Hateful; bad; odious; atrocious; offensive, and not very funny.

HEIRLOOM Any family possession used to promote envy and bickering from one generation to another.

HELIOS The sun-god, who drives a four-horse chariot through the heavens, wears shades, and is reputed to be the finest surfer in Greek mythology.

HELIX Anything having a spiral form, such as a staircase or a screen pass.

HELL   The fiery abode of evil spirits, where Satan and his band of devils constantly torment their inmates by promising them marshmallows every Tuesday, and never delivering.

HELLENIST   A Greek scholar or, more loosely, anyone who eats at Greek restaurants.

HELMET   A covering for the head worn by soldiers to keep the brain from splattering all over the place when a bullet enters it.

HELP   To assist and furnish with relief; as, I was glad to help. 2. To butt in and make things worse; as, I was only trying to help.

HEMATOSIS   The very complicated process by which blood is formed, as distinguished from the relatively simple process by which it is shed.

HEMISTICH   An incomplete line of verse, as one written by an avant garde, post-Impressionistic, neo-Romantic, experimental poet.

HENOTHEISM   The worship of one God with the acknowledgment of the existence of other Gods, in contrast to monotheism, which is the denial of the existence of any God but one's own, as well as the religious rationalization for hating and mistrusting those who damnably choose to worship a non-existent God.

HENPECK   To improve the business prospects of one's husband by giving him as many reasons as possible to stay late at the office.

HERCULES   The heroic son of Zeus, whose hands alone could strangle a lion, whose feet alone could kick down an iron door, and whose breath alone could kill an ox.

HERD   A number of large animals assembled together, often to hear a political speech.

HERE   In this place; as, it's here. 2. In this place, hopefully; as, it's around here somewhere. 3. In this place, you think; as, I know I put it here.

HEREDITARY   Descending from an ancestor to an heir, in the form of money, property, or a disease.

HERESY Religious opinion opposed to the authorized doctrinal standards of any particular church, and tending to promote thought.

HERMIT A person who does not socialize and who watches a lot of television.

HERMIT CRAB A person who does not socialize, watches a lot of television, and is ornery.

HERO A decorated military person, an outstanding athlete, or someone who makes one smash movie.

HERRING An extremely unhappy and abused fish. Not only is it puny among other fish in the ocean, but also, when caught, it faces the unenviable prospect of being smoked, pickled or salted.

HETEROGRAPHY Spelling differing from standard current usage, as in heterograffy.

HETEROSEXUAL Pertaining to sexual passion for a member of the opposite sex, preferably of the same species.

HETEROTAXIS Abnormal arrangement of the parts of the body, geological strata, etc., as in having a rock where your brain ought to be.

HEXAHEDRON A polydron of six faces, one for every mood.

HEXAPOD Having six feet and a whopping bill from the podiatrist.

HEYDAY A time of joy and high spirits, followed by hangover day.

HIBERNATE To pass the winter in a torpid state, as do many animals and Congress.

HIDE The skin of an animal on its way to extinction.

HIDEOUS Horribly ugly and shocking and dreadful and revolting and awful and disgusting and downright yukky.

HIERARCHISM A strange, contradictory mixture of politics and sanctity within a church government.

HIERATIC Consecrated to sacred uses; sacerdotal; of, or pertaining to, bingo.

HIGH Lofty; elevated; prone to giggle.

HIGHBROW A person who has had a browlift operation.

HIGH SCHOOL A place which harbors illiterate youths.

HIGHWAY A crawlway during the rush hour and a speedway at any other time.

HIGHWAYMAN A toll collector on the turnpike.

HILL A natural elevation of land lower than a mountain but higher than a breadbox, unless it's an ant hill, which is lower than a breadbox but higher than an ant.

HILLBILLY A club belonging to a policeman from West Virginia.

HIPPOPOTAMUS A huge herbiverous mammal, seldom seen outside its native environment, Disneyland.

HISTORIAN An enchanter of small schoolchildren, who provides for them accounts of national events the way everyone wishes they'd really happened. 2. A disenchanter of adults, who writes books which refute the accounts of events in grammar school history books.

HISTORY A record of civilization and the events occurring before, during and after its wars.

HITCHHIKE To travel by rule of thumb.

HOARSE Having a grating voice, as when any loyal sports fan leaves the arena.

HOAX A so-called practical joke, which is generally not very practical and certainly not very funny.

HOBBY An activity that diverts and relaxes the mind, such as mixing martinis.

HOLD To stay on a telephone listening to nothing for as little as a few seconds or as long as it takes the switchboard operator to remember which blinking button is yours. There are reports that people have actually collapsed and died while waiting for their calls to go through.

HOLE   A cavity in the ground into which one may, for any number of reasons, bury one's head, remembering to leave room for one's foot, which has usually been put in one's mouth.

HOLIDAY   A day set aside for eating much, drinking much, and meaning little.

HOME   A building where you can eat and sleep and walk around in your underwear. 2. The place to which a person returns to recuperate after a bout with independence.

HOMESICK   Missing the joys of unrestricted complaining. 2. Suffering the effects of rude waitresses and beds that aren't broken in.

HOMEWORK   Work that is done during commercials.

HOMILETICS   The art of preaching for profit.

HOMINY   A dixie kernel.

HOMOSEXUAL   One whose attraction to members of the same sex is regarded as deviant in societies which place great stock in all matters of morality, except the morality of minding one's own business.

HONEST   Honorable; truthful; in business and politics, characterized by cheating within the accepted bounds.

HONESTY   The quality of stating what you really think, despite the liabilities. 2. The practice of telling people the truth, even though it is obvious from their looks and the way they nod their heads that they don't believe a word of it. 3. The next best thing to a well-planned and perfectly executed lie.

HONEY   A term of endearment, especially between husband and wife; sweetie pie; baby doll; lambykins.

HONEYMOON   The period of time between the wedding ceremony and real life.

HONOR Tribute or esteem bestowed upon someone who usually claims to be unworthy of receiving it, but who accepts it anyway in order to prevent someone even less worthy from receiving it.

HOODLUM An adult juvenile delinquent.

HOPE Trust that something desired will be obtained eventually, even if one has to sink to total despair before obtaining it.

HOPEFUL Having a capacity for hope in direct relation to a capacity for disappointment.

HOROSCOPE A chart based upon the aspect of the stars at a particular time, such as at the moment of a person's birth, used to concoct all sorts of information about the person's character, equally attributable to all people, but made to sound very special and unique to the individual, because otherwise the information would not be worth the money that is wasted on it.

HOROSCOPY The practice of studying the stars and their effect upon the wallets of the gullible.

HORRIBLE Exciting horror, shock and, when it does not affect you personally, relief.

HORROR Great aversion and repugnance, sufficient to warrant condemnation but not cessation; as, the horror of war.

HORSE An animal with enough sense not to bet on men racing.

HORTICULTURE The art of keeping the neighbors' pets away from your plants.

HOSPICE An inn for travelers kept by a religious order, which means that there are Bibles in the rooms.

HOSPITAL An institution in which the lucky patients are healed and released, while the unlucky ones are kept and subjected to unnecessary drugs, unnecessary surgery and unmitigated expense.

HOSTAGE A person who is held captive at gunpoint, often by freedom fighters.

HOSTESS The woman with the "mostest," which means with the most tired feet, the most strained smile, and the most frazzled nerves.

HOSTILITY   An act of open ill will, exchanged between enemies who are getting along or friends who are not.

HOT   Having a temperature high enough to make steam, to cause a burn, or to get a girl into serious trouble. 2. Excited by music; as, hot to trot.

HOTBED   A boxspring, a mattress, and an electric blanket.

HOTEL   A large building which provides accommodations for business, social and illicit affairs.

HOUR   A period of time, the duration of which depends entirely upon what one is doing. In school, it lasts about three days; at an amusement park, about seven minutes.

HOUSE   A building, similar to a home in appearance, but substantially unlike one in spirit.

HOUSEBROKEN   Pertaining to a child who has finally stopped scribbling on the walls.

HOUSEFLY   An insect athlete trained in an event known as slamskirting, which involves zipping into a house an instant before the screen door closes.

HOUSEKEEPER   The person in a house who fixes the beds, dusts the furniture, and curses the last one to use the bathtub.

HUG   An embrace, usually between two fully clothed people, but on occasion between two unclothed people, the embrace then being called a bare hug.

HUGE   About the size of an elephant, or even two elephants, or in the case of a building, several hundred elephants.

HUMAN   Relating to, or characteristic of, beings who are distinct from other creatures in their ability to misuse language.

HUMANITARIAN   One whose diet is comprised strictly of humans.

HUMBLE   Not proud; not boastful; not pretentious; unlikely to receive credit for accomplishments.

HUMDRUM   Dull and monotonous and dull and monotonous and dull and monotonous, etc.

HUMILIATE To reduce someone to a low position in the eyes of others, and in so doing, to reduce oneself to a lower position.

HUMILITY Freedom from pride, arrogance, and promotions.

HUMOR The sixth sense, sometimes regarded as the sick sense, in people, which deals with the mental faculty of appreciating or expressing the comical aspects of existence, such as the one about the three traveling salesmen, the farmer's two daughters, their cow, a large container of whipped cream and a tractor.

HUMORIST A person who uses humor to communicate an idea, in place of fists.

HUN A term used by inner city waitresses to address their patrons; as, what'll it be, hun?

HUNCHBACK An assistant to a mad scientist.

HUNK A man as seen through the eyes of a nymphomaniac.

HUNKY-DORY Peachy-creamy.

HUNT To pursue for the purpose of capturing, as in the case of escaped convicts, or killing, as in the case of convicted animals.

HUSBAND A man who has taken a solemn vow of jealousy.

HYDROGEN BOMB An enormously destructive bomb, which was originally designed to be so horrible that it probably would never be used, and then more were made to increase the horribleness so that it definitely would never be used, and then more were made for the same reason, and so on.

HYPOCHONDRIAC Someone who has a high susceptibility for imaginary diseases. 2. A person who works at being sick.

HYPOCRITE A lie, personified.

I Everybody's favorite pronoun, followed closely by me and mine.

IBIS A kind of wading bird, the female of which is commonly known as a lady in wading.

ICBM Insanely conceived ballistic missile.

ICEBOUND Regarding the fiancée of a man who can afford expensive jewelry.

ICE-SKATE To fall down on ice, get up, take two gliding steps and fall down again.

ICONOCLAST A destroyer of idols, otherwise known as a gossip columnist.

IDEA Any turmoil in the mind, ranging from a brainstorm to a slight drizzle. 2. A mental phenomenon, viewed by many as an ailment, the remedy for which is two aspirin.

IDEALIST One who eats seaweed and dreams of lobster, while a realist settles for tuna fish.

IDEOLOGY The manner of thinking peculiar to a given class or society, which provides a framework for the arrogance of its members and from which is formulated the language of propaganda.

IDIOT A very stupid person, such as the one who invented the ketchup bottle.

IGLOO An Eskimo house made of snow blocks, for which there is no commonly accepted market value. This causes a severe problem for real estate tax assessors.

IGNORANCE   Bliss, but bliss of which there is no knowledge.

IGNORE   To disregard willfully, in the hope that whoever or whatever it is will be quiet, go away, or drop dead.

I'LL   The contraction of I will, which just as often means I might.

ILLITERATE   Unable to read. 2. Permitted to watch unlimited television.

ILLUSION   A false image, such as the smile on the face of anyone other than the winner in a beauty contest.

IMAGINARY   Real, but not really real, in the sense that the reality exists only in the mind, and although the reality in the mind is real reality, it is not as real as it would be outside of the mind, where really real reality exists.

IMBIBE   To drink alcoholic beverages, usually for one of the following reasons: to avoid being called anti-social, to have an excuse for acting obnoxiously, to throw up, to enjoy and appreciate dull conversation, to become suddenly funny, or to make driving home a challenge.

IMITATE   To forfeit one's original style in order to copy the style of someone else. This is a foolish and wasteful undertaking, except in the field of popular music, where a great deal of money is to be made by people who copy.

IMMATURE   Pertaining to the attitude and behavior of the other person in all matters of disagreement.

IMMEDIATELY   Without delay; as, I'm cashing this check immediately. 2. When I get around to it; as, I'm mailing your check to you immediately.

IMMIGRANT   Someone who exchanges the disagreeable certainties of life at home for the agreeable uncertainties of life in another country. 2. A person who is seeking the opportunity to pay higher taxes. 3. One who flees oppression in search of pollution.

IMMORAL   Contrary to the moral law, which states that some people have the right to impose their standards of decency on other people.

IMMORALITY Anything that is forced upon responsible adults. 2. Exposing children to sex, violence, alcohol and pre-sweetened cereal.

IMMORTAL One of the gods of ancient Greece or Rome, who lived forever, kept in great shape and, incredibly, never needed dentures.

IMP A mischievous little child who is so cute that you'd just like to eat him up, or better yet, you'd like to get your dog to eat him up.

IMPARTIAL Forgoing bias until all the facts are in; as, an impartial jury.

IMPEACH To charge a public official with the grave offense of allowing the newspapers to find out about his private dealings.

IMPEDE To stop in progress; as,

IMPEDIMENT A speech disorder, as in the form of heckling or commotion during a public address.

IMPENETRABILITY The law of matter which holds that two bodies cannot occupy the same space at the same time, except on a subway train during rush hour.

IMPENITENCE The refusal to add hypocrisy to the list of one's sins.

IMPERIALISM The policy of seeking to extend the empire of a nation by acquiring resentment.

IMPERIUM Supreme power; absolute domain; the realm of oil companies.

IMPIOUS Failing to genuflect before entering a bank.

IMPLANTATION The insertion of a Southern estate.

IMPONDERABLE Able to live in a small body of water.

IMPORTED Enriched with sufficient status when packaged to justify a higher price than that of a domestic product of comparable quality.

IMPORTANT Ranking somewhere in significance between the end of a high school football game and the end of the world.

IMPOSSIBLE Pertaining to that which hasn't happened yet and to that which will never happen as long as those who can make it happen believe that it can't ever happen.

IMPOSTOR One who deceives others by pretending to be someone else. 2. One who deceives others simply by being himself.

IMPOVERISH To place on social security.

IMPRACTICAL Pertaining to any solution of a problem that conflicts with one's own.

IMPRESSIONISM An art form which involves wearing designer clothes, driving an expensive car, and bragging a lot.

IMPRIMATUR An official approval of a book, signifying that there is nothing in it that will offend people, except perhaps those people who would appreciate reading about all sides of an issue.

IMPROBABLE About as likely as having two car inspections in a row without any major repairs. 2. About as likely as having one.

IN Up to date and faddish; as, faded jeans are in or the doctor is in.

INABILITY Merely an excuse not to keep trying.

INACCESSIBLE Accessible, but not wishing to be bothered.

INACCURATE Of or like a weatherman.

INADEQUATE Insufficient, especially in the sense that; as, this definition is inadequate.

INALIENABLE Unable to be made into a creature from outer space.

INANIMATE Like or resembling a clerk in a bookstore.

INAPPROPRIATE Not in keeping with what is considered proper by the majority of people; as, it is inappropriate to spend more than an hour a day thinking.

INAUDIBLE Not able to be heard, which is the way many people prefer their children, although this is a common mistake, for it is often the case that when children are not able to be heard it is because they have just broken something or are in the process of breaking something.

INAUGURATE To give the public one last chance to see a newly elected official before the reins of power take hold of him.

INBREEDING The attempt of a sickly, stupid, unattractive family with strong chins to prevent, by marrying one another, the unfavorable prospect of having children with weak chins.

INCA One of a large tribe of South American Indians, most widely known for having Spanish swords sticking in various parts of their bodies.

INCANTATION The use of magic spells or verbal charms, such as "Abracadabra," "Presto chango," or "You are the best looking woman in this bar."

INCAPABLE Unable to get dressed up like Superman.

INCENDIARY Of or pertaining to the malicious burning of property, as opposed to the friendly burning of property.

INCEST The act of taking the concept of brotherly love a little bit too far.

INCH The amount of anything that a person gives in order for another person to take a yard.

INCINERATOR Someone who advocates the abolishment of the motion picture code.

INCLEMENT Pertaining to weather that is bad enough to prevent one from making it to work but not quite bad enough to prevent one from making it to the bowling alley.

INCOMPARABLE Matchless; as, he could not light his cigarette because he was incomparable.

INCOMPETENT Having the necessary qualifications to head a government office.

INCOMPLETE Lacking something, as in the case of a definition which uses itself as an example of what it is lacking.

INCOMPREHENSIBLE Ont acpebla fo inbge mopcherdnede.

INCOMPRESSIBLE R e s i s t i n g   c o m p r e s s i o n.

INCONCEIVABLE Of or pertaining to a sexual relationship in which a pregnancy cannot occur.

INCONSEQUENT Not sequence in.

INCONSIDERATE Taking measures to insure the absolute privacy of someone else's feelings, by completely disregarding them.

INCONSISTENCY The act of saying one thing today and another thing tomorrow that conflicts with it and another thing the next day that conflicts with both earlier statements; hence, the act of talking like a politician.

INCONSOLABLE Having just returned from Las Vegas.

INCONSPICUOUS Not wearing flippers, red socks, a kilt, green elbow pads, a gorilla mask, epaulets, or a Dewey for President button.

INCREASED Without a line in one's pants.

INCUBUS An evil spirit, supposed to take sexual liberties with women at night, generally without even asking them out for a drink first.

INDECENT Morally offensive use of a camera; as, indecent exposure.

INDELICACY A grilled cheese sandwich, or something along that line.

INDEPENDENCE Freedom from control by others. 2. Freedom which results from controlling others. 3. State of having sufficient money and social standing to be free from control by others. 4. State of having sufficient moral courage to resist the desire for money and social standing in exchange for control by others.

INDESCRIBABLE Defying description; as, her long, billowing, satin gown with white lace and a pink hem embroidered with small, bright, red roses made of velvet was indescribable.

INDIAN GIVER A Hindu Santa Claus.

139

INDICT   To charge with an offense, although most people prefer to charge with a credit card.

INDIFFERENT   See APATHETIC. 2. Or don't see APATHETIC.

INDIGESTIBLE   Cooked by a husband whose wife is in bed with a cold.

INDIGNATION   Anger generated by something that is base or disgraceful, which often renders the person feeling this anger so righteous and so pure that he feels totally justified in taking combative action that is at least equally base or disgraceful.

INDISPENSABLE   Designating a person who cannot be replaced, except by another person.

INDIVIDUALITY   That quality which distinguishes one person's clothes, home decor, and choice of radio station from another's. It may, in rare cases, also include a person's way of thinking.

INDOLENT   Avoiding exertion; indulging in relaxation; occupying the office of a senior vice president.

INDUSTRIAL   Pertaining to a country with large numbers of factories and endangered species, the chief among the latter being factory workers.

INEDIBLE   Cooked by the same husband whose wife is still in bed with a cold.

INEFFICIENCY   An apartment that is not one room.

INERT   On a couch watching a baseball game.

INEXACT   Not precisely correct, as the 1811 Overture.

INEXHAUSTIBLE   Having a clogged muffler.

INEXPENSIVE   Costing half as much as something that lasts twice as long; costing half as much as something that works twice as well; costing half as much as something with a designer label, which has twice the prestige.

INEXPRESSIBLE   Not capable of being expressed and, therefore, unlikely to arrive by the next morning.

INFALLIBLE Inhuman; unearthly; inspiring absolute confidence right up to the point of ultimate disaster.

INFANCY The period of life when one first realizes where one is, which certainly explains why so much of it is spent crying.

INFANTRY Soldiers who march on foot, provided their feet are still attached to legs.

INFECT To expose to society.

INFERNO A hell-like region, such as any big city in July or the seashore on Memorial Day.

INFIDELITY The result of a cheap radio or stereo system.

INFINITE Without limits of any kind, said of God or of a child whose parents do not believe in discipline.

INFINITY Somewhat longer than the 1963 version of *Cleopatra*.

INFLATION An economic state designed to get people to stop worrying about insignificant things, such as whether or not they can afford a home, and to start worrying about important matters, such as how they're going to pay the food bill.

INFLEXIBLE Safely imprisoned in one's attitudes, protected from the threat of new ideas and sheltered from the horrifying prospect of having one's mind set free.

INFLICT To impose something painfully unwelcome; as, to inflict an invitation to a commencement ceremony.

INFLUENZA A common bronchial disease which usually confines those affected to bed for several days, although it can sometimes cause such discomfort that it is actually worse than going to work.

INFORMAL Pertaining to an occasion at which people are not required to wear gowns and tuxedos; as, an informal garage sale.

INFRANGIBLE Not capable of being broken up, except by ferocious tickling.

INFURIATED Having failed to see the funny side of the situation.

141

INGENIOUS Characterized by the combination of cleverness, shrewdness and ingenuity or stupidity, disorganization and luck.

INGRATE A person who returns a pat on the back with a punch in the stomach. 2. Someone who believes that, since it is better to give than to receive, he is doing his family and friends a favor by consistently making them better people.

INGRATITUDE The one gift that children give to their parents which can, when real effort is put into it, approach the magnitude of the gifts they receive.

INGURGITATE To eat with the kind of grace and courtesy that serves as a living proof of Darwin's Theory of Evolution.

INHABITANT One who is, or dresses like, a nun.

INHERITANCE The money, property and possessions that are left by a person after death to be divided among his heirs, who frequently take time out from their grieving to bicker about who got what and how much, each being convinced that he or she was more loving and devoted to the deceased than the others and therefore is entitled to material compensation proportionate to the aforementioned love and devotion.

INHUMAN Unlike this human. 2. But exactly like that human.

INHUMANITY State or instance of treating one's fellow human beings like one's fellow apes.

INITIATION See INHUMANITY.

INJECTION A fearsome medical procedure which produces such anxiety that the mere contemplation of it can cause some people, including grown men who have been to war, to feel faint and weak in the stomach. See NEEDLE.

INJURY The thing to which an insult is added in order to complete the damaging process, so that the person subjected to it will be spared the added confusion of wondering whether the initial harm was done on purpose.

INK A magic potion, used by literary wizards to cast spells which transform ordinary readers into enchanted voyagers. 2. A fluid with all of the lethal properties of a snake's venom, injected by the fangs of critics, hacks, and gossip columnists.

INNOCENT   Not caught.

INNOVATION   Anything that is still too new for researchers and psychologists to determine how damaging it is.

INNUENDO   A coward's insult.

INORGANIC   Designating a wide array of candy and snack items, produced chemically and given catchy names and colorful labels to arouse the interest of small children, as well as adults of nominal intelligence. They are generally useful for destroying unwanted teeth and have the same nutritional value as their packaging.

INQUISITION   A religious campaign of the sixteenth century designed to demonstrate that the best way to help heretics to find the truth is to torture and kill them.

INQUISITIVE   Disposed to cause embarrassment to one's parents, especially in public.

INSANE   Characterizing someone who loses his mind temporarily, as a criminal who becomes deranged just long enough to commit a crime and then recovers, or loses his mind completely, as any juror who falls for this line of defense.

INSECT   A small, crawling, leaping or flying creature, whose sole purpose for existing is to provide people with something convenient to kill in between hunting trips and wars.

INSECURE   Inhabiting the kind of planet where nothing is quite certain, where everything is a gamble, and where the more one has the more one risks losing.

INSIGNIFICANT   Unimportant and trivial, as the price of gasoline to a pigmy.

INSOMNIA   Prolonged inability to clear one's conscience.

INSPECTOR   A person who conducts official examinations of the contents of plain white envelopes, as well as buildings, facilities, operations, etc.

INSPIRATION An animating influence of a spiritual nature, the anticipation of which is the principal occupation of lazy artists. 2. An infusion of compelling creative power resulting from the preternatural enlightening of the mind or the simple stealing of another person's ideas.

INSTALLMENT The act of getting a horse into its compartment.

INSTANT A period of time one half of a moment less than a flash.

INSTINCT A natural and unreasoning tendency to action; as, the name-calling instinct of politicians.

INSTRUCTOR A teacher at a college who ranks somewhere between a professor and a blackboard.

INSTRUMENT A contrivance for inflicting pain or for making music or, in the case of certain ungifted players, for doing both at the same time.

INSULT A hurtful remark delivered by an unthinking friend or a thinking enemy. 2. A remark aimed at strengthening the bond between enemies.

INSURANCE A business which operates by offering a client the comforting thought that, just in case a fire ravages his home, killing his wife and children and destroying all of his valuables, he will be financially compensated.

INTEGRATION The act or process of bringing people of different races together, so that they can avoid contact with one another on a much more intimate level.

INTELLIGENCE Applied common sense. 2. The desire to ask the right questions. 3. The capacity to find the right answers.

INTENTION A person's aim or desired goal, the realization of which can sometimes become so dominant in the person's mind that reason, practicality, and regard for the feelings of others are abandoned; as, the mother could not understand how she possibly could have ruined her son's honeymoon, for she had the very best of intentions.

INTERESTING Regarding a person who says things with which you agree.

INTERMINABLE Lasting six and a half times longer than one's cousin's piano recital.

INTERN A medical person who is practicing practicing.

INTERPELLATE To question formally, as at a prom.

INTERPRETER A person who explains the meaning of something, such as a poem, for the benefit of people who do not possess their own interpretive mechanism, such as a brain.

INTERROGATION A set of questions delivered in what is frequently a hostile and intimidating manner by an attorney in a courtroom, evidently designed to discourage people from witnessing crimes.

INTRANSIGENT A well-bred man who refuses to travel.

INTRICATE Confusing and involved enough to be avoided at all costs, since failure to do so may involve one with a lawyer, at all costs.

INTRINSIC So much a part of one's nature, say cultural anthropologists, clinical psychologists and sociologists, that one has the perfect scientific excuse not to do anything about it; as, the intrinsic aggressiveness of man.

INTROSPECTION The act of looking into one's own mind and examining one's own thoughts, an operation which is considered dangerous if conducted more than once a month.

INTUITION The power of knowing without reasoning, commonly attributed to mothers, who are thought to be endowed with this extraordinary gift at the moment when a child is born, from which point mothers usually have neither the time nor the energy to reason. The power, however, tends to decrease with age, although many mothers continue to make use of it long after their children are grown, in most cases with considerably less success.

INVISIBLE Regarding the things that the poor are entitled to have in unlimited quantity.

INVOCATION   The act of asking God not to pay any attention to anyone else who may be requesting the same thing that you want. 2. In time of war, calling upon one's deity to compete with one's enemy's deity in bringing about victory.

IODINE   An antiseptic that stings when applied to a cut, so that little children who hurt themselves when no adult is watching get to cry and receive their allotment of sympathy during treatment.

IONOSPHERE   The layer of the earth's atmosphere polluted with technical hardware. It is beyond the stratosphere, which is the layer of bus fumes.

IOU   I outsmarted you (by taking your money and leaving you with this little piece of paper).

IRATE   Enraged; as, an irate husband is a man who is enraged to be married.

IRRATIONAL   Not endowed with enough reason to see how absolutely sensible your side of the story is.

IRRESISTIBLE   Fattening.

IRRESPONSIBLE   Thinking of life as a joyride, in somebody else's car. 2. Having an ample supply of foolish friends who don't know when they're being used or masochistic friends who do.

ISHTAR   The Babylonian goddess of love, who was also the Assyrian goddess of war. Neither people saw a conflict in her roles.

ISOCRACY   A government in which everyone has equal political power and babies are delivered by storks.

ISOLATIONIST   One who believes that government should totally dispense with foreign policy and concentrate all of its efforts on making the domestic situation twice as bad.

ITERATE   To say or do more than once, as distinguished from reiterate, which is to say or do more than more than once.

IVORY   A rackful of billiard balls on a table thousands of miles from a rotting elephant carcass.

IXION A mythological king of Thessaly, who was punished by Zeus for loving Hera by being tied to an eternally revolving wheel at Tartarus. In his case love did, in a manner of speaking, make the world go round.

JABBER To transmit via the mouth the verbal essence of a thoughtless mind.

JACK A mechanical device kept in the trunk of a car, which is designed to be so simple to operate that even the most inexperienced female driver can use it to change a tire, often in a mere two or three hours.

JACKAROO An apprentice on a sheep station, who has to acquaint himself with every kind of music that sheep like before he can become a disc jockey there.

JACK-OF-ALL-TRADES An official who oversees the swapping of baseball cards.

JADE A wench, specifically a socket wench.

JAHVE A court game, similar to rackets but much easier on the ears.

JAIL An environment wholly conducive to plotting and planning, where criminals go to contemplate future crimes.

JALOPY The kind of a car that captures a boy's heart in a minute and his father's garage for six months afterwards.

JAM To make music that usually sounds as good as whatever it is you've been smoking.

JAMSHID A mythological king who was punished for his excessive boasting by being banished to Texas, where he is compelled to spend eternity listening to the excessive boasting of his neighbors.

JANITOR   A person whose business is teaching apartment dwellers to be self-sufficient, mainly by making himself scarce whenever there is a leaky pipe, a broken refrigerator, etc.

JANUARY   National Date Correction Month, when everybody everywhere at least once makes the mistake of putting the wrong year on a letter, a check, or a homework assignment.

JAPETH   The son of Noah who was in charge of cleaning the ark. He was a very thorough worker and he never took a moment's rest until he was sure his job was dung.

JARGON   The technical language of a science or profession designed to make things sound more important than they are. It is particularly useful in impressing politicians, who are always anxious to allocate funds for projects that are important sounding.

JAW   The part of the face which shares with the nose the distinction of being broken most often in fistfights.

JAWBREAKER   An accomplished participant in fistfights. See JAW.

JAY   A person who is so gullible that he will believe anything, even the truth.

JAYWALK   To cross a street suicidally, or at least with the intention of losing a limb.

JAZZ   A kind of music which, if it can be defined, isn't it.

JEALOUS   Operating under the delusion that a person can be, or ought to be, completely fulfilled in every aspect of life by one, and only one, other person. 2. Selfishly, and often justifiably, distrustful. 3. Insecure, and loving it.

JEANS   The contribution of the farmer to the annals of high fashion.

JEER   To have heard, according to usage in large northeastern cities; as, jeer the latest?

JELLY   A food preparation which, joined with peanut butter, comprises the most successful and long lasting marriage in the history of lunch.

JERK   Someone who brings potato chips to the movies; someone who wears white socks with a suit; someone who has to squeeze every fruit and vegetable in the produce department.

JESTER   A person who purposely plays jokes on people with pleasing results, not to be confused with a city councilman.

JET   A slow rocket.

JEWELRY   Personal ornaments worn on the body to weigh it down, to give it sparkle like a Christmas tree, or to make it more attractive to covetous people.

JIFFY   The time it takes for the average television set that has been sitting in the shop for two weeks to be repaired.

JIG   A dance which is so lively and irregular that it requires a performer who is in condition; specifically, in drunken condition.

JIHAD   A religious war waged to uphold a principle, such as the principle of the sanctity of human life.

JILT   To cast off a lover unfeelingly, and in so doing to render him a service by relieving him of contact with a person capable of such an act.

JINGLE   A catchy little tune used in commercials, having a quality that infiltrates the brains of unwary people and induces them to hum the tune unconsciously while walking or riding the bus, resulting in acute embarrassment and higher sales.

JINGOISM   The practice of confusing patriotism with barbarianism, stemming from the belief that a country best maintains its self-respect by doing all it can to reduce the self-respect of other countries.

JINX   Anything which causes an overly superstitious person to have bad luck—such as his brain.

JITTERBUG   A dance that is performed by many people who disdain the popular dances of today and who long for a return to the time when dancing was respectable and graceful, as when boys respectably flipped girls over their shoulders and gracefully slid them between their legs.

JOB   Something that is done to make money, as opposed to a career, which is something that is done to make a lot of money.

JOCASTA   The mother of Oedipus, whose marriage to her son led to Freud's assertion that every boy secretly wants to murder his father and marry his mother, or murder his mother and marry his sister, or murder both his parents and marry the lady next door.

JOG   To grimace in gym shorts and running shoes, while pulling the legs beneath oneself in an awkwardly rhythmic motion.

JOKE   Everything in life, if you think about it long enough. 2. Nothing in life, if you think about it too much.

JONAH   A prophet who lived in a large fish for three days because he thought it would make an interesting Bible story.

JOSH   To tease in a good-natured way, so that a person's feelings are hurt good-naturedly.

JOURNALIST   A person who gives you the who, what, where, when, how and why of a story, but can still leave you asking the question, "Huh?"

JOY   A state of bliss, such as that which parents experience from the day their baby is born to the first sleepless night.

JOYLESS   Having the imprudence to be born in a country where there is nothing to eat.

JUDGE   A public official whose main job is to make sure that there are enough criminals allowed back on the streets to keep life interesting. 2. A man of the bench who cannot be bought, although there is often the possibility of a short-term lease.

JUDO   The Japanese art of knocking people down and throwing them all over the place while grunting.

JUKEBOX   A coin-operated record player located in restaurants, for the purpose of disrupting the conversation at nearby tables, and in bars, for the purpose of insuring that those patrons who do not already have a headache from what they are drinking are given no unfair advantages over those who do.

JULY   National Get Away To It All Month, when everybody rushes to the nearest resort area to spend a quiet, relaxed vacation amidst the noise and confusion of millions of other quiet, relaxed vacationers.

151

JUNCTION   The place where railway lines meet, but whether anything serious develops from there is up to the individuals.

JUNE   National Weep at a Wedding Month, when people who enjoy crying in church have plenty of opportunities.

JUNGLE   The total lack of civilization and the overgrowth of vegetation. 2. The total lack of vegetation and the overgrowth of habitation.

JURY   A group of people assigned to a trial, whose ability to mete justice is in direct proportion to their ability to perceive the truth despite the degree to which lawyers try to twist it.

JUST   Conforming with one's own ideas of what is right and conflicting with one's adversary's.

JUSTICE   The administration of that which is fair and equitable to everyone, with no special consideration given to the rich and the powerful, unless of course they get into trouble.

KABALA An occult science, differing from psychiatry in the sense that its practitioners profess to understand things much less mysterious than the human mind.

KALIF A Moslem leader known for his beautiful gardens; hence, a kalif flower.

KAMIKAZE A Japanese pilot, whose strange but effective method of losing weight was to dive his plane into a ship. This was the first of the so-called "crash" diets.

KANGAROO An animal that can actually knock out a human being with its feet, although there are usually several individuals in any gym class with similar capabilities.

KANTIANISM The doctrine that a thing in itself is unthinkable, with its attributes merely applied by the mind, and that therefore something which is apparently confusing, such as Immanuel Kant's philosophy, is not really confusing but is only perceived to be confusing.

KARMA The belief that people who are diseased and poverty-stricken had it coming to them and they should be ashamed of themselves for the way they led their previous lives.

KAY King Arthur's foster brother and a knight of the Round Table. Yet another glowing example of political patronage jobs in Camelot.

KAZOO An instrument made especially for people with an excessive absence of musical ability.

KEG A container holding enough beer to prevent the average fraternity party from degenerating into a civilized affair.

KENNING A descriptive poetical name used in place of the usual name of a thing, as "childish mudslinging" for "political debate."

KETCHUP A condiment vaguely resembling blood, commonly smeared by messy children all over their clothes for the purpose of giving their mothers heart failure.

KHAKI Cloth used in military uniforms because it absorbs blood well, allowing for cleaner and dryer battlefields.

KICK An early mode of communication between members of opposite sexes; a pre-kiss.

KID A child who is old enough to know better, but not yet old enough to know worse.

KIDNEY A bean-shaped organ used primarily as a model for swimming pools. Its secondary use is in the human body, where it collects urine, a fact which many pool owners, particularly those with a lot of children, find unpleasantly appropriate.

KILL To play God, usually without preparing for the part or paying royalties. 2. To deprive oneself of the kind of peace enjoyed by one's victim.

KILT A type of skirt worn in Scotland as a symbol of the equality of marital roles. In Scottish households, no one wears the pants in the family.

KIN All of one's relatives taken as a group, although it is rare to find someone who can take more than a couple of them at a time.

KINDERGARTEN A school where a child is taught to make things that look remarkably like the things all of the other children in the room have made. This teaches him the values of observation, imitation and cooperation, as well as the relative unimportance of imagination.

KINDNESS The act of treating people as though you were getting paid for it.

KING The head of a country, who attains the position from a birthright and who therefore differs from elected officials in the sense that the public never really gets the chance to evaluate him on his ability to make empty promises and to verbally abuse an opponent.

KINGPIN   A wrestling hold invented by Henry VIII.

KINKY   Regarding twisted rope or hair, or a relationship making use of either.

KIP   The hide of a small beast, usually in youth, worn by a larger beast, usually in high heels.

KISS   The coming together of lips, spirits, bodies, lives, beings, emotions, faiths, desires, hopes and trusts. 2. An oral procedure for the exchange of germs.

KITCHEN   A room for preparing dyspepsia, high blood pressure and obesity.

KLEPTOMANIAC   A person who steals without knowing why, as opposed to a professional thief, who steals without knowing why not.

KNIFE   An instrument with so many functions that the belief among some that the elimination of its use in stabbing people would detract from its popularity is largely groundless.

KNIGHT   In medieval times, a man of great chivalry and valor. In modern times, any entertainer whom the Queen finds amusing.

KNOT   An interlacement of rope, string, ribbon, etc. designed to discourage people from biting their nails.

KNOWLEDGE   The accumulated information gained from experience and education, which some people use like bricks to build walls around their attitudes and others use like a hammer to knock down the walls.

KOWTOW   To treat a person with such outlandish respect that one undermines one's own dignity and therefore, by inference, the dignity of the person respected.

K RATION   Concentrated army food comparable to three meals, not including breakfast, lunch and dinner.

LABEL   A word or phrase used to describe a group of people, who think and act exactly the same and who express exactly the same degree of outrage over not being regarded as individuals.

LABOR   The first, and frequently the least severe, pain induced by a child and endured by a mother.

LABORATORY   A place where cancer is administered to rats.

LABYRINTH   A place full of intricate and confusing passageways in which a person may wander aimlessly for hours or even days, originally used by early Greeks to entertain visiting relatives.

LACCOLITH   A mass of igneous rock that intrudes between sedimentary beds and makes a good night's sleep practically impossible.

LADY   A woman who asks for a glass with her beer. 2. A woman who wishes she had more to regret in the morning. 3. A woman who takes longer to get dressed than it takes to learn the clarinet. 4. A woman who chews gum one stick at a time.

LAISSEZ FAIRE   The theory that the government has no business messing up affairs which the trade unions are perfectly capable of messing up on their own.

LAKE   A large body of water completely surrounded by styrofoam cups and cigarette butts.

LAMB   A person who is meek and innocent enough to be devoured by a wolf in chic clothing.

LAMPOON A malicious satire upon a person, for the sole purpose of revealing his faults. The faults of the writer are self-evident.

LANCELOT One of the few knights of the Round Table who was not related to King Arthur. He came close, however, by having relations with Queen Guinevere.

LAND Any place on the earth's surface that does not promote drowning.

LANGUAGE The words and word combinations used by a large group of people, so that they can express themselves in commonly accepted terms and thus be misunderstood comprehensibly.

LANSQUENET A card game that is so complicated that only people who have no time for card games can understand how to play it.

LAPSE A miscarriage, as of justice, which victimizes a person, as of the lower class, due to some fault, as in the legal system.

LARCENY The theft of personal property, which, when the property is valuable, is classified as grand, at least for the person who stole it.

LARES Ancient Roman household gods, among whom were Spatulus, the god of cooking utensils, and Tupperwarius, the god of leftovers.

LARGE Designating a size of clothing determined unscientifically according to the whims of manufacturers. What is large in the eyes of some is medium to others, while a third group categorizes the size as extra large. This is evidently the way clothing manufacturers have fun, although the enjoyment is generally not shared by people who are either swimming or suffocating in their clothes.

LARGEHEARTED Taken advantage of by the smallhearted.

LARVA An insect in its pre-pest stage.

LARITHMICS The scientific study of population and its effect upon the number of people living someplace.

LARYNGITIS An inflammation of the larynx, resulting in the inability to speak above a whisper, viewed by the person who has it as an affliction but often by the people occupying the same household as a blessing.

LASCIVIOUS Pertaining to someone who wants the only thing that a person who will have anything to do with him has to give.

LAST Being the final one until the next final one; as, she told him that this was absolutely the last time she would lend him money.

LATE Showing a high level of low regard for others. 2. Not in time to avert worry but too early to be given up for dead. 3. Possessing a seemingly unlimited supply of imaginative, and often amusing, excuses.

LATIN Pertaining to the people of Latium, all traces of whom have disappeared, with the exception of a unit of their currency which still exists, known as the Latin quarter.

LATITUDINARIAN Someone who holds that people should believe what they want to believe, even if what they want to believe is what someone else wants them to believe. 2. Someone who believes in the freedom to choose enslavement.

LAUGHTER One of the few truly universal human expressions and one of the only ones that helps prevent people everywhere from blowing each other's brains out. 2. The cynic's single greatest stumbling block.

LAUNDRY A place where people send their clothes to have the buttons removed.

LAVATORY A room where women go and mysteriously lose track of time. Although it takes the average woman just over twenty minutes to powder her nose, there are recorded cases of those who have spent over three hours in this activity and even instances of women who have gone to freshen up and never returned.

LAW The body of rules in a community, which are only as good as they are enforceable, and which are only enforceable if they make sense, and which only make sense if they apply equally to everyone, and which only apply equally to everyone if the ability to hire a shrewd lawyer plays no part in the application of justice.

LAWYER A person who makes guilty people look innocent and innocent people look guilty and innocent people look innocent and guilty people look guilty, and all of this with a straight face.

LAXATIVE A medicine that affects the bowels in almost exactly the same way that a scandal affects a gossip's mouth, and with similar results.

LAZY Inclined to expend as much energy avoiding work as most people expend working. 2. Not disposed to use one's brain as a means for producing one's own thoughts, but instead as a mechanism for adopting the thoughts of others.

LEADER One who takes advantage of people who are not disposed to use their brains. see LAZY (2).

LEANDER An ancient Greek, who was an ardent Hero worshiper.

LEARN To get it through one's thick skull.

LEASE A long and confusing legal document, designed to prove to apartment dwellers that there is absolutely nothing wrong with people signing papers they don't understand.

LECHER A man with the amazing ability to keep his eyes and hands roaming, while his mind remains permanently fixed in the gutter.

LECTURE An oral punishment delivered by a parent to a child, which is frequently worse than a physical one, but which serves as a primer for the more agonizing punishments awaiting the child in certain high school and college classrooms.

LEECH A bloodsucking worm, the most slimy and repulsive being one of the human variety.

LEFT A political body comprised of members who seek to replace old programs that don't work with new programs that don't work—but don't work in progressive ways.

LEG One of two qualifications for the position of private secretary.

LEGEND A story from the past which may or may not have really happened, such as the legend of the 1978 gasoline shortage.

LEISURE   Television time. 2. Time devoted to the arduous task of trying to find something to do. 3. That incredibly brief period between Friday's relief and Monday's grief.

LEMON   A car suffering from repair shopitis, a common malady in which the car actually believes that the repair shop is its mother. 2. A citrus fruit that is sometimes imported and used for foreign ade.

LEND   To allow someone to use a belonging with the understanding that it will be returned in a reasonable period of time, preferably under five years, keeping in mind that borrowers as a breed tend to have abnormally weak memories.

LEO   The fifth sign of the zodiac, representing people who feel a longing desire to chase an antelope.

LEPRECHAUN   A little fairy who is said to reveal the place where treasure is hidden if caught. The only problem is that the people who see them are generally in no condition to catch them.

LESS   That quantity of any natural resource which people of reason recognize as being sufficient for sensible living, while the other 99 percent of the population ascribe to the opposing viewpoint.

LETTER   A written communication, which is one of the nicest things in the world to receive and one of the most flattering, since it requires more thought and effort than a thousand phone calls.

LEVEL-HEADED   In agreement with you, and the more agreeable the leveler.

LEXICOGRAPHER   A person suffering from a rare mental condition which impels him to write a dictionary.

LIAR   Someone who attempts to improve upon the truth by making it sound more realistic. 2. Someone who twists the facts for his own benefit, as distinguished from a lawyer, who twists the facts for the benefit of his client. 3. Someone who says something false in order to hurt someone else, as opposed to someone who says something false in order to avoid hurting someone else.

LIBERAL   Derogatorily said to have a bleeding heart by those who take a peculiar amount of pride in the fact that theirs are made of stone.

LIBERTY   Freedom from everything except death, taxes, and an occasional run-in with an insurance salesman.

LIBRARIAN   A person who goes to college to study whispering and how to say, "Sh-h-h."

LIBRARY   A quiet, generally uncrowded building, since the only people who go there are the ones who can read.

LIE   To regard the truth with the same disdain that one regards one's integrity. 2. To deceive oneself.

LIEUTENANT GENERAL   A commissioned officer ranking between a general and a specific.

LIFE   The brief period of time between birth and death, one third of which is spent sleeping, one third working, one sixth waking up, going to work, coming home from work and going to bed, one twelfth worrying, going to the doctor and doing laundry, one twenty-fourth filling out forms, one forty-eighth grocery shopping and walking the dog, one ninety-sixth waiting in line, one hundred and ninety-second selecting carpet and applying antiseptic, one three hundred and eighty-fourth trying on shoes, and the other three hundred and eighty-fourth spent doing what you feel like doing.

LIFER   One who, through crime, sentences society to pay for his sustenance for the rest of his life.

LIFELESS   In front of a television set.

LIGHT   Anything that helps one to see more clearly, as the emission of the sun, the moon, the mind, etc.

LIMBO   The place where theologians say the souls of unbaptized infants go, since they cannot possibly get into heaven, not having had the opportunity to be instructed by theologians in the proper method of applying for admission.

LIMERICK   A poem that makes little sense;
That is not very deep or intense;
That is often quite dumb
And regarded by some
As a rhythmical, rhyming offense.

LIMITS   Restrictions placed on children's behavior, which help them to define their world and which spare them from assuming the terrifying responsibility of controlling their parents.

LIMNOLOGY   The scientific study of biological conditions in lakes and ponds and of the ways that fish, frogs and other organisms can make constructive use of styrofoam cups and beer cans.

LIMOUSINE   A large chauffeur-driven sedan, which is most commonly used to transport people to the airport or to the cemetery. Most prefer the former trip, although with the latter you get the vehicle all to yourself.

LINE   The shortest distance between two points, if it is straight, or the longest, if it is the one a taxi driver is taking.

LIPS   The outer rims of the mouth, used primarily for kissing, smiling, pouting, and making conspicuous marks on the neck that cause embarrassment in gym class.

LIQUEUR   An alcoholic drink served after dinner, for which cough syrup may be substituted without detection.

LIRA   The monetary unit of Italy, which is worth as much as an Italian merchant can dupe a tourist into thinking it's worth.

LISTEN   To make sense out of sound by keeping the mind as open as the ears and allowing the process of reception to register before engaging the process of transmission.

LISTLESS   Indifferent; spiritless; inclined to be the death of the party.

LITERATURE   All writing that has not become dated a week after it was written. 2. All writing that has not become dated a hundred years after it was written. 3. All writing that will not have become dated forty-million years after it was written.

LITHOLOGY   The study of rocks, which attracts few students, because there is not a single piece of the work that isn't hard.

LITTER   The result of an attempt by city dwellers to add an element of a country feeling to their environment, by making it look like a pig sty.

LITTERATEUR A person who reads magazines that don't have any pictures in them.

LITTLE Twice as large as tiny and three times larger than itsy bitsy or teensy weensy.

LIVABLE Pertaining to conditions that are perfectly fine for someone else.

LIVE To make what little sense one can from a situation that defies rational analysis and to survive in that situation to the best of one's ability, for reasons that no one knows.

LIVER A meat that is regarded by children as a punishment inflicted by their mothers to get back at them for making noise, not cleaning their rooms, etc.

LOAN Money that a person borrows for the purpose of buying something now and paying and paying and paying and paying for it later.

LOATHE To dislike a person to such an extreme degree that the effect on your nervous system is generally worse than anything the person could have done to cause you to dislike him in the first place.

LOBOTOMY An operation performed on certain actors to prepare them for their roles on prime time television shows.

LOCOMOTIVE An absolutely crazy reason for doing something; as, he murdered his wife, but he must have had a locomotive.

LODGE The members of a secret society, who meet regularly in order to wear funny hats and to avoid talking to their wives.

LOGIC The canon of rules for valid reasoning, one of which stipulates that if A) emotions are not subject to reason and B) beings with emotions constructed the rules of reasoning, then C) the rules of reasoning are unreasonable.

LONESOME Insufficiently acquainted with oneself to appreciate the company of others. 2. Sufficiently acquainted with oneself to appreciate the company of others.

LONG About the length of time it takes to do anything one dislikes doing.

LONGER   About the length of time it takes to get up the energy to do anything one dislikes doing.

LONGEST   About the length of time it takes putting off doing anything one dislikes doing.

LONG-WINDED   Characterizing a person who could listen to himself talk all day, which is about twenty-four hours longer than anyone else would care to listen to him.

LOON   A bird known for its insanity (crazy as a loon), although there is some question as to the mental competence of the scientist whose studies led to this conclusion.

LOOPHOLE   A small opening through which corporations and large businesses manage to squeeze their tax exemptions. It is large enough to sprain the law, but not to break it.

LOOSE   Pertaining to someone whose presence in a bar has everything to do with thirst but little to do with drinking.

LOSER   Anyone whose enjoyment of a game hinges solely upon its outcome.

LOST   On the little back road that definitely looks familiar and most certainly leads to the main highway.

LOVE   A feeling of utter emotional incompetency, coupled with the unsuppressed desire to perform embarrassing acts, such as frolicking naked in a field of daisies or writing sonnets of dubious literary merit. The feeling runs rampant among human beings, with the marked exception of psychology majors.

LOYAL   Equally opposed to anarchists who would overthrow the government and politicians who would undermine it.

LUCIFER   An archangel who was invested by God with great pride and rebelliousness, and then condemned to hell for exercising it.

LUCK   The key ingredient in any success, followed distantly by talent, skill and hard work. 2. That element pervading all of human experience which makes life as interesting as it is unfair.

LUDICROUS   Exciting laughter, especially from incongruity, as when a used car salesman says to a customer, "Let me be perfectly honest with you."

LUGGAGE   Those suitcases or bags which indicate that a couple is checking into a hotel primarily to get some sleep.

LUNCH   In school, a meal comprised of two bites of a bologna sandwich and dessert. 2. In business, three martinis with a side order of food.

LUST   The desire to put off falling in love with a person's mind until better acquainted.

LUTIST   A person who makes lutes for the three people in the world who want one.

LUXURY   Anything which costs a lot of money, designed to produce a feeling almost as good as walking through a forest or listening to a robin. 2. Anything which feels as though it ought to cost a lot of money, such as watching a sunset or wading in the ocean.

LYCANTHROPY   A mental illness in which the person thinks he is Lon Chaney, Jr.

LYNCH   To hang a murderer without giving him his legal right to spend the next three years in appeals courts.

LYSSOPHOBIA   A fear of insanity that is so obsessive it can drive a person crazy.

M. A. Master of Anything, if sufficiently pompous and surrounded by high school graduates.

MACHINE Any of a wide array of mechanical contrivances which help to free people from many mundane tasks and shackle them to many mechanical contrivances. 2. Any device with just enough moving parts to scare the average user into not trying to fix it himself.

MACKEREL A fish that has not changed throughout history, because it takes extreme care in selecting a mate exactly like itself; hence the expression, wholly mackerel.

MACROPHYSICS The branch of physics that deals with objects that can be seen, as opposed to objects hidden in a closet.

MAD Angry over nothing; as, "What are you mad at me for?" 2. Justifiably angry; as, "I'm mad at you."

MADHOUSE Any house about twenty minutes after the father has said, "Now let's all sit down and discuss this thing calmly and rationally."

MAFIA A group of persons whose proliferation of crime differs from that of politicians in the sense that it is organized.

MAGAZINE A periodical which features a wide variety of written material, from articles to advertisements to short stories to advertisements to interviews to advertisements to poetry to advertisements to advertisements to advertisements.

MAGICIAN   Someone skilled in the art of illusion, as a lawyer who can shake a client's hand and rifle his wallet at the same time, while smiling. 2. Any woman who knows how to use make-up effectively.

MAGISTRATE   A public official who helps to stem corruption among motorists and policemen by fixing traffic tickets, which makes bribing the officer who issues the ticket unnecessary.

MAGNETIC POLE   Someone from Krakow with enormous sex appeal.

MAID   The wife of a man who was spoiled by his mother.

MAIL   Something that arrives in one's mailbox promptly on time, as a bill, several days late, as a personal letter, or sometime in the remote future, as a check. 2. Any of a nauseating array of solicitations, their main purpose being to promote exercise daily between the mailbox and the trash can.

MAJOR   That which distinguishes a party attended by college students, where the most popular questions are, "What's your major?" and "What's your sign?" from a party attended by non-college students, where the most popular questions are, "What's your sign?" and "What's your sign?"

MAJORITY   That number among any group of people that is the easiest to manipulate; as, (whoever rules) the majority rules.

MAKE-UP   A substance applied to the face, which is fundamental to women attracting men in the evening and scaring the daylights out of them the morning after.

MALADJUSTED   Unable to cope with the insanities of one's environment. 2. Out of kilter with socially acceptable misbehavior.

MALCONTENT   Any thinking citizen who has not already cynically resigned himself to the gross ineptitudes of bureaucracy.

MALICE   Portable ill will that can be taken anywhere, although it has the extraordinary capacity to become gradually quite heavy, so that the person carrying it is pulled down by it, often into the closest available ditch.

MALIGN   To refer to one's opponent in a political compaign.

MALL   A shopping area with a large number of different kinds of stores, so that people who are prone to buy things impulsively can get all the things they don't need in one trip.

MALPRACTICE   The treatment by a surgeon or physician in a manner contrary to standard medical rules, which stipulate that treatments should never result in physical injury to the patient, but that all injuries should be strictly confined to the patient's bank account, dignity, and psychological well-being.

MAMMAL   Any of a large number of animals that milk their young, although humans are the only animals that continue to milk one another beyond infancy.

MAN   A primate more widely known for his assertions of intellectual superiority than for any behavioral pattern to fortify those assertions. 2. The only animal who keeps a history of his past, which is almost as thorough as his failure to learn from it.

MANAGER   The person in a hotel or store whose skill lies in the ability to tell customers exactly the same thing that a clerk has already told them, but in such a manner that they go away thinking that they were right in considering the clerk incompetent.

MANATEE   A sea cow, also known as a dowager with a yacht.

MANEGE   A riding academy or, in other words, a school where students are harassed by criticism and ridicule.

MANIAC   A raving lunatic, which is a lunatic who liked the play much more than the other lunatics.

MANICHEAN   Pertaining to the religious system formulated by the Persian teacher Mani, who believed that matter is inherently evil and that, therefore, all a person has to do to lead a good life is to abstain from contact with things.

MANICURIST   A person who makes up hands so that they look too nice to be used for anything.

MANIPULATE   To control others for one's own purpose, thereby realizing some minor gain while simultaneously condemning oneself to the company of weak, stupid and gullible people.

MANKIND   The human race, so called because most of the participants are too busy rushing toward the finish line to appreciate the scenery along the way or to develop even the foggiest notion of where they are running or why.

MANNA   Any food-like substance that miraculously falls from heaven, bird droppings excluded.

MANSION   A house in which the bathrooms outnumber the neighbors.

MANTIC   Gifted with prophetic powers, such as the power to foretell how many suckers will pay to have their fortunes told in an average week.

MANUSCRIPT   An author's guts, bound and ready for the editor's scalpel.

MANY   Quite a few, as in the number of one's fine points. 2. Several, as in the number of one's faults.

MAP   A puzzle designed for the entertainment of drivers and passengers. The easy part of the puzzle is figuring out what the road markings mean; the hard part is figuring out how to fold the thing back into its original shape when finished using it.

MARATHON   An event in which non-smokers demonstrate their superior ability to collapse in the street.

MARCH   National Jump-the-Gun Month, when people without coats who are so sure that spring is just around the corner catch pneumonia.

MARIJUANA   A weed that is smoked in order to produce a feeling similar to that experienced by a person who has just thought of something.

MARKET   A place where one is robbed and the thief is not even present; he has a clerk.

MARKS   The indicators of a successful or misspent educational experience, highly regarded by employers and given by teachers in a variety of subjects, which do not include honesty, integrity and common sense.

MAROONED   Born on Earth.

MARRIAGE   A social institution dedicated to the proposition that any man and any woman who can stand looking at each other go into the bathroom every morning deserve a tax break.

MARS   The Roman god of young widowhood.

MARTIAN   A little green man, who differs from Earthlings in that he has the good sense to avoid contact with them.

MASCARA   A preparation designed to discourage women from crying in public.

MASK   A covering for the face, such as make-up, which is commonly used by plain women to transform themselves miraculously from unattractive to hideous. 2. The false, fake face of a phony, feigning feeling.

MASOCHIST   A person who is fit to be tied.

MASQUERADE   An assembly of persons wearing masks, as at any beauty contest or televised awards presentation. See MASK (2).

MASSACRE   The cruel and atrocious killing of a number of human beings, differing from a war in that the victims need not all be young men in order to qualify.

MASSEUR   A person who generally gets along well with people and who seldom rubs them the wrong way.

MASTER   The husband of a wife who has allowed herself to be reduced to canine status; the owner of a dog.

MASTHEAD   A marijuana-smoking lookout on a ship.

MATADOR   The man who puts an end to the bull, as a moderator at a political debate.

MATERIALISM   A disease in which the victim finds himself spending more time accumulating things than he does enjoying them.

MATHEMATICIANS   That group of people who receive a society's greatest esteem, due to the fact that, more than any other group, they are the ones who really count.

MATINEE   A movie shown in the daytime for people with nothing else to do, known among theater employees as the matinee idle.

MATRIARCH   A kind of family doctor, whose prescriptions include large doses of guilt, which she dispenses to her patients in order to spare them from succumbing to the affliction of emotional independence.

MATTER   The substance composing a physical object, thereby distinguishing it from a non-physical object or a metaphysical verb.

MATURE   Pertaining to one's own attitude at all times, especially when confronted by the stupid, childish, stubborn, biased and overbearing attitude of someone else.

MAUSOLEUM   A magnificent tomb reserved for a person who can afford to decompose in style.

MAXIM   A saying of a proverbial nature; as, Don't make fun of the way my toes are all bunched together until you've walked a mile in my shoes.

MAY   National Crams Month, when term papers are due, final exams are taken, and coffee sales are way up.

MAYOR   The person in any city or borough whose sidewalk is always clean, whose street has no potholes in it, and whose trash is collected on time each week.

ME   The objective case of I and one of the most vital words in the language, without which the average person would be severely limited in his topics of conversation.

MEAL   That portion of food designed to curb one's appetite between snacks.

MEANING   The middle ground between the speaker's beating around the bush and the listener's jumping to conclusions. 2. A parcel mailed from the mind to the mouth, where it is forwarded to the mind of another, its condition upon delivery varying according to first, second, or special fourth class vocabulary and the care with which it is wrapped.

MEASLES   A perennially popular disease among children, because it not only prevents them from going to school but it also produces red spots on the skin, which make the sickness very official looking and evoke both sympathy from family and envy from friends.

MEAT   One of the four basic food groups in the typical American diet, the other three being potatoes, soda and cookies.

MECHANIZE   To replace human agents with mechanical agents; to put human agents in charge of mechanical agents; to render human agents and mechanical agents indistinguishable.

MEDDLE   To poke one's nose into somebody else's business, evidently to avoid the smell of one's own business.

MEDICINE   The science which seeks to relieve the pain and hardship of illness by means of astounding cures and to promote the pain and hardship of cures by means of astounding bills.

MEEK   Wise enough to realize that the only kind of revenge which makes any sense is that not taken, since those who cause injury to others invariably end up injuring themselves, and doing a much better job of it than anyone else could.

MEGALOMANIA   A serious mental disorder, suffered by people whose delusions of grandeur interfere with their ability to lead otherwise normal lives of obscure mediocrity.

MELANCHOLIA   Extreme depression of spirits, sometimes caused by the complete absence of any delusions of grandeur and the unquestioning acceptance of a normal life of obscure mediocrity. See MEGALOMANIA.

MELIORISM   The doctrine that the world keeps getting better as time goes on, a belief held devoutly by people who are in line for a large inheritance.

MELODRAMATICS   The conduct of people who place their emotions on a pedestal, where their brilliance will not be marred by the dim light of their intellect and common sense.

MELODY   The part of a piece of music that can be taken into the shower. 2. A succession of notes that form a tune, commonly employed by composers who have not dedicated their lives to being misunderstood.

MELPOMENE   The mythological Muse of tragedy and the patron saint of the six o'clock news.

MEMORY   A panoramic cinema of the past, including scenes that have been edited throughout time and footage that has been spliced out, usually because it detracts from the hero's image of himself on the screen.

MENDACIOUS   Uncomfortable with the truth, as is a rodent with the mange.

MENOPAUSE   Nature's way of rewarding women who have waited the better part of their lives for a legitimate reason to be moody.

MENTALITY   Mental power, or, in many cases, mental power failure.

MENU   A roadmap to the land of obesity.

MEPHISTOPHELES   One of the chief devils, whose foremost responsibility in the promotion of human suffering is to make sure that the people who write television commercials are never blessed by God with an original idea.

MERCENARY   A soldier who does not need an excuse like patriotism to partake in the sheer joy of killing people.

MERCY   Compassion for someone who deserves punishment but who has never been shown compassion before, as distinguished from stupidity, which is compassion for someone who has seen it and taken advantage of it.

MERETRICIOUS   Of or pertaining to a woman who has to take it lying down.

MERIT SYSTEM   The system of promoting employees according to their competence, particularly their competence at marrying into the employer's family.

MESS   A quantity of food or a confused mixture of things or, in the case of a housewife who was married only for her looks, both.

METAL   A substance which is either precious, like gold or silver, or merely adorable, like tin or copper.

METAPHOR   A figure of speech suggesting a resemblance between two things, as levity is the soul of wit.

METAPHYSICAL   Concerning abstract thought and its many practical applications to abstract existence.

METEMPIRICS   The philosophy dealing with things transcending the field of experience, such as a comfortable subway ride.

METEOROLOGIST   One who scientifically guesses the weather.

METICULOUS   Paying strict attention to every detail but one—that of being bearable.

METRIC   A system of measurement designed solely to confuse Americans.

MEZZO-SOPRANO   A singer whose vocal range prevents her from getting to die at the end of an opera.

MICROBAROGRAPH   An instrument for recording small and rapid change, as that of a candy store owner with quick hands.

MICROCOCCUS   A kind of bacteria that lives on dead material, such as the script of a kung fu movie.

MICROSCOPE   An instrument used to invade the private lives of bacteria and protozoa, either for purely scientific research or to satisfy the crazed perversions of science-minded voyeurs.

MIDAS   A king of Phrygia, whose wish that everything he touched be turned to gold was granted by Dionysis. This worked out great for the king until the first time he had to go to the bathroom, after which he begged the god to take his favor back.

MIDDLE   In the place where he stands who would make no true friends and no lasting enemies.

MIDDLE-AGED   Being aware of growing old but being too young not to give a damn.

MIDWIFE   A woman who works strictly on a C.O.D. basis.

MIGRANT   A laborer who has escaped the oppression of picking potatoes in his native country for the opportunity of picking lettuce in a free one.

MILITARY   Of or pertaining to the men and machinery that combine to make wars work. The former supply the blood, which adds a splash of color to the otherwise drab uniforms, and the latter provide the means for killing at a distance, to insure that there is nothing personal intended.

MILK   A drink that will never attain the same popularity among children as other drinks until somebody can figure out a way to make it cause cavities.

MILLIONAIRE   A person who can afford not to impress people. 2. Someone whose failure to shave on a given morning is called an eccentricity instead of a slovenly affront to social decorum.

MIND   The center of thought, commonly believed to reside in the brain, although considering the way some people think, there is persuasive evidence that it may, in certain cases, actually be located quite a bit lower in the anatomy.

MINE   Not yours, and don't you forget it.

MINERVA   The Roman goddess of citizenship, whose moral standing was open to question because she was constantly getting involved in civic affairs.

MINK   A small, semi-aquatic animal, which some people would like to see left alone to live in the wilderness, but the prevailing practice is to defur to a higher authority.

MINOR   Someone who can't wait to grow up, so that he can wish he were a kid again. 2. A person who has not yet reached the age of regret.

MINOTAUR   A mythological monster that was half man and half bull. Its modern counterpart, most frequently found in bars, is half man and all bull.

MINUTE   One-tenth of a clerk's coffee break; one-thirtieth of a manager's coffee break; one-sixtieth of an executive's coffee break.

MIRACLE   An occurrence which defies the laws of nature, such as the time in Detroit when a television movie actually went for fifteen minutes without a commercial.

MIRROR   A reflective glass used in the bedroom for preparing oneself the night of a party and in the bathroom for repairing oneself the morning after.

MISANTHROPE   One who hates everything about mankind except for mankind's most hateful attribute, the ability to hate.

MISBELIEVE   To believe what the members of a religion other than one's own believe.

MISCONCEPTION   A possible result if she forgot to take her pill.

MISER   One who unselfishly permits others to partake of the joy of giving.

MISERY   A distressful state that is said to love company, but only if the company knows when to leave.

MISESTIMATE   To estimate in the manner of a car mechanic.

MISFORTUNE   The kind of thing that happens the day after you tell yourself that you've finally got it made.

MISGIVING   A premonition that something bad is going to happen, often felt by people whose houses are about to be robbed but whose helpful friends have convinced them that their feelings of apprehension are silly, that of course they remembered to lock the door, and that it would be stupid to go back and check.

MISLAY   To put right over there. 2. Or was it over there?

MISOGYNY   A serious mental condition marked by the hatred of all women, even the ones who drive trucks.

MISOLOGIST   Someone who harbors a hatred of reasoning and is prepared to back it up with plenty of good reasons.

MISONEIST   Someone who bears a hatred or intolerance of anything new, such as a grandchild.

MISS   A semi-obsolete title for an unmarried woman, which has been replaced by Ms. in some circles, by way of making a statement, or by one's first name, by way of making a friend.

MISSIONARY   A person who is dedicated to bringing the truth to people who somehow managed to survive for centuries without ever once realizing that the things they believed in were utter nonsense.

MISTRESS   A woman who has a married man all to herself at night and the bathroom all to herself in the morning.

MISUNDERSTAND   To open the ears, close the mind, and ready the mouth.

MITHRIDATISM   The act of taking poison in increasing doses as a means of building an immunity to it, as in the case of people who start out with talk shows and gradually work their way up to situation comedies.

MNEMONICS   The act of improving your memory, which is important for a number of reasons, but I can't recall offhand what they are.

MODEL   A pro poser.

MODERNIZE   To cover with aluminum siding; to replace with something made out of plastic; to remove anything remotely quaint or charming.

MODESTY   That quality possessed by people who do not wish to draw attention to their good deeds and accomplishments, provided that someone else draws attention to them.

MONASTERY   A place where monks go to escape from kids who play their radios on the bus.

MONDAY   The day when most people unhappily return to the jobs which chose them.

MONEY   The means whereby some people attain their dreams and others lose track of them. 2. The best thing in the world to have, next to an appreciation of those things which are priceless.

MONKEY   An animal who has been taught to speak sign language and whose first message was: "Nobody's going to make a human out of me!"

MONOGAMY   Marriage that is opposed to more than one spouse at a time, based upon the conviction that it's hard enough to decide what to watch on television the way it is.

MONSTER   A grotesque movie creature of high intelligence, as exhibited by the fact that it always goes after beautiful women.

MONTH   A page of a calendar, a paragraph of a year, a sentence of a life, a comma of history, and a period of time in which Handel wrote "Messiah."

MOON   An extraterrestrial repository for scientific litter.

MORAL   Pertaining to anything that does not interfere with another person's right to pursue his own ideas of what is good and proper.

MORDRED   The nephew of King Arthur, who was also a knight of the Round Table and yet another sparkling example of political favoritism in Camelot.

MORE   Still less than an envied neighbor has. 2. Sufficient to render a pleasantly full stomach into an upset one. 3. Just enough to satisfy a present urge but never enough to satisfy subsequent urges. 4. Pertaining to the amount of anything desired by people who never seem to find the time to appreciate fully what they already have.

MORGAIN   A sister of King Arthur, and one of his few relatives who was not a knight of the Round Table.

MORON   The principal character in a popular series of jokes; as, why did the moron mix ice cubes with his pimientos? See PUNCH LINE.

MORTAL   Relieved of the thought of an eternity of vacuuming and endless car inspections.

MORTGAGEE   A person who belongs to a house for 25 or 30 years, after which the house belongs to him and his children have all grown up and left and he is ready for a smaller place.

MORTICIAN   A person whose business is dying when people aren't.

MOTEL   A place that offers free movies in the rooms, so that any married people who happen to be staying there have something to do, too.

MOTHER   The only person brave enough to go through a kid's pockets. 2. A woman who is said to be happiest when she is giving birth to her children, although there is ample evidence to suggest that there is a time when she is even happier: when everyone at the table is having seconds.

MOTORCYCLIST A motorist who renders a vital public service by providing overheated car drivers with a target for their hostilities, thus sparing the car's passengers from potential abuse.

MOUNTAIN A natural elevation of earth, which people climb in order to prove to themselves that there is more to life than keeping up the mortgage payments—but not much more.

MOUSE A little rodent with substantial cartoon credentials.

MOUTH The opening in the head into which food is placed, which in no way accounts for the absolute garbage that sometimes comes out of it.

MOVIE A carnival ride for the mind, in which a screen becomes the landscape of a world both familiar and foreign, where time loses its grip and dreams take hold of reality.

MULE An animal with the unfair reputation of being stubborn, when what it is actually doing is patiently resisting the efforts of anyone who is stubbornly insisting that it move.

MULTIPLICATION That branch of mathematics which requires that all children not owning pocket calculators must learn their times tables.

MURDER An act which ranks the guilty party lower than any animal, since the victim is not even used for food. 2. The one crime for which there can be no just punishment, as it is an insult to the victim's life to equate it with that of a murderer.

MUSEUM A building that assembles the past, presents it to the present, and preserves it for the future.

MUSIC The art that reaches the soul through the ear and lifts it to a kingdom where beauty and order reign.

NAG   To turn one's tongue into a whip and use it to lash the nerves of one's spouse, child or other unfortunate being; to demonstrate that even deafness has its advantages.

NAIVE   Gifted with a lack of perception about the world that allows one to take comfort in non-existent ideals.

NAKED   In your birthday suit, which is the only suit in your wardrobe that is constantly undergoing alterations. 2. Unprotected by the shield of a designer label.

NAME   Something that is received at birth, retained in life, and relinquished at death, unless the owner did something worth remembering, in which case it is revived, and either revered or reviled. 2. The title by which the average person is well-unknown.

NAPKIN   A square piece of cloth or paper, which some people place on their laps and others under their collars. The former tend to have food stains on their shirts; the latter, on their pants.

NARCISSIST   One who believes in an I for an I.

NARCOTIC   A kind of drug intended for people who are extremely extravagant, as well as inefficient, since a single bullet is far more effective and economical.

NARROW-MINDED   Pertaining to a person who is as stubborn and stupid as you would be if you weren't so tolerant of obstinate, thick headed people and unwilling to put labels on them.

NASTY   Foolishly willing to sacrifice a priceless portion of one's goodness in exchange for the petty satisfaction of getting even with somebody; spiteful to oneself.

NATAL   Dating from birth or, if not dating, at least seeing on a casual basis.

NATION   A large group of people connected by a commonly misunderstood and misused language, a common belief that it's every man for himself, and a common fear and mistrust of other nations.

NATIONALITY   The credential for admission into a banquet hall filled with song and dance and a rejoicing in the differences among people. 2. The credential for admission into a tomb filled with bias and scorn and a disdain for differences, where the proud and the arrogant celebrate their hatred in exclusive darkness.

NATURAL   Not yet available in artificial form.

NATURAL GAS   A wild and swinging party attended by nudists.

NATURE   The major stumbling block in the path of progress. 2. The system that is responsible for birds not having the sense to stay away from oil slicks and whales foolishly swimming in the vicinity of harpoons.

NAUGHTY   Adorably mischievous, as one's own child. 2. Maliciously troublesome, as the kid next door.

NAUSEA   The overwhelming desire to go to a different restaurant next time. 2. The feeling which overtakes children on the turnpike exactly midway between rest stops.

NAVEL   The part of the body designed to store lint, the exact use for which science has yet to determine.

NAVY   The branch of the military designed to save cemetery space.

NAZISM   The political doctrine advocating the predominance of a superior race, which differs from inferior races in its uplifted capacity for bestial behavior and its transcendent mastery of intolerance.

NEAR   Not far at all, if you're asking someone else to go there for you; at a great distance, if you have to go there yourself; too far and out of the question, if someone else is asking you to go there.

NEARBY   Close at hand, unless it is on the floor, where it is close at foot.

NEBUCHADNEZZAR An ancient Babylonian king, whose practice of lynching criminals from trees amid magnificent plants and flowers originated the famous Hanging Gardens of Babylon.

NECESSITARIANISM The doctrine that the will is not free, which anyone who has ever gone to a lawyer to make one out knows to be quite true.

NECESSITY Anything that is essential to existence itself, as bread to the poor or caviar to the rich. 2. The mother of retention; the mother of prevention; the mother of convention.

NECK The part of the body that keeps the head from falling down the throat and being eaten alive.

NECROMANCER A person who claims to be able to communicate with the spirits of the dead, provided that only one condition is met: that the survivors of the deceased party be incredibly stupid.

NECROPSY A post-mortem examination, which most dead people consider grossly unfair since they cannot possibly be expected to pass under the circumstances.

NEED A desire under the influence of envy.

NEEDLE An instrument of terror which is used by doctors and nurses to stab patients, resulting in physical pain and emotional trauma that is often worse than the ailment which necessitated being stabbed in the first place.

NEEDLESS See UNNECESSARY. 2. On second thought, don't bother. It's USELESS.

NEFARIOUS So heinously wicked that only self-righteous hypocrites can serve for comparison.

NEGATIVISM The doctrine that nothing in the universe is certain, except of course for the doctrine that nothing in the universe is certain. 2. The doctrine of a person who is absolutely sure that he is never absolutely sure.

NEGATIVIST Someone who is uncertain about everything, especially the meaning of the preceding definition.

NEGLIGEE A garment that a woman puts on so that she can take it off so that she can get it on; an undressing gown.

NEIGHBOR Someone whose vacuum cleaner interferes with your television reception and whose kids cut across your lawn and whose car takes up two spaces at the curb and whose radio plays music that is too loud and too lousy. 2. Someone who can become so involved in telling you what's wrong with the people across the street that she barely has time to go across the street and tell them what's wrong with you. 3. Someone who doesn't say beans to you until she wants to borrow a cup of them.

NEMESIS The Greek goddess of retribution, whose efficiency in rectifying offenses deprived the ancient Greeks of the pleasure and stimulation of holding grudges, which contributed to their complacency and the eventual demise of their civilization.

NEOARSPHENAMINE A synthetic form of arsenic useful to people who intend to commit artificial murder.

NEOLOGISM A new word, such as neoneologism.

NEONEOLOGISM A word that is so new that even neologists don't know it yet.

NEOPHYTE A heathen who has been converted into a sinner.

NEPHEW Someone to whom an aunt or an uncle is merely another person that you have to go and visit when you'd rather be out somewhere riding your bike.

NEPOTISM A promotion policy based on family relationship rather than merit, intended to maintain a healthy level of resentment within a company.

NERVOUS Alive in the modern world without a drink, a pill or anemia.

NESSUS A centaur who attempted to ravish the wife of Hercules. When Hercules found out, the centaur explained that he was only horsing around and Hercules killed him, not so much because he loved his wife but because he hated bad puns.

NEST EGG Money that a person puts away so that, in case his hot water heater explodes, he can get a new one in time for his car to break down.

NETWORK One of the major television companies responsible for providing programs which promote family togetherness through collective mental atrophy.

NEUROTIC Possessed by overpowering feelings of anxiety, often springing from the demented notion that one is living in a pressured society.

NEUTRALITY The status of a nation that does not have a surplus of young men to waste. 2. The policy of refusing to participate in a war which never would have started if the warring parties had subscribed to a similar policy. 3. The policy of a country that is not always ready to blame some other country for the problems it can't solve on its own because it is too busy building bombs.

NEW AND IMPROVED Pertaining to an old product that wasn't very good to begin with to which an advanced ingredient has been added that makes it almost as good as it was claimed to be in the first place.

NEWS Who (was murdered), what (burned down), where (the latest earthquake occurred), when (the bus fares are going up), and why (the mayor belongs in jail).

NEWSBOY A kid with the uncanny ability to hit a bush with a folded-up newspaper.

NEWSPAPER All the news to give you the blues. 2. Tomorrow's waste paper. 3. A daily case history of the world's mental condition.

NEWTONIAN A believer in gravity.

NEW YEAR'S DAY The first hangover of the year, followed by the first gluttonous meal, followed by the first upset stomach. 2. A day ideally conducive to the breaking of resolutions.

NICE Pleasant and forgettable; as, it certainly was a nice party. 2. Inoffensive and unremarkable; as, he sure is a nice guy. 3. Sweet and unattractive; as, she's really a nice girl.

NICKEL A coin that can purchase exactly five times the amount of that which a penny can purchase; namely, nothing.

NICOTINE   The toxic alkaloid in cigarettes which gradually kills the smoker, but not until the tobacco industry and the government tax system have gotten what they want out of him.

NIECE   A person who is as spoiled and pampered as her aunts and uncles are single and childless.

NIFTY   Very stylish, assuming that one's sense of style is about ten years in advance of one's slang.

NIGGER   A black person who acts like a white person who uses this term.

NIGHT   The perfect time to take advantage of the darkness all around you to see the light that is within yourself.

NIGHTCAP   The last drink of the night or the last drink of them all, depending upon who's driving.

NIGHTFALL   The loss of one's footing after dusk.

NIGHTMARE   A dream in which the invisible monsters of your sub-conscious mind take shape and chase you all over the place, assuring you that the morbid fears of your waking hours are not unfounded.

NIHIL OBSTAT   Permission granted by religious officials to publish a book that does not contain any ideas which might induce the reader to challenge, and thereby strengthen, his faith.

NIHILISM   The doctrine that social conditions are so intolerable that they should be destroyed completely and replaced with something tolerable, such as chaos.

NIMBUS   A band of radiant light surrounding the heads of gods, saints, middle linebackers and other venerable personages.

NIMIETY   Redundancy. 2. Redundancy.

NINCOMPOOP   A ninny; a ninnyhammer; a sillywilly; a stupydoopy. 2. Anybody who uses one or more of the aforementioned words.

NINE   The last year before one hits what sociologists call the double-digit period of life, which is the hard part.

NINETEEN The last of the teen years, during which the average person begins to become all of the things he spent the preceding six years condemning, so that by the end of the following six years he will have become ideologically neutralized and a productive member of society.

NIOBE The wife of Amphion, who spent so much time excessively boasting about her numerous children that Zeus turned her into stone, an act which evoked a great outpouring of praise to him among her relatives and neighbors, whose prayers he answered.

NIRVANA A state of freedom from pain, worry, fear, and static cling.

NIT-PICK To make an annoyingly big deal out of an insignificantly small detail, as when the engineer of the Titanic suggested that perhaps they should slow down a bit.

NITROUS OXIDE A gas which produces laughter and which some people suspect is secretly dispersed among live audiences of televised situation comedies, explaining their ability to laugh at inane humor. The other possible explanation is that they are morons.

NO A word that children hate to hear almost as much as they love their parents for saying it.

NOBODY Somebody, with an ego problem.

NOCTAMBULIST A person walking in his sleep, who can be distinguished from a person going to work in that he is usually not wearing a jacket.

NODULE A rounded mass of irregular shape, commonly known to frequent confectionery shops and bakeries.

NOISY Urban.

NOMADISM A wanderful life.

NOMINEE The person chosen as the best qualified to slander a person of the opposing political party, who is running for office with equal qualifications.

NONCOMBATANT A person involved with the military, such as a surgeon or a chaplain, who, in times of war, does not have to fight anything except his conscience.

NONCONDUCTOR   A musician or a member of the audience at an orchestral concert.

NONCONFORMITY   The refusal to accept acceptance in return for abandoning awareness.

NONDESCRIPT   Of the kind of policy that a liberal candidate advocates when compaigning in a conservative area; of the kind of policy that a conservative candidate advocates when campaigning in a liberal area; of the kind of policy that a moderate candidate advocates when campaigning in any area.

NONEDUCABLE   Incapable of being taught by someone who is incapable of trying hard enough to teach; capable of being taught by someone who doesn't know the meaning of this word.

NONENTITY   A person of no account, who prefers instead to keep his money hidden in the house somewhere.

NONFLAMMABLE   Not flammable, as confused with not inflammable.

NONINFLAMMABLE   Not inflammable, which does not have to be confused with anything because it is confusing enough by itself. This confusion has never bothered most linguists, although it has occasionally caused some people to get burned up.

NONINTERVENTION   The state or habit of a country that concentrates on mismanaging itself and does not become concerned with the mismanagement of other countries.

NONRHYMING   Unlike this definition, intact,
But quite the opposite, in fact.

NONSENSE   His sense; her sense; their sense.

NON SEQUITUR   A conclusion which does not follow from the premise and which therefore only applies to people who take the dog out more than once a day.

NOODLE   A paste made with egg which imaginative cooks include in a wide variety of recipes; as, that's using your noodle.

NOON   The time of day when many people take a break from work to go and have a few drinks or a marijuana cigarette. This is known as the twelve o'clock high.

NORMAL Pertaining to people who behave the way you want them to behave. 2. No more or less crazy than anybody else.

NOSE The part of the body that smells or, in odor words, the scent sense.

NOSTALGIA A yearning to return to a time when everything was just great; namely, 5,000,000,000 B.C.

NOTE A musical word in a language of love.

NOTHING

NOTHINGNESS See NOTHING. 2. Hear NOTHING. 3. Taste NOTHING. 4. Smell NOTHING. 5. Feel NOTHING.

NOTORIOUS Unfavorably well-known among a large enough portion of the general public to make a comfortable living from natural curiosity and the secret attraction most people feel toward offensive characters.

NOUN The name of the subject in a sentence, which can be a common noun (clerk or bookkeeper) or a proper noun (socialite or lawyer). Less used are the collective noun (trashman) and the abstract noun (philosopher).

NOVEL Prodigious prose with a prolonged plot and probably a problem-prone protagonist.

NOVELIST A professional prosaic protractor.

NOVEMBER National Diet Prevention Month, when the turkey is stuffed and so is everybody around the table.

NOVOCAIN An anesthesia that helps to deaden the pain of the music in a dentist's office.

NOW At the moment when a vehicle starts to move; as, now we're getting somewhere. 2. At the moment when you've finished reading every outdated magazine in sight; as, the doctor will see you now. 3. About ten minutes before the phone rings; as, now is the perfect time to take a bath. 4. In about an hour; as, she should be home any minute now.

NOWHERE In the place where nothing and nobody are, despite the fact that no one knows how nothing can be there with nobody, since nothing can get there and neither can nobody. 2. The abode of the double negative.

NUCLEAR Pertaining to a type of energy that produces lower electric bills, as well as the distinct possibility that people living in the vicinity of a reactor may one day not have to worry about electric bills at all.

NUDISM A cult dedicated to the naked truth.

NURSE A person with white legs who inserts things into sick people and expects them to be mind readers by asking questions like "How are we feeling today?" 2. A doctor's accomplice in the wealth care field.

NUT A dried fruit that is one of the more expensive foods, only available to people who are willing to shell it out.

NYMPHOMANIAC A female whose needs are not hidden,
Which explains why she's often bedridden.

O   See ZERO. 2. On second thought, never mind. It's really nothing.

OAF   One of the people who always manage to be just ahead of you at an information counter.

OAK   A tree that is a symbol of strength because it is very hard, as is the head of many a person who is determined never to display weakness.

OAR   One of two long wooden implements used to propel a boat and, since they are identical, it doesn't matter which one goes on which side. It is clearly an either-oar situation.

OASIS   A place in the desert that is to a thirsty man what a library is to a thinking one.

OATMEAL   A hot cereal that mothers claim is supposed to stick to your ribs, which is such a revolting thought that it is no wonder many children are hesitant to eat it.

OBDURATE   Hardened against displays of tender feelings for fear of being stepped on by others, and so stepping on oneself.

OBEDIENT   Complying with the laws of an authority, provided that that authority complies with the higher laws of mercy, understanding and justice.

OBESITY   The condition of people who get so much exercise opening and closing the refrigerator door that it is a mystery that they are as out of shape as they are.

OBFUSCATE   To confuse and bewilder, as by the use of confusing and bewildering words, such as obfuscate.

OBITUARY   A column in the paper that names the people who have died, which is not to be confused with the critic's column, in which people named only wish they were dead.

OBJECTIVISM   A theory developed by subjective, personal, emotional beings which stresses a view of reality that is objective, impersonal and unemotional.

OBLIGATION   The duty that every person has to himself not to make promises he can't keep. 2. Any contract or agreement by which a person is bound and through which a person quickly learns when he has bitten off more than he can eschew. 3. Something that binds a person to his own sense of responsibility and decency.

OBLIVION   A vast desert in which those human grains of sand who choose to ride a gust of wind in search of fame, fortune and adventure eventually come to rest alongside the other grains who were simply swept along, unaware that the grains who will be remembered are those who neither rode nor were swept, but who chose instead somehow to rise above their sandhood and defy the wind.

OBNOXIOUS   Regarding a person who finds himself so interesting that he considers it his civic duty to inflict his wealth of information upon the rest of the community.

OBSCENITY   Anything that deliberately offends or hurts people, as the imposition of the moral code of one individual upon another individual.

OBSCURANT   One who strives to hinder the progress of knowledge, as a teacher who has all the answers.

OBSCURE   Easily understood to be vague, by anyone who understands that the first step toward understanding something that is vague is to understand that it is vague; as, yet another obscure definition.

OBSERVANT   Taking mental notes for an exam called life.

OBSERVATORY   A building in which scientists go through hell trying to understand the heavens.

OBSESSION   Persistent preoccupation possessing predisposed people, posing potential personality problems; as, obsession with the letter "p."

OBSOLETE   Replaced by something that causes cancer, destroys the ozone layer, depletes energy resources, or tilts the natural balance of the environment.

OBSTACLE   Anything that gets between a person and his goal, for which he should be grateful, because without it his goal would not be worth attaining.

OBSTETRICIAN   A doctor who treats two people (a pregnant woman and her baby) for the price of one (television set).

OBSTINATE   Pertaining to a person who stubbornly refuses to yield to your arguments, which naturally represent the very essence of reason and logic, even after you have stubbornly and unyieldingly exhausted every means at your disposal of pointing out to him the errors in his thinking.

OBTAINABLE   Losable.

OBVIOUS   So evident that even a person who can't ride a bicycle can understand it; as, there is an obvious flaw in reasoning in this definition.

OCCASIONAL   See NOW. 2. And THEN.

OCCASIONALISM   The philosophical doctrine that the interaction of the mind and the body can be explained quite simply, unless you happen to be an occasionalist.

OCCIPUT   The part of the head which is usually facing one's accusers, generally at a distance.

OCCULT   Designating a science which makes use of knowledge that is so secret and so mysterious that it can be grasped only by people whose minds have the capacity to consume it fully, being as devoid as possible of conventional knowledge.

OCCUPANT   The person in a house who gets the mail that nobody else wants; a potential sucker for a mail order deal of a lifetime.

OCCUPATION   The thing that a person does so that nobody can accuse him of being a bum except his spouse.

OCCURRENCE Something that actually happened, or if historically speaking, may have happened, or if described by the neighborhood gossip, happened differently, or if depicted in a Hollywood movie, probably didn't happen.

OCEAN One of the large bodies of water which cover three-fourths of the earth's surface, serving as nature's primary defense against condominium builders.

OCHLOPHOBIA Morbid fear of Times Square on New Year's Eve, Mardi Gras, and white sales.

OCTAMETER Containing eight feet, as mixed doubles at Wimbledon.

OCTARCHY Government by eight rulers and a tape measure.

OCTOBER National Loose Leaf Month, when the people with the biggest trees and the biggest lawns have the biggest backaches.

OCTOPUS A dibranchiate cephalopod having eight arms, the male of which is reported to be murder on a first date.

OCTOSYLLABLE A line of eight syllables; as, Hey, baby, how about a drink?

OCULIST A doctor who treats your eyes, provided you can see your way clear to pay his bill.

ODDS A means of gauging the relative stupidity of gamblers.

ODIN The mythological god of poetry and war, whose motto was: The pen is mightier than the sword, and vice versa.

ODONTOLOGY The science of teeth and the most frightful methods of treating them.

ODOR Any smell emanating naturally from the human body, which naturally must be artificially masked in order to function naturally in society.

OEDIPUS The adopted son of the king of Corinth, who bought a row of houses in Thebes and converted them into a series of apartments, which later became known as the Oedipus Complex.

OFFENSE The members of a football team who do most of the scoring, which explains why quarterbacks get more dates than middle linebackers.

OFFICER The term used to address a policeman who is standing next to your vehicle holding a ticket book and a pen, as distinguished from the wide array of terms used to address him after he's handed you a ticket and gotten back into his patrol car.

OFFICIOUS Butting in where one is neither wanted nor needed, although it cannot be said that it is none of one's business, since one's business is being a pain.

OFF-THE-RECORD A politician's way of saying, "And now I'm going to tell you what I *really* think."

OGRE A hideous giant of folklore who eats human beings, as well as an occasional certified public accountant.

OIL The substance that keeps car owners in the red and Arabs in the driver's seat. 2. The blood of industry.

OIL SLICK A leak from a super tanker used to control local populations of fish and birds.

O.K. See ALL RIGHT. 2. If you'd rather not, it's OKAY.

OLD Advanced in years and in opportunities to expand and explore; as, there is no such thing as "growing" old; there is, however, such a thing as "not growing" old.

OLD-FASHIONED An advertising term used to denote an attempt to attain artificially the quality, taste or feeling that a given thing used to have naturally.

OLEOMARGARINE The all-purpose, economical spread
For those who like butter but don't have
the bread,
And for those with the bread to buy butter
with ease
Who can't afford buttery calories.

OLIGARCHY A form of government in which the power is vested in a small group. It is the same as a democracy, except that fewer people have to be bought in order to accomplish the group's ends.

OLYMPICS   A series of games between the United States and Russia, with other countries sending along participants to add an international flavor to the proceedings.

OMISSION   Act or instance of   ; also, state of being 2. A thing which is

OMNIPOTENT   Unlimited in power and authority, as God, the head of a labor union, etc.

OMNIPRESENCE   The quality of being present everywhere, except for high school locker rooms, which even God can find hard to take.

OMNIVOROUS   Eating everything; as, omnivorous in-laws.

ONTOLOGY   The branch of knowledge that investigates the nature of being, in terms of the relationship between existence and reality and the intrinsic manifestation of the essence of life as it inherently relates to being in its most existential sense. 2. The science of reality, which is forever seeking new ways to take itself seriously.

OOLOGIST   A person who studies birds' eggs, which sounds like easy work until you think about climbing to the tops of all those trees.

OPEN-MINDED   Pertaining to a person who is considerate of divergent opinions, including the ones he knows are wrong.

OPERA   A musical drama usually sung in a foreign language, so that the audience has little sense of plot, as did the composer.

OPERA HOUSE   An aria area.

OPERATION   The surgical removal of a patient's savings.

OPHIOLATRY   The worship of serpents, which dates back to the earliest recorded hisstory.

OPINION   A stance or an attitude about a given subject which each person is entitled to express and each other person is entitled to ignore.

OPINIONATED   Shackled to an opinion, as a dog is chained to a fence.

OPPONENT   A person who is either a worthy adversary, in which case he deserves one's respect; or an unworthy adversary, in which case he is beneath one's contempt; hence, a personal attack upon one's opponent is, by definition, a personal attack upon oneself.

OPPOSITE   A synonym of antonym; as, opposite and antonym are synonyms and a synonym is the opposite of opposite. Therefore, if opposite itself is a synonym, then opposite is the opposite of opposite. 2. What the first part of this definition is to proper reasoning.

OPPRESSION   The use of power to crush the spirits of people, so that they are almost as unhappy as their leaders are unfit. 2. Authority by those who are too insecure to see the sense in sensitivity and too stupid to understand the power of justice.

OPTIMIST   Someone who still cares enough to become disgusted, who still thinks enough to become depressed, and who still feels enough to cry.

ORACLE   The medium by which ancient Greeks and Romans received divine revelation, the modern counterpart for which is Sunday morning television.

ORANGE   A citrus fruit which is placed in children's lunch boxes so that it will blend colorfully with the apples and grapes in the cafeteria trash can.

ORATORY   The art of speaking in public without . . . uh . . . uh . . . hesitating or using words what ain't, you know, properly correct and all.

ORCHESTRA   A group of musicians who gather together to celebrate sound, to blend beauty, and to prove that, if there isn't a God, there ought to be.

ORDEAL   A painful experience, such as shopping for Christmas presents. 2. An intensely painful experience, such as paying for Christmas presents. 3. A very intensely painful experience, such as returning Christmas presents.

ORDINARY Regarding people who, in their self-appraisal, choose the easy way out.

ORGAN A very large musical instrument, most commonly found in a church or in a suburban split-level home, the difference being that somebody plays the one in the church.

ORGANIZE To play a toccata and fugue.

ORIENTAL RUG A Japanese toupee.

ORIGINALITY The foremost and finest trait of a true artist, be he flutist or florist, writer or wrestler, juggler or janitor. 2. The state or quality which results in being unappreciated, misunderstood or detested, generally for about twenty years.

ORNAMENT A woman who looks absolutely radiant with her mouth closed; the wife of an ambassador.

OROGRAPHY A college course dealing with the study of mountains which is graded on a slope.

ORTHOCHROMATIC Sensitive to green, as a banker.

ORTHODONTIST A doctor who gives you a million dollar smile, which you proudly display right up until the day you get his bill.

ORTHODOX Correct in theological opinion, in the opinion of those deemed qualified to make such determinations by those whose opinions they have deemed theologically correct.

OSCINE A bird that sings, as distinguished from a hummingbird, which is one that can't remember the words.

OSCULATE To kiss, in a way that sounds absolutely horrible and scandalous; as, Were you aware that your daughter was osculating right there on the front porch last night?

OSTENTATION A display intended to impress those on whom the beauty of simplicity is lost, they being too sophisticated to appreciate any but the inferior forms of beauty.

OSTRACISM The act of those who exclude anybody from anything, so that someday their children may be similarly excluded.

OTHER Different or distinct; as, he went on the other train. 2. Alike or indistinguishable; as, he voted for the other candidate.

197

OUCH A word which a person instinctively utters when he is slightly injured, his expressions becoming progressively more colorful with the severity of the injury.

OUIJA A board used to obtain messages from the other world, which are of a practical value about the equivalent of the intellects of those obtaining them.

OUT A secret place known only to teen-agers, where they go to congregate for hours on end to the complete mystification of their parents; as, "Where are you going?" "Out."

OUTCLASS To refrain from attempts to appear classy.

OUT-OF-DATE Alone on a Saturday night.

OUTRAGEOUS So offensive, so heinous and so atrocious that it has all the ingredients of a box office hit.

OUTSPOKEN Likely to have a small number of faithful friends and a large number of respectful foes.

OVEN A chamber for broiling a chicken or steak,
For baking a casserole or a cake;
Everyone loves it—they really do mean it,
But nobody loves it enough to clean it.

OVERCAST To put too many actors in a play.

OVERCHARGE To lead an army toward the enemy from the top of a mountain.

OVERCOAT To paint the same wall more than twice.

OVERCOME To travel some distance beyond one's destination.

OVERLAP To spend too much time sitting on the upper legs of another person.

OVERSPEND To go food shopping.

OVERSTUFF To bring the family to grandmom's house for dinner.

OWL A bird which has the reputation of being wise, probably because it only comes out at night, when most of the really scary creatures are asleep.

PACIFIER   Something that is placed in an infant's mouth to prevent him from expressing his outrage over what his instincts tell him has got to be some kind of a mistake.

PACIFIST   A person who believes in the unamended version of the Fifth Commandment.

PACKAGE   Any item which, for a modest fee, the post office will gladly drop on the floor for you several times.

PACK RAT   A Boy Scout who informs on his fellow scouts.

PAD   The apartment of someone who still thinks that beads hanging in a doorway are groovy.

PAGANISM   The religion of those who recognize none of the three one and only Gods (Christian, Mohammedan, Jewish), but choose instead to worship a false god who doesn't even have a good corporate image.

PAIN   Physical or mental distress, provided in abundance throughout life for the purposes of building character, justifying life in the hereafter, and, most importantly, allowing individuals to experience as frequently as possible the exquisite pleasure of self-pity.

PAINTER   The only creative artist who has no trouble at all with his work, since he does it easelly.

PAINTING   Worlds on canvas skies;
Sheer music for the eyes.

PALACE The home of a sovereign, such as a king, a queen, a Hollywood producer, etc.

PALEFACE The name given by American Indians to the white man, due to the ashen complexion which generally accompanied his contemplation of the tomahawk.

PALMISTRY The practice of studying the palm of a person's hand and reading his future; namely, that he is about to be taken by a con artist.

PALPABLE Capable of being touched, but usually not until after dinner and a movie.

PALPITATION The rapid beating of the heart, as when one is in love or when one is in trouble. They are frequently the same thing.

PALTER To talk or act insincerely, or as though one were running for office.

PAMPER To wait on hand and foot, often with the result of being slapped and stepped on, respectively.

PANDORA A mythological woman who was given a box by Zeus which she opened, allowing to escape all human ills, such as greed, envy, detergent commercials, etc.

PANIC A sudden, overpowering fright concerning financial affairs, most commonly experienced in the aisle of a supermarket.

PANNE A soft fabric with a dull start but with a lustrous finish.

PANSOPHIST A person who thinks he knows everything about everything, when the only thing he probably knows better than anybody else is how to pick stupid friends.

PANTHEISM The doctrine that God and the universe are inseparable, based upon the dictum: "What man has joined together let no God put asunder."

PANTHER The leopard, the cougar, or, if not sufficiently confused already, the jaguar.

PANTOMIMIST An actor who speaks with gestures to those who can hear with eyes.

PAPER   The bare landscape upon which the writer plants the seeds of imagination, ingenuity and technique, and the reader reaps the fruits of knowledge, adventure and enjoyment.

PAPHIAN   Pertaining to illicit love, such as that of a wife for her husband's paycheck.

PARABLE   A short narrative containing a spiritual truth, which is almost as often told as it is seldom applied.

PARACHUTE   An umbrellalike apparatus which operates perfectly so much of the time that, on those extremely rare occasions when it fails to open, the person wearing it doesn't complain.

PARADE   An outdoor procession commonly featuring a number of off-key marching bands and girls in sequined costumes throwing batons high into the air and dropping them in the street.

PARADISE   The place where righteous souls go after death to escape their in-laws. 2. A place without doctors, telephones or frozen pizza.

PARADOX   A statement or proposition seemingly self-contradictory, and yet sufficiently absurd to be true.

PARAGOGE   The addition of an unnecessary syllable at the end of a word, which, from a grammatical standpoint, couldn't be worser usage.

PARAGRAPHIA   A mental disorder marked by the inability to express ideas coherently in writing, frequently suffered by critics of humorous dictionaries.

PARAKEET   A small bird that can learn to speak, but only as poorly as its owner.

PARANOIA   The chronic sensation that someone or something is out to get you, most commonly suffered by people who regularly watch the nightly news.

PARAPHRASE   A familiar phrase rendered in other words, as "If at first you don't succeed, blame it on your parents."

PARAPSYCHOLOGY   The science which seeks to explain the mysterious process of the transference of thought without speech and its relationship to the more common, yet far more mysterious, process of the transference of speech without thought.

PARASITE　Someone who believes in give-and-take relationships—you give and he takes.

PARATROOPER　A falling target attached to a parachute.

PARCHEESI　A game that is also called parchesi or parchisi or pachisi. It is the only game in the world that has more names than it has players.

PARDON　To judge that a person's remorse is greater than his offense and his resolution to reform is stronger than his susceptibility to repeat.

PARDONER　One who believes that the extending of mercy is contagious and that one who has been forgiven is more apt to forgive.

PARENT　A person with at least one reason to long for the past, at least one reason to strive for the present, and at least one reason to believe in the future.

PARENTHESIS　(or) used together (like this) by way of comment (or explanation).

PARK　A place where one goes to escape the exhaust fumes of buses and confront the exhaust fumes of campers. 2. An area in the city where empty beer cans and wine bottles are preserved in their natural state.

PAROLE　The period between when a prisoner is released from prison and when he is caught again.

PARONOMASIA　A play upon words, which is a punny way of putting something, or in golf, a funny way of putting something, or in home repairs, a putty way of filling something, or in gardening, a frilly way of potting something.

PARONYMOUS　Having an identical root, as two fans for the same football team.

PARRICIDE　A rather extreme method of getting out of cleaning one's room.

PARROT   A bird traditionally named Polly that always wants a cracker, although research has shown that the only birds that say this are the ones owned by women and that what they are actually saying is "Polly wants to crack her," denoting that the birds are as sick of listening to these women as are their husbands.

PARSIMONIOUS   So intent upon saving money as to end up missing the point of it.

PARTICIPATE   To risk making a fool of yourself in order to be alive, while those who laugh at your efforts languish in the deadly world of the spectator.

PARTICIPLE   An adjective form of the verb, modifying a noun; as, reading the definition, the reader identified the participle but, finding nothing funny about it, he paused, wondering what it is doing in this dictionary.

PARTING   The act of combing the hair away from a dividing line, an unemotional procedure for most people but considered quite sad by some, including Shakespeare, who said, "Parting is such sweet sorrow."

PARTNER   One of two people, who enter into business together so that each will have someone to blame if the business falters, someone to accuse of being a crook, and someone to gripe about every night at the dinner table.

PARTURITION   The act of giving birth, although most women in labor will assure you that it's no act.

PARTY   One of the two major political groups in the United States, the members of each of which dedicate themselves to thwarting the efforts of the opposing group to get anything done, while at the same time all of them are forever preaching to the people about a unified nation and sacrificing personal interests for the common good.

PASIPHAE   The wife of Minos, who gave birth to the Minotaur. She is the only character in Greek mythology who is known for certain to have been full of bull.

PASSION   An intense emotion which makes the body hot and leaves the mind out in the cold.

PASSIVE   Overcoming the fear of being dead by living as though one already were.

PASSPORT   A document granting permission for a tourist to go and be swindled by the merchants of another country.

PAST   The realm of regret and the domain of despair, where people go to dwell in the darkness of what could have been, their eyes closed to the light of what is, as are their minds to the promise of what could be. 2. The so-called "good old days," which are only as good as one's memory is weak and only as old as the loss of one's dreams.

PASTIME   A means of employing one's mind without getting it out of bed.

PASTRY   A cake or a pie with a crust of dough paste
That's a treat for the tongue but a woe for the waist.

PAT   The miraculous procedure of increasing a person's height by several feet through the simple application of the palm of one's hand to his back.

PATERNITY   A kind of legal suit brought against a male whose mistake was lust but whose crime was stupidity.

PATIENCE   A quality that is labeled a virtue by those who would like others to wait forever for the things they already have.

PATIENT   A person confined in a hospital, whose name (patient) derives from the fact that he spends 95 percent of his time calmly lying in his bed, wondering whatever became of his doctor.

PATRIARCHY   A matriarchy in which the father is permitted to settle minor controversies and to make proclamations.

PATRIOTISM   The love of one's country and the desire not to see it destroyed by the proliferation of hatred for those of another country. 2. An excuse for national arrogance, extending from the absurd notion that the heightened capacity for mistrusting and misunderstanding other cultures is a legitimate basis for a superiority complex.

PATRONIZE   To treat in a condescending way, as though one equated superior intelligence with inferior behavior.

PATULOUS E x p a n d e d.

PAUSE To..................................hesitate.

PAWNBROKER A person who deals in the by-products of misfortune.

PEACE A period of temporary sanity, during which the leaders of countries quietly and tranquilly develop their campaigns of fear, designed to lure their unwary followers into unspeakable atrocities. 2. An unearthly state of affairs, possible only on a planet where love and rationality pay higher dividends than hatred and stupidity. 3. Merely common sense in its purest form.

PEACH A fruit that is and always was
Distinguished by its ample fuzz.

PEDANT A person who monopolizes a social gathering by expounding at length upon the many books he has read, among which was not, unfortunately, one on the art of conversation. 2. Someone with the absolutely amazing ability to be both a knowledgeable person and an ignoramus at the same time. 3. A person who has yet to learn that true knowledge breeds humility.

PEDESTAL A place of elevation where a man will sometimes put a woman, in order to facilitate the process by which she can step all over him.

PEDIATRICIAN A doctor who casually rids
The pains that are suffered by kids.

PEDIGREED Rapacious desire for feet.

PEDOLOGY The science which deals with soils, considered by many to be the most important of all sciences, and there are sufficient grounds for this.

PEGASUS A winged horse that flew across the sky, causing outrage among the ancient Greeks, who could tolerate bird droppings falling on their heads, but they had their limits.

PEN The tool with which the literary carpenter transforms the blueprints of his imagination into a concrete form, the inventiveness of his architectural designs and the quality of his raw materials determining the stability and durability of the finished structure.

PENANCE A means of absolving the conscience of past sins so that the way is clear for the reception of future ones.

PENDULOUS Swinging freely, as most Californians.

PENITENT Feeling sufficient sorrow for an offense to regret sincerely having to repeat it.

PENNY A coin that was worth saving in Benjamin Franklin's day.

PENOLOGY The branch of criminology which deals with the rehabilitation of convicts by teaching them practical skills that are of great use to people without criminal records.

PEOPLE Human beings, many of whom like to distinguish themselves from animals on the grounds that they can think and the animals cannot. The question, however, is not so much whether they can think but whether they do think.

PEPPER A pungent condiment which, when large quantities of it come into contact with the tongue, is effective in deterring small children from cursing. In adulthood, the opposite is true.

PERCEIVABLE Capable of being perfectly misunderstood.

PERCHANCE Possibly,
Poetically.

PERCIPIENCE The faculty of perception, otherwise known as the professors of the philosophy department.

PERCUSS To swear at someone thoroughly.

PERDITION Damnation of the soul, commonly resulting from the ostentatious and hypocritical condemnation of other souls.

PERFECT Pertaining to a man who does exactly what his wife wants; as, the perfect husband. 2. Pertaining to a woman who does exactly what her husband wants; as, the perfect wife. 3. Flawless; as, a perfect fool.

PERFECTIONIST A person whose greatest flaw is his inability to accept a flawed world. 2. Someone who can't understand for the life of him why everyone else can't follow his example and be unbearable. 3. Someone who is never content with anything, particularly his nervous system.

PERFIDY The act of teaching a person to be more careful about whom he trusts the next time, if indeed there is a next time. 2. The function of the fink; the realm of the rat; the jurisdiction of the jerk.

PERFUNCTORY Performed in the manner of a person whose job is nothing more than a life sentence for the crime of indifference.

PERIAPT A charm worn to ward off all afflictions, except the affliction of superstition.

PERIL An opportunity to test one's courage in facing danger and one's common sense in deciding whether to avoid it or to try to conquer it. 2. In the parlance of overly protective parents, exposure to the risk of being alive.

PERIPATETICS The philosophy of Aristotle, who made his students walk around with him when he taught, the practice resulting in the origin of two important things which have survived to this day: the concept of thinking on one's feet and somnambulism.

PERIPHRASIS The use of many, many, many, many, many words when one can express the same thing without the use of many, many, many, many, many words.

PERISHABLE Pertaining to those items of food in a bachelor's refrigerator that look like the creatures in a grade B science fiction movie.

PERJURE To commit the foolish crime of trying to outsmart a lawyer, who is the first person in the world to discern the circumvention of the truth, being an expert at it himself.

PERMISSIVE Of the philosophy that anything goes, and under this philosophy, the first thing that usually goes is sanity. 2. Regarding parents who allow their children to do what they like, and more often than not, what they like to do the most is to take advantage of their parents.

PERORATE To speak. 2. And speak. 3. And speak.

PERPETRATE To do something offensive; as, to perpetrate a first down.

PERPLEXING See DISTURBING, but do not see PUZZLING or ENTANGLED. 2. See COMPLICATED and PUZZLING, but do not see INVOLVED. 3. See ENTANGLED and INVOLVED, but do not see COMPLICATED and DISTURBING unless you have already seen PUZZLING. 4. Confusing.

PERSECUTOR One who relieves God of the bothersome task of punishing those who hold unpopular religious beliefs, such as the belief that no one holds a monopoly on religious truth.

PERSEPHONE The mythological goddess of the infernal regions, who used to throw such a hell of a party that even the condemned souls were said to have had a damned good time.

PERSEVERANCE The noblest human quality of all, without which nothing worthwhile would ever have been accomplished, no dream realized, no barrier surmounted, no frontier blazed, and no triumph relished.

PERSON An insignificant microspeck in the cosmos, one cell of whose brain holds more mysteries than a galaxy of stars. 2. A member of a species of the most intelligent and stupidest creatures on the earth, who are smart enough to strive (unlike apes) but too dumb to strive together (unlike ants).

PERSPECTIVE A particular viewpoint; as
      Her problems overwhelmed her
      And she couldn't be objective;
      If only she could conquer
      Her hysterical perspective.

PERTINENT Related to the matter in hand, especially a member of its immediate family.

PERTURB To disturb greatly in mind; to disquiet profoundly; to show someone the front page of a newspaper.

PERUKE A fancy wig worn by men of the past and considered utterly absurd and outlandish by today's men, who prefer instead the quiet simplicity of studded earrings.

PERVERSE Deviating from what is right, and making the most of what is left.

PESSIMIST Someone who cheerfully accepts the conditions of life as unchangeable, whose attitude is that you can't fight city hall, and whose philosophy is that a life lived passively is a life lived happily.

PESTICIDE Anything that is effective in keeping the kid next door away.

PET One of a large variety of animals much beloved of humans, more than for any other reason because of their lack of emotional sophistication; that is to say, they have not yet learned how to use affection as a weapon.

PETROGRAPHY Systematic rock classification, as hard, soft, punk, etc.

PETROL The British word for gasoline, illustrating once again that Britons have a serious problem speaking English.

PETROLOGY The science of studying rocks, which study begins by going to a quarry and filling one's pockets and hands with as many specimens as possible, the scientific process known among petrologists as getting stoned.

PETTY Pertaining to a policeman who is frivolous and trivial; hence, a petty officer.

PEW A wooden bed inside a church, cleverly designed in the shape of a bench so that many people can sleep at one time without wrinkling their suits and dresses.

PHARMACIST A licensed drug pusher; a doctor's accomplice, whose job is to insure that a society which operates on the theory that there is a pill for every ill receives its perpetual fix.

PHEASANT A brilliantly colored bird, although not brilliantly colored enough for some people, who feel that what is missing is just a little splash of deep red. This is easily accomplished by the insertion of a bullet.

PHENOLOGY The science of the migration of animals, which can become so confusing to students that they sometimes don't know if they're coming or going.

PHILANDERER   A man who makes love to women just for the fun of it, and definitely not just for the hell of it.

PHILANTHROPIST   A person who is unreasonably wealthy and simply overflowing with love for all men, particularly the poor suckers who worked for him and helped him to make his fortune.

PHILANTHROPY   A means whereby a millionaire can ease his conscience, get a foundation named after him, and save a nice bundle of tax money, all at the same time.

PHILOLOGY   The study of literature, which can be quite interesting as long as one doesn't read too much into it.

PHILOSOPHY   The science which investigates the fundamental truths underlying reality, one of which is that no one in the real world can understand a word of it.

PHILTER   A potion supposed to be able to excite love; loosely, a double scotch on the rocks.

PHOEBE   The Greek goddess of wild nature; hence, the patroness of teenagers at the seashore.

PHONETICS   The science of sounds, which seeks to explain the entire spectrum of eary phenomena.

PHONICS   The science of sounds, which seeks to explain these phenomena from a specific vocal point.

PHONOGRAPH   A machine scientifically designed to transfer dirt from the surface of a record to the tip of a needle.

PHONY   A person who pretends to be what he is not, frequently in order to impress people who are too busy pretending to be what they are not to appreciate his effort.

PHOTOGENIC   Regarding anyone who appears in at least half of the family pictures without his eyes closed or his mouth hanging open.

PHOTOGRAPH   One of a hundred reasons to stay away from neighbors who have just returned from a vacation. 2. An exposure that exposes the vanity in everyone.

PHRASE   A short pithy expression, such as "He who laughs last is usually the more ruthless."

PHRENOLOGY   The study of the shape of skulls, one of a series of studies that come under a variety of different headings.

PHYLUM   A group whose members share a common descent, as the people exiting a bus and transferring to the subway.

PHYSICIAN   A medical doctor, who differs from a surgeon in that he doesn't have to cut you open to get what he wants out of you.

PHYSICS   The science of matter and motion
And the incomprehensible notion.

PIANO   A musical instrument that presents a great many problems to the beginning player, but they can usually be hammered out.

PICA   The craving for unnatural food, as chalk, clay, popsicles, etc.

PICCOLO   A small flute that is played just for the shrill of it.

PICNIC   An outdoor party for the purpose of bringing insects and people closer together, in the spirit of mutual potato salad.

PICTURE   Something that says a thousand words, but whether or not those words make any sense depends upon the artistic language of the creator and the visual vocabulary of the beholder.

PIE   A pastry that encourages the dietetic vice
Of thinking, "It won't hurt to have just one more little slice."

PIG   An animal that is always in a good mood and under no circumstances can become disgruntled. 2. A person who is very stylish.

PIGEON   A bird noted as an exterior decorator, specializing in statues, although it will occasionally consent to do a hasty number on a person sitting in a park.

PIGHEADED   Stubborn and obstinate, unlike oneself, who is steadfast and resolute.

PIKE An elongate fish that is not very loyal and will sometimes attack its own mate; hence, a turnpike.

PILGRIM One who travels to some holy place of devotion, as a doctor on his way to the bank.

PILLAR A steadfast supporter of the social order, so called because he generally has a will of iron, a backbone of steel, and a head of brick.

PILLBOX An ingeniously designed concrete structure with a dual function, serving both as a small fortress for one or more machine gunners and, upon the insertion of a hand grenade, as a tomb for their remains.

PILLOWCASE An assignment for a private investigator, who has been hired to track down a spouse suspected of marital infidelity. 2. An incident for the homicide department involving an apparent suffocation in bed.

PILOT The person on an aircraft who points out all of the landmarks you can see from the other side of the plane.

PIMP A kind of waiter, who satisfies a customer's appetite by serving him whore d'oeurves.

PIMPLE A blemish on the skin, particularly dreaded by teenagers, since it forces them into a tight squeeze.

PINBALL A game that pits the machine's highest score against the player's ability to waste time.

PINCERS An instrument used by a person who wants to have a truly gripping experience.

PING-PONG A game similar to tennis, except that in this game the resolution is tabled and the players do not say "Ugh" when serving.

PINNA A winglike part, as that of an actor who spends most of the play watching from offstage.

PINOCHLE A card game that is avoided by normal people because it is an established fact that any person who takes part in this game isn't playing with a full deck.

PIONEER   A person who paves the way so that others can come and pave the streets.

PIOUS   Holier than thou and considerably closer to God, assuming that God favors the attention of humorless, obsequious bores.

PIPELINE   A row of customers waiting to be served in a tobacco shop.

PIRACY   Artistic theft, which differs from the routine practice of copying exactly the same thing that everyone else is copying in the sense that what is stolen is worth stealing.

PISCATORIAL   Pertaining to fishing and the net profits thereof.

PISTOL   A small firearm which affords its owner numerous distinct advantages over a rifle: it can be concealed easily in public to avoid annoying inquiries by the police, it can be kept in a drawer at home to encourage the natural curiosity of small children, it can be introduced conveniently into family arguments to bring them to more lasting resolutions, it can be fired repeatedly to insure that the victim does not get back up and start more trouble, and it can be used easily to commit suicide without the mess and acrobatic ability required with a larger gun.

PITY   A feeling of deep compassion, occasionally extended toward another but never so earnest and sincere as when directed toward oneself.

PIXILATED   Having attained the ideal level of mental unbalance, recognizing that the best way to keep from going totally insane is to be a little insane all the time and that a little craziness can amuse and enrich many people while a lot of craziness can only amuse and enrich one psychiatrist.

PIZZA   A tomato pie that's covered with mozzarella cheese
Or a frozen imitation that looks like a disease.

PLACEBO   An inactive medicine which is prescribed merely to give the patient a sense of social belonging, a feeling that he is not being left out, that he is in fact sharing with his neighbors the common experience of being on drugs.

PLAGIARIZE   To insult one's mind in the most flagrant way possible by proclaiming through the ideas of another its absolute incapacity to function on its own.

PLAGUE   The destruction of a large number of surplus human beings by a highly contagious disease, the responsibility for which is generally attributed to God, who is thought to be upset about something or other.

PLAINTIFF   One who brings a suit to court in the hopes of having it custom-fitted to his specifications, even if it means suing the pants off the defendant to do it.

PLAN   Any scheme which would have gone off without a hitch if it weren't for the intervention of reality. 2. A mental arrangement for a future disappointment.

PLANET   One of the nine celestial bodies revolving around the sun, of which only Earth shows any apparent signs of unintelligent life.

PLANETARIUM   A place where small schoolchildren are taken so that those among them who are afraid of the dark can partake in a valuable learning experience, that of being mocked and humiliated by the other students.

PLANETOID   A body resembling a planet, as Sydney Greenstreet.

PLANT   Anything that grows in the sun and the rain
And is none the worse off for lack of a brain.

PLASTER OF PARIS   A nineteenth-century French designer.

PLASTIC   One of the five basic elements and the substance destined for eventual use in replacing everything that presently exists, including children. Scientists predict that, by the year 2025, entire families will be made of plastic and that plastic replacement organs will be so commonplace they will be available in department stores.

PLATE   The thing that separates the food from the table and that defines the area in which a person may safely place his fork without being considered strange.

PLATFORM   The principles declared by a political party every four years, which are usually adopted without much difficulty since they only have to last until the end of the election.

PLATITUDE   An utterance that is applicable to any occasion and meaningful to none. 2. A trite-and-true statement.

PLATONIC   Regarding love without perspiration.

PLATOON   A military unit led by a young officer with a commission and trailed by a dark figure with a scythe.

PLAY   The food of the theater, which is planted and grown by the playwright, prepared and served by the actors, consumed and digested by the audience, and regurgitated and reviewed by the critic.

PLAYBOY   A guy whose idea of a major challenge is to make it from his swimming date to his lunch date to his tennis date to his dinner date to his nightclub date without forgetting any of their names. 2. Someone who is too busy seeking pleasure ever to find it.

PLAYWRIGHT   A person whom you can't take anywhere in public, because you never know when he's liable to create a scene.

PLAZA   A public square, such as the park commissioner.

PLEA   The answer that a defendant is advised by his lawyer to make to the charge against him, which depends upon whether or not the evidence will support a lie.

PLEASURE   Anything your doctor tells you you can't have.

PLEDGE   A person in college who is willing to risk humiliation, arrest, personal injury and even death by taking part in an initiation ceremony, so that he can earn the right to join a society of drunkards. What a person that stupid is doing in college is hard to say.

PLEIADES   The seven daughters of Atlas, who were transformed into a group of stars, but none of them ever landed a contract with a major studio.

PLENTY   More than enough to satisfy one's need
But not enough to satisfy one's greed.

PLEONASM   Redundancy of language in writing. 2. Redundancy of language in writing.

PLESIOSAUR   A marine reptile, not to be confused with a navy frogman.

PLOD   To walk heavily, as after Thanksgiving dinner.

PLOT   A literary work's main story or a secret plan or a small piece of ground; as, a plot about a plot to seize a plot.

PLOW   A farm implement that is easy to use, once you get into the groove.

PLUM   A fruit that is related to the peach, prune and cherry
But is barely an acquaintance of the apple and strawberry.

PLUMBER   Someone who clears your drain and then drains your wallet.

PLUMP   A term used by well-meaning matchmakers to describe a person with a weight problem to a prospective date, who with an ounce of brains recognizes what the term really means, and as for arranging a date, fat chance.

PLURALISM   The philosophical theory that there is no single ultimate reality, but rather a number of ultimate realities, each ultimately real. No one knows what this is supposed to mean, but some pluralists have stated that a simplified way of thinking of it is that there is an ultimate reality for every day of the week.

PLUTOCRACY   A government that is ruled by the wealthy; hence, any government.

PLYMOUTH ROCK   A kind of popular music originating in the south of England.

PNEUMATIC   Pertaining to a kind of vigorous exercise performed by military recruits that causes them to breathe heavily and expel a lot of air; hence, a pneumatic drill.

PNEUMATICS   The branch of physics treating of the compressive properties of gases, which is a field that attracts few researchers because most of them can't deal with that kind of pressure.

PNEUMATOLOGY   The belief in specters, which many people consider to be a big farce, but that's only because they don't know how to get into the spirit of the thing.

PNEUMONIA   A disease marked by the partial loss of credibility among mothers, who are forever telling their kids during the winter that they are going to catch it, and none of them ever do.

POCKET   A small pouch sewn in a garment, specifically designed for the insertion of the hands of one's doctor, lawyer, accountant, Congressman, etc.

PODIATRIST   A doctor whose business is to treat
The problems solely of the feet.

POET   A person whose writing may be very good and occasionally may even be understood; as
Some poets are awfully obscure;
What they're talking about no one's sure;
Each symbol and allusion
Adds more to the confusion
And the readers don't read—they endure.

POETRY   Writing that rhymes
Or doesn't rhyme, at times,
In fact, it may contain a line that has only one
Word
In it, or a line that is so long that it seems absolutely
perverse
And if that's the case, it's more than likely free verse,
Which may be easy to understand or terribly hard
And if it's the latter, it's generally avant-garde;
If it's funny or has a satiric bite,
It's referred to, in poetic circles, as light,
Which leaves only one category additional
And that, of course, is the stuff called traditional.

POIGNANT   Painfully moving; as, she had just gotten used to her apartment when she was informed that she had been transferred to another city and would be poignant.

POINT   A needle; as, the doctor assured her that she would barely feel the injection and, since he had never lied to her before, the point was well-taken.

POISON   A substance that can prove fatal if ingested and is therefore no laughing matter, although in Ancient Rome it was sometimes administered to a person just for a gag.

POKER   A card game which enjoys immense popularity because it is a game that is 80 percent luck, unless one is winning, and then it is 80 percent skill.

POLAR CIRCLE   A very exclusive set of Eskimo socialites.

POLAR LIGHTS   Arctic cigarettes with less tar and nicotine than regulars.

POLE VAULT   A burial chamber for someone from Warsaw.

POLICEMAN   A person who arrives at the scene of a crime, usually after it has already been committed, and tries to subdue and arrest the offender, so that he will be prevented from committing any more crimes from the time he is taken into custody until he is let back out on the street again.

POLICY   A settled course adopted and followed by the government, until a crisis occurs, at which point it's anybody's guess what will happen.

POLITICIAN   A person who will promote
Anything to get a vote.

POLITICS   The science of government, established to boost the average citizen's self-esteem, by offering him elected officials as a basis for comparison. 2. The science of determining and implementing the most efficient means of squandering the public's money.

POLKA   A dance that was originated in Bohemia by people who discovered that if they hopped around in as lively a manner as they could the sound of the accordion was not as painful.

POLL   An opinion survey which indicates absolutely nothing except the belief among the people who made it that all housewives with a husband, two kids and a garbage disposal think alike.

POLLUTE   To exploit the environment for the purpose of enriching one's children and poisoning one's grandchildren.

POLLUTION Industry's contribution to the environment in reciprocation for its use of natural resources.

POLO A game that is played almost exclusively by the very rich, since the typical sportsman cannot possibly afford to be saddled with all the added expenses involved.

POLTERGEIST A ghost that used to be a hippie activist in life, which accounts for why it likes to rap so much at night.

POLYANDRY The state of a woman who leads a varied life
As wife and wife and wife and wife.

POLYGAMIST A mysterious man with many wives;
The mystery is how he survives.

POLYGENESIS The anthropological theory that two or more branches of the human race evolved independently, which explains the existence of ballet dancers and used car salesmen.

POLYGLOT Un confusion de languages.

POLYHEDRON A figure formed by many plane faces, as when a team of homely cheerleaders make a pyramid.

POLYNOMIAL An expression of two or more terms, as a tribute to the presidency of Franklin Roosevelt.

POLYPHEMUS A cyclops who captured Odysseus and his companions and put them in a cavern, where he could keep his eye on them.

POLYPHYLETIC Derived from two or more ancestral races, such as the ancestral relay and the ancestral hurdles.

POLYPTYCH A number of panels folding together, as when two or more game shows are cancelled simultaneously.

POLYSULFIDE A compound of more than one atom of sulfur with a radical, as occurs any time a political anarchist lights a cigarette.

POLYSNYDETON Repetition of conjunctions in close and orderly but separate or distinct succession.

POLYTHEISM The belief in many false gods, as distinguished from monotheism, which is the belief in one of many one true Gods.

POMICULTURIST   One who specializes in fruit culture and who frequently takes an apple with him to the opera.

POMP   An elaborate display of magnificence and wealth, such as a royal parade, designed to brighten the spirits of the thousands of unemployed people who have come to watch.

POMPOUS   Overcome with one's position of importance in the world, the way a goldfish might convince itself that its bowl is the Atlantic Ocean.

PONDER   To weigh every aspect of a problem very slowly and thoroughly so that, when the mistake is made, there is no doubt in your mind that you are an absolute idiot instead of a careless fool.

POOL   A swimming area which a person has built on his property in order to discover how many friends he didn't know he had. 2. A tank of water aboard a singles' cruise ship reserved for engaged couples and others who are prepared to take the plunge.

POOR   Underprivileged, which is to say, lacking in certain privileges, such as the privilege of eating.

POP   A small explosive report, as one written by an investigative journalist who has uncovered a little information about a big scandal.

POPCORN   One's father's outworn jokes.

POPE   A bishop whose future couldn't be any brighter;
After all, he's the one with the biggest miter.

POPPYCOCK   Empty talk, as a conversation about boxes with nothing in them.

POPULACE   The masses, including those on drugs, sometimes known as the high masses.

POPULAR   Having such an enormous talent that even people who are tasteless like what you do. 2. Having such an enormous lack of talent that only people who are tasteless like what you do. 3. Having no ideas worthy of offending anyone.

PORCUPINE   One of a variety of spiny rodents which are so lovable and affectionate that many people have been known to get stuck on them.

PORNOGRAPHY Any written or graphic material that stimulates people strictly from the neck down.

PORPOISE A large marine mammal, which is considered by many to have a very high intelligence, although its apparent lack of fear and suspicion toward humans is an indication to the contrary.

PORT A place where thousands of sailors have tens of thousands of imaginary girlfriends.

PORTATIVE Capable of holding, as anyone who tries to call a bus terminal for ticket information.

PORTENT An event which portends ominous things to come, such as an election.

PORTION An amount of food which, if it tastes good, is a helping, and if it doesn't, is a hindrance.

PORTMANTEAU WORD A word formed by arbitrarily combining twords.

PORTRAY To represent a character dramatically; as, the senator is about to portray a concerned individual.

POSE To present oneself before others with the intent of self-flattery and with the result of self-mockery.

POSITIVISM The system of philosophy which excludes everything but natural phenomena, asserting that unnatural phenomena, such as all assertions made by philosophers, do not exist and are therefore not a part of reality or, at best, a part of reality that is ultimately unrealistic.

POSSESSIVE Intent upon taking away someone's freedom as punishment for the crime of being in love with you.

POSSIBLE Within the grasp of anyone who believes that the idea of human limitations is just an excuse and that there can be no such thing as failure for one who continues to make an attempt, that one can fail only when one stops trying.

POSTDATE To go out with somebody after you have just been out with somebody else.

POSTERITY   The people whose job it will be to figure out how to convert all those excess nuclear warheads into food.

POSTHUMOUS   Regarding the kind of fame reserved for people who lived ahead of their time and died before it.

POSTMISTRESS   A woman whose affair with a married man has led to his leaving his wife and marrying her.

POST OFFICE   The department of government noted for its efficiency in delivering urgent mail, such as bills and solicitations from mail order houses. Less important mail, such as checks and personal letters, is another matter.

POSTPONE   To mail corn bread to someone, frequently without a reasonable explanation.

POSTPRANDIAL   Following a banquet; as, a postprandial headache, a postprandial stomachache, a postprandial hangover, etc.

POT   The colloquial term for marijuana, which is sometimes smoked exclusively in the bedroom (chamber pot). It makes certain people who smoke it feel like big wheels (pot shots), while others complain that it gives them an upset stomach (pot belly).

POTATO   A vegetable that's tasty, cheap and goes with any meal; Now if only they could make one that you didn't have to peel.

POTENTIAL   That which would-be great people set as a goal to reach, and which great people set as a goal to surpass.

POTHOLE   A pit in the street that has not been filled because there was very little money left in the local budget, and what was left had to go for more important things, such as raising the salary of the street commissioner.

POVERTY   The state of people who are free of the anxiety of having their silverware stolen. 2. The state of people who do not have to worry about making mind-boggling decisions, such as whether to play tennis or go sailing. 3. The state of people who have no place to go but down, about six feet.

POWER   A controlling influence over others, the possession of which can drive people to the point that they relinquish control of themselves, since no one can take over another person's mind without losing a part of his own. 2. The ability to control, which itself controls in direct proportion to the individual's desire for it.

POWERLESS Pertaining to the average citizen, who is too busy worrying about the mortgage to be bothered with incidentals, such as taking some responsibility for the kind of world in which he lives.

PRACTICE Repeated action; as, practice makes purfect. 2. Repeated action; as, practice makes perfict. 3. Repeated action; as, practice makes perfect.

PRAGMATISM An American movement founded by a group of philosophers who theorized that the function of thought is as a guide to action and that, therefore, the function of philosophers is to spend less time sitting around theorizing and more time going out and doing something.

PRAISE To glorify God, usually in a loud voice and with such obvious devoutness that one draws attention, and frequently praise, to oneself.

PRANK A mischievous little act designed to make the victim laugh, particularly if he can get his hands on the mischievous little neck of the prankster.

PRATTLE To demonstrate that the ability to speak has no intrinsic correlation to the ability to say something.

PRAY To humble oneself before God and accept totally that His will be done, in all matters, that is, except the one under petition.

PREACH To compensate in discourse for what is lacking in example.

PREADAMITES People who believe that there were men before Adam, although they concede that he was the first one with connections in high places.

PREADOLESCENT Pertaining to the period when boys start taking baths on their own because they actually want to smell good and girls start refusing to wear their old clothes because they aren't sexy enough.

PRECAUTION A measure taken beforehand to insure that, when everything goes wrong anyway, your disgust will be fully justified.

PRECENTOR The member of a church choir who leads the other singers, generally chosen because of a vocal ability to awaken people suddenly.

PRECIOSITY Overrefinement of language, practiced by individuals who use their vocabularies more as a vehicle to impress people than as a tool to communicate with them.

PRECIPITIN A specific antibody developed to respond to a foreign protein, such as one from Argentina.

PRECISELY Exactly; as, the president told the reporters at the press conference precisely what he might do if and when he decided whether or not to act on the issue.

PRECOCIAL Designating birds that are covered with soft fluffy feathers and do not adapt well to confinement in cages. In short, these birds are down and out.

PRECONCEPTION The act of starting a family before the wedding ceremony.

PRECURSOR A host who execrates his guests before they arrive.

PREDATE Just to have a friendly conversation or maybe go for a short walk.

PREDECESSOR A male parent who plays golf, otherwise known as a forefather.

PREDICAMENT Any trying situation, such as tasting a vegetable you've never had before.

PREDISPOSE To put out the trash the night before it is due to be collected.

PRE-EMPT To disrupt the emotional and psychological well-being of a huge portion of the American public by cancelling a regularly-scheduled t.v. show and replacing it with something that nobody wants to see, such as a presidential address.

PREFABRICATE To make up a lie while on your way to meet the person to whom you are going to tell it.

PREGNANT Anticipating the joys of motherhood, if a wife, or its horrors, if a girlfriend.

PREHENSILE Adapted specifically for seizing; as, the prehensile fingers of a politician.

PREJUDICE The act or process of depriving oneself of the opportunity to meet different people, to appreciate different ways of looking at things, and to understand different aspects of a commonly shared experience called life.

PRELUDE Musically, a strain that precedes the principal theme, as when the conductor overexerts himself in the opening bars.

PREMATURE Pertaining to the grey hairs on a person who is still full of life and who certainly is not ready to dye yet.

PREMEDITATION The act of getting into the lotus position and putting the thumbs and index fingers together.

PREMONISH To give a warning beforehand, which is the recommended way to do it, because to give a warning afterward is usually not a whole lot of help.

PREOCCUPATION The job of someone who is still in school.

PREPARE To cut off the skins of some apples well in advance of baking a pie.

PREPOSITION A word placed in front of a noun to indicate that another noun or a pronoun is in, under, over, through, for, against, with, by, to, of, around, beyond, between, beside, before, after, from or toward it; as, a preposition-ridden definition.

PREPOSTEROUS So contrary to common sense that it is only sensible to people with uncommon sense; as, what kind of preposterous reasoning do you call that?

PRE-RAPHAELITE A modern painter whose works suggest early methods; hence, any painter who paints in the morning.

PRESAGE All of the ingredients that go in a roast before the spice.

PRESCHOOL   Designating the period in a child's life when he thinks learning is fun, having yet to be convinced that it is work.

PRESCRIBE   To designate drugs as a convenient alternative to common sense, preventative measures and natural remedies.

PRESENT   The moment between this moment and this moment, which is just long enough to decide to climb Mount Everest, to wonder why snow is white, to think of something you've never thought before, to grow.

PRESENTIMENT   A feeling that something is going to happen, which is an extremely strong possibility.

PRESERVATIVE   A substance added to food to keep it from decay, which is more than can be said for what it does to the body that eats it.

PRESIDE   To make up one's mind beforehand which opinions one is going to embrace in a controversy.

PRESIDENT   A person entrusted with enough power to drive even a totally sane person crazy, much less a politician.

PRESS   All of the people who gather and present news collectively, so called because of the way they go about getting information.

PRESSURE   The headache of getting ahead.

PRESUME   To take it for granted that other people will be so delighted to discover that a superior mind anticipated their thinking for them that they will be grateful when they learn later what it is you knew they would have thought.

PRETENDER   The guy who worked behind the bar before the guy who now works behind the bar.

PRETERITION   The Calvinistic doctrine that God chooses only certain people for salvation and leaves the others to work in department stores.

PRETERNATURAL   Strange and inecksplickabull; as, the preternatural spelling of the word "inexplicable."

PRETZEL   A snack food for people who like their drinks with a twist.

PREVIEW   An advance film clip containing ten seconds of unbearably exciting action from a movie containing fifteen seconds of unbearably exciting action.

PREY   An animal that is hunted for food by a carnivorous animal, as distinguished from one that is hunted for sport by a barbarous animal.

PRIAPUS   The Greek and Roman god of virility, so designated because of his hairy chest, his wavy hair, and his ability to pick up girls just by snapping his fingers.

PRIDE   A reasonable degree of self-esteem concerning one's accomplishments or an unreasonable degree of self-esteem concerning one's accomplishments; hence, a confusing degree of self-esteem concerning one's accomplishments.

PRIG   Someone who will not overlook a single detail of a single thing, the way a human being might.

PRIM   Regarding a person who is almost as absolutely proper as he makes others feel absolutely uncomfortable.

PRIMA DONNA   The female singer in an opera company charged with the disposing of flowers after a performance.

PRIMARY   An election in which less than a third of the voters choose the candidates whom less than half of the voters will put in office.

PRIMITIVE   Pertaining to any group of people who have not yet learned a civilized method of destroying their environment. 2. Designating people who are so backward they don't even know how to make bombs.

PRIMORDIAL   First in order, as the most meticulous housekeeper on the street.

PRINCIPLE   A most important and fundamental rule of conduct, for it entails a commitment between a person and his conscience, which is an authority much more difficult to elude than religion or government.

PRISONER   Anyone confined on a planet without knowing the reason.

PRIVACY   One's right to mind one's own business and leave the neighbors guessing.

PROBABILISM   The doctrine that certainty is impossible, and you can be certain of that.

PROBATION   The legal procedure which allows a convicted criminal to rejoin society provided he can convince a panel that he has reformed and is truly sorry for his offense, his remorse often being so genuine that one can actually imagine him becoming upset over his next crime, especially if it's a murder.

PROBLEM   Something that is never as bad as it seems and is always worse than it seems after it is over.

PROCESSION   The part of a wedding ceremony in which the bridal party proceeds slowly up the aisle in order to give members of the congregation the opportunity to get clear pictures of the backs of the heads of other members of the congregation.

PROCRASTINATE   To put off until tomorrow what you put off until tomorrow yesterday.

PROCREATOR   One who is in favor of God.

PROCUMBENT   Lying with face down, evidently ashamed of the deception and rightfully so.

PROCURER   One who is on the side of medical research.

PRODIGAL   Given to reckless spending and an uncontrollable craving for designer jeans.

PROFANE   To violate something regarded as sacred, as to put a dent on somebody's new car.

PROFANITY   Language used regularly by people whose mouths are described poetically as verbal garbage disposals.

PROFESSOR   A teacher in a college or university who specializes in a particular area of knowledge, unless he works in a country ruled by a sovereign, where is is expected to teach a great number of subjects.

PROFICIENT   Not second-rate, but first,
By virtue of being well-versed.

PROFITEER   One who is too keen a businessman to allow a minor obstacle, such as ethics, to stand in the way of good business.

PROFOUND   Intellectually deep, as a philosopher inside the Grand Canyon.

PROFUSION   In support of nuclear weapons.

PROGENITOR   A direct ancestor, as a grandfather who tells you exactly what he's thinking.

PROGNOSTICATION   The act of prognosticating, which is fine as long as you don't do it with somebody's wife.

PROGRAM   To arrange your life the way you would arrange data cards in a computer, being careful not to let anyone fold, spindle or mutilate your schedule by trying to inject it with spontaneity.

PROGRESS   The heightened awareness that a self-propelled robot which totally runs the household but also eats the children is no advancement. 2. A tiny step on the road to world improvement, as opposed to a giant leap on the road to world destruction. 3. Any new technology that does not cause cancer, endangered species or the involuntary rearrangement of the internal organs.

PROHIBITION   Any law that attempts to prevent people from doing what they are going to do anyway; hence, a law designed to encourage the average citizen to become a criminal and to lend gangsters a legitimacy which they don't deserve.

PROJECTILE   A body projected by an exterior force, as a dull-witted actress with a slick agent.

PROLETARIAN   A member of the lowest class in a community, usually a first grader.

PROLOGUE   An introductory act, as the one put on by a guy who's trying to impress his blind date.

PROLONG   T o   d o   l i k e   t h i s

PROLUSION   A trial performance, generally given by one of the lawyers although a witness will also occasionally put on a show.

PROMISCUITY   The indiscriminate desire to contract an embarrassing disease.

229

PROMISE   A pledge to another, which is worth precisely as much or as little as the person making it.

PRONE   Inclined to do something, as while leaning against a lamp post.

PRONOUN   A word used instead of a noun, as in the following categories: if he refers to a jealous husband, it is called a possessive pronoun; if she refers to an aunt, it is a relative pronoun; if we refers to a married couple, it is a reciprocal pronoun; if they refers to the police, it is an interrogative pronoun.

PROOF   A combining form of the adjective proof; as, he was so confident of his position in the company that he considered himself fireproof.

PROPAGANDA   Any concerted effort to offer a public service to the handicapped; namely, by providing free opinions to people who have lost the use of their brains.

PROPHECY   The forecast of an event set to occur far enough in the future that no one will remember what the forecast was.

PROPHET   One of the people who received direct divine revelations, back in the days when God was still making personal appearances.

PROPITIOUS   Favorably disposed, as in a large plastic bag tied at the top.

PROPOSER   Someone who models for a living.

PROPOUND   Opposed to the metric system.

PROPRIETOR   An owner of a place of business; also, in a wider sense, a fat owner of a place of business.

PROPRIETY   A rule of what is fitting, as opposed to what will have to be let out at the waist.

PROSE   Writing that meets only one condition:
That its form not be that of this definition.

PROSELYTISM   The act of a person who knocks on your door and asks if he can shove his religious beliefs down your throat for about an hour.

PROSTITUTE   A woman of low moral character, whose services can be purchased by a gentleman of high moral character.

PROTAGONIST   The principal character of a drama, who comes face to face with an antagonist and, if the writer of the drama expects to make any money out of it, defeats him.

PROTEST   The expression of a group of people who gather in a rally or a march to draw attention to a social wrong and to be labeled fanatics by the people who will accept the credit for correcting the wrong once the so-called fanatics have been proven right.

PROTOCOL   The rules of etiquette of the diplomatic corps, which stipulate that one should never arrange a formal dinner on the day after one's embassy has been bombed.

PROUD   Inferior in class to those whom one considers inferior in rank.

PROVEN   Satisfactorily in keeping with one's beliefs.

PROVERB   A profound maxim that is biblically oriented, as He who lives by the dollar dies by the dollar.

PRUDENCE   The ability to pretend that the world is a reasonable place and to act accordingly.

PSEUDOCARP   Anyone who thinks he's a fresh-water minnow.

PSEUDONYM   An assumed name adopted by an author so that he can convince himself that his anonymity is self-imposed and not the result of an overwhelming lack of interest in his work. It is also useful for confusing his bank teller.

PSYCHASTHENIA   A neurotic condition characterized by phobias, obsessions, the desire to write and so forth, and so forth.

PSYCHIATRIST   A mind doctor, who charges you so much to listen to your problems that you need a second one just to help you deal with the anxieties associated with paying the first one.

PSYCHIC   A person who can sense nonphysical forces, such as gullibility and doltishness.

PSYCHOANALYSIS   A treatment which consists of delving the subconscious in search of repressed desires, which can take years, especially if one of the repressed desires is the desire to become emotionally dependent on a psychoanalyst.

PSYCHOLOGY The science which explores all aspects of the mind, including the unknowable aspects, which comprise all aspects of the mind.

PSYCHOMETRY The act of divining information about a person through contact with an object that has been in his possession. For instance, if the object is a five dollar bill that the person has handed to a psychometrist for services rendered, it may be divined that he is a dupe.

PSYCHOPATHY A mental disorder in which the affected individual is emotionally unstable, unduly conceited and suspicious, lacking in common sense and social feeling, and devoid of self-control and truthfulness. Other than that, he may be perfectly normal.

PSYCHOSIS Any serious mental derangement, such as the uncontrollable urge to wear graduation gowns in restaurants.

PUBERTY The period of life when all the trouble starts.

PUBLIC That group of people most easily identified by their dilated nostrils, which are the result of being led around by the nose and being infuriated.

PUBLISHER A person with a head for what's good to publish, An eye for what's ripe and a nose for what's rubbish.

PUDDLE A small pool of water used by motorists to redesign the clothes of passing pedestrians.

PUGILIST A person who is paid according to his ability to cause physical injury to other people. If he can also cause blood, his earnings will skyrocket.

PULL To push in reverse.

PULSIMETER An instrument that registers precisely how irregular a pulse is, as the first step toward getting to the heart of the problem.

PUMA   Another name for a cougar, which is another name for a catamount, which is another name for a panther, which is another name for a mountain lion, which is a large cat with an identity crisis.

PUN   A kind of play on words that some people enjoy immensely, while others consider it absolute punishment.

PUNCH LINE   The final part of a joke; as, he wanted to have chilly peppers. See MORON.

PUNCTUAL   Respectful of the time of other people and, therefore, respectful of the people themselves. 2. Mindful of the fact that people who make other people wait are actually stealing a part of their lives, a crime every bit as serious as stealing their money.

PUNISHMENT   A corrective measure which helps to prevent future offenses, when administered with mercy and justice. 2. A noncorrective measure which helps to insure future offenses, when administered with vindictiveness and anger.

PUNK   A person whose mouth is bigger than his brain and whose behavior serves as ample proof of the evolution of the species.

PUNSTER   One who is addicted to the sound of other people's groans.

PURE   Free from guilt; hence, not in contact with one's mother.

PURGATORY   A place of temporary punishment after death, thought by theologians to resemble a dentist's office.

PURIST   A person who is oversolicitous about purity in language and who regards writers of humorous dictionaries as the lowest form of reprobate miscreants.

PUSH   To pull in reverse.

PUSHER   A murderer who kills on the installment plan.

PUZZLE   Something which perplexes, such as an absurd and utterly pointless argument between two angry people. This is known as a cross-word puzzle.

PYGMIES   A group of people who are very small, the reason being that they refuse to grow up and act like adults. All they ever want to do is climb trees and chase animals around the forest with little spears in their hands.

PYRAMID   A figure comprised of four triangular faces meeting at a point, which is said to have mysterious powers; specifically, the power to make people who manufacture and sell pyramid-shaped objects quite wealthy.

PYROMANIAC   A person who is eager to acquaint himself with an environment similar to the one that awaits him in the hereafter.

PYRRHONISM   The doctrine of Pyrrho, founder of a school of skeptics in ancient Greece, who asserted that he had made great strides in the area of revolutionary thought, but his students doubted this.

QUADRAGENARIAN Concerning the age when a person begins to wonder if maybe those grey hairs aren't premature, after all. 2. Concerning the age when optimists decide they look distinguished.

QUADRANT An arc of 90° or, if in the shade, about 75°.

QUADRATURE The process of making square, otherwise known as growing up in the Midwest.

QUADRENNIAL Lasting four years, as the regret of the American electorate.

QUADRILINGUAL Using four languages, as two parents, a son and a daughter.

QUADRIPARTITE Consisting 2. of 3. four 4. parts.

QUADRUMANOUS Having four hands, as two couples: as, "Two couples, quadrumanous?" she said.
"You must be some sort of a joker."
"A riddler would be more to the point," said he.
"The couples are playing strip poker."

QUADRUPLE To convert an average person's monthly salary to a professional athlete's weekly salary.

QUAFF To drink deeply, as in a mine shaft.

QUAGMIRE A position of extreme difficulty, as that faced by anyone attempting to find what it is that makes this definition so interesting and amusing.

QUALIFIED Related to the boss. 2. Having an influential father. 3. Equipped with the skills to do a job, the confidence to sell oneself, and the tolerance to put up with the boss's relatives and the people with influential fathers.

QUALM A conscience attack, the best remedy for which is a heaping dose of rationalization, washed down with a good stiff drink.

QUANDARY See PERPLEXITY. 2. Or maybe it would be better to see PREDICAMENT. 3. Or maybe both. 4. Or maybe neither. It's a DILEMMA.

QUARREL An exchange that helps to bring people together, specifically in the area of the fist and the jaw.

QUARRY An animal that is hunted by a human that is blunted.

QUARTERMASTER The person who makes change at a pinball arcade.

QUATRAIN A poetical stanza
Which one defines
As having, like this one,
Exactly four lines.

QUEEN The wife of a king, whose job it is to produce future kings, or the daughter of a woman who failed to do her job, who assumes the throne on the grounds of brotherlessness and rules a country of disappointed subjects, the resultant inferiority complex rendering her paranoic, unable to find true love, and perfectly suited for the subject of a sappy Hollywood movie.

QUEER A slang term for homosexual. 2. Peculiar, as any person who uses a slang term for homosexual.

QUESTION Anything asked, right?

QUOTATION A notable statement that is worth repeating, such as Denson Wagner's famous line: "I may not know much, but what

I do know I think I've forgotten." Or the classic quip uttered by Lillian Moss: "The only thing that keeps me from being happy is my situation in life."

QUOTE   To repeat what somebody said or, more commonly, what somebody said somebody said.

RA   The great sun god who enjoyed immense popularity until Helios came along, driving his fiery chariot across the sky and proving conclusively that a traditional god was no match for a god with a gimmick.

RABBIT   An animal with high hops for the future.

RABBIT'S FOOT   The foot of a rabbit, considered a good-luck piece, despite the fact that it certainly didn't work for the rabbit.

RABBLE   A gang of people who are of one mind, which is about all their combined mental capacity requires.

RACE   A contest of speed, as the annual Scandanavian Marathon, in which the object is to cross the Finnish Line.

RACISM   The assumption that some races of people are superior to other races in their ability to be arrogant, prejudiced and deluded.

RACIST   One who is addicted to the track.

RACK   A medieval chiropractic device on which people discovered that the simple technique of pulling the bones from their sockets helped them to clear their minds and thereby to form more rational beliefs and opinions, in keeping with the operator of the device. This technique gave birth to the expression, stretching the truth.

RADAR   A radio detecting device, especially one that can locate both FM tuners and small transistor models.

RADDLE   To twist together, as at a wedding reception.

RADICAL   Someone who expects major political changes to occur overnight, as do bad dreams. 2. A person who has all the answers but little idea of the questions.

RADIO   An apparatus previously used to receive broadcasts in the privacy of one's home but presently employed as a portable public nuisance, played at full volume on buses and street corners by people whose deep psychological need to fill their heads with deafening noise is directly linked to the void that otherwise exists.

RADIOACTIVE   Awakening in the morning to the sound of one's favorite station.

RADISH   A pungent vegetable, the harvesting of which poses certain questions that some gardeners find difficult to solve, but it's really quite simple once you get to the root of the problem.

RADIUM   A radioactive element that is constantly breaking up, although it is unclear just what it thinks is so funny.

RAFT   A vessel of logs constructed by a person who is trying to get off of an island and back to civilization—convincing evidence that being shipwrecked causes insanity.

RAGS   Clothing worn by people who have been spared the suffering and anxiety associated with one of the most serious problems facing the rich, the need for more closet space.

RAIL   Any of a large group of wading birds related closely to the crane and distantly to the bulldozer.

RAILROAD   A means of transportation that people in the business claim is the safest available, but that's just one of their standard lines.

RAIN   To a farmer, it's a blessing;
To a surfer, it's depressing;
To a commuter, it means umbrellas;
To an umpire, it means "That's all, fellas."

RAINFALL   The loss of one's footing during a downpour.

RAINPROOF   Conclusive evidence that a crime took place while a thunderstorm was in progress.

RAISE   An increase in pay designed to keep the average worker just close enough behind the cost of living that he can remain comfortably in debt.

RAISIN   A little shrunken shriveled grape
That failed to keep itself in shape.

RAKE   To break your back for an hour gathering all the leaves in your yard into a neat pile so that five minutes after you go inside your kids can scatter them all over the yard again.

RAKE-OFF   A commission that a public official rakes from an illegitimate transaction, and that ain't hay.

RALLY   An extremely serious medical condition among tennis players, comprised of a series of strokes.

RAM   An animal immortalized by Gershwin in the famous song, "I Got Plenty O' Mutton."

RAMBLE   To go from place to place without a goal, as a hockey player in a bad slump. 2. To write in a pointless fashion, as with an unsharpened pencil.

RANCH   A place where sheep are kept for shear profit and cattle so that even people who are in error need not miss steak.

RANCID   Having a rank smell, as that of a lieutenant general.

RANGE   A region famous for its musically gifted animals, especially noted as the place where the deer and the antelope play.

RANK   One of the two things that an army spy must submit to the enemy if he is captured, the other being the folder of secret papers that he stole; hence the expression, rank and file.

RANT   The explosive discourse of a mental dud.

RAPACIOUS   Desirous of everything and deserving of nothing.

RAPIDS   The part of a river that most appeals to photographers, whose picture-taking adventures there are popularly known as shooting the rapids.

RAPIER   A sword that is used in the sport of fencing, which is an activity that requires great care in choosing opponents, since some people can become carried away and really play it to the hilt.

RAPT   Transported with emotion, as in the case of someone who is crying on a train.

RAPTURE   Ecstatic joy, as that experienced by a wife who is pregnant or by a bride who is not.

RARE   Less common than a smile on the face of a supermarket cashier and more common than an effective president.

RASCAL   A base person, which is any player who is not a pitcher, catcher, shortstop or outfielder.

RASH   Given to acting hastily, said of the Keystone Kops (if you call that acting).

RAT   An animal which cities provide free of charge to ghetto children in order to enrich their appreciation of nature.

RATHE   Poetically speaking, this is to say
The early portion of the day.

RATIFY   To sanction formally, as at a wedding.

RATIONAL   Pertaining to a person who thinks the way you think. 2. Using reason when possible, retaliation when profitable, and retreat when practical.

RATIONALISM   The philosophical theory that reason is a source of knowledge totally superior to the senses, which explains why the only people who can understand this theory are those who have totally taken leave of theirs.

RATIONALIZE   To demonstrate the awesome power of mind over motive.

RATTAN   A climbing palm; as, she slapped his rattan when she felt it reach the hem of her skirt.

RATTLESNAKE   A venemous snake, similar to the critic but more civilized in the sense that it gives a warning before it strikes.

RAVEL   To do the opposite of what you would not do if you were unraveling.

RAVEN   A black bird best known Poe-etically.

RAW   Pertaining to the jokes of a comedian who is crude and vulgar; hence, raw material.

RAZE   To remove something utterly, as opposed to removing it without saying anything.

REACT   To perform in a play that has survived the opening night.

READ   To enter the world of the word, where the mind is monarch, where the boundaries are horizons yet unseen, and where time is an ocean as swift as a river and as still as a lake.

REALIST   An idealist three months after graduating from college. 2. Someone who faces facts, such as the fact that he has forgotten how to dream.

REALITY   A security blanket which those without vision wrap around themselves in complacent comfort. 2. A broad wall of stone in the visionary's path, through which he must slowly and diligently chisel a tunnel if he is ever to see the light on the other side.

REAR   To raise children, so called because of the place that gets most of the disciplinary attention.

REASON   That attribute of sound thinking that makes man different from the other animals. The difference is that the other animals have it.

REASONABLE   Regarding one's own attitude in all matters of disagreement.

REBATE   A refund paid by a manufacturer to a customer for purchasing a product that is overpriced in direct proportion to the amount refunded.

REBEL   To denounce at fifteen the values that one will adopt at twenty.

REBIRTH   The act of waking up in the morning, to a person who considers each day a life in itself.

REBORN   Born again, as a born again agnostic.

REBUFF   To shine your shoes once more.

RECALCITRANT   Having twice as much respect for constituted authority as for oneself; having no respect for constituted authority.

RECEIPT   The supermarket's counterpart to a bank robbery note, except that in the supermarket it is presented to the victim after the crime has been committed.

RECEIVE   To give someone else the satisfaction of giving.

RECEPTIONIST   A person whose job is to tell you that someone who is in is not in or that someone who will see you in an hour will see you in a moment.

RECESS   A period of intermission in school or in Congress, the difference being that in school it does not take up more time than the lessons.

RECIDIVISM   The practice of going back and committing the same crime after imprisonment, unmistakable proof that prisons are so successful at helping convicts to form lasting relationships that they just can't stand being away from their friends for very long.

RECIPROCAL   Equally shared by both sides; as, a reciprocal bathing suit.

RECITAL   A musical entertainment, when given by a professional instrumentalist; a musical detainment, when given by a relative's kid.

RECKLESS   Pertaining to people who have taken a crash course in how to drive.

RECKONING   A computation, as of corpses; hence, dead reckoning.

RECOIN   To use the only clever phrase you ever invented every chance you get.

RECONCILIATION   The act of bringing back into harmony, as a reunion of barbershop quartets.

RECONDITE   2. Hidden from sight.

RECONSIDER To decide to decide
After every side has been descried.

RECORD A disc from which music is reproduced by a needle that is connected to a tone arm that is connected to a turntable that is connected to an amplifier that is connected to speakers that are connected to the psyche.

RECOVER To bring oneself back to a normal state; as, to recover from high school.

RECREATION Any diversion that helps to take one's mind away from the things that take one's mind away.

RECRUIT A soldier who can remember the taste of real food.

RECTIFY To take anything that somebody else has done and do it your way.

RECTILINEAR Characterized by straight lines, as Bud Abbott.

RECURRING Appearing again; as, a recurring nightmare. 2. Appearing again; as, a recurring definition.

RECURVE To put on a girdle.

REDETERMINE To make up one's mind once and for all again.

RED FOX A really good-looking Russian woman.

REDISCOVER To find something for the first time for the second time.

REDOUBTABLE Capable of not being believed more than once.

REDRESS To make amends, namely by putting on a nicer outfit.

REDSKIN A North American Indian, so called in the nineteenth century because of the lavish amounts of blood generally coating his body.

REDUNDANCY The use of an excess of words to convey an idea that could be conveyed just as easily with the use of fewer words and without the use of all the extra words which do nothing substantially to aid in the conveyance of the thought and which, in fact, actually detract from its conveyance by interfering with the simplicity of expression that is best served by a nominal number of words and is in no way served by the senseless inclusion of superfluous verbiage.

RE-ECHO   The echo of an echo of an echo of an echo of an echo, etc.

REED   Musically, any thin, elastic tongue of cane or wood in current usage.

REEDBUCK   A fawn-colored African antelope, of which the females are always hornless and the males are always horny.

RE-EDUCATION   The process of going to work after having gone to school.

REEFER   A marijuana cigarette, the use of which has become so prevalent at all levels of society that its legality is under consideration by authorities, and most users think it's high time.

REEL   A small windlass that is connected to the part of a fishing rod near the handle with one end of the line attached to it and the other end attached to the hook, which is a wound about way of putting it.

RE-ENLIST   To demonstrate a preference for the military life or a total loss of sanity, assuming that there is a difference between the two.

REFECTORY   A dining hall in a monastery, otherwise known as a monk mess.

REFEREE   A person who is blind and inept, when he penalizes a member of your team. 2. A person who is alert and competent, when he penalizes the opposition.

REFINERY   Showy clothes that are worn two seasons in a row.

REFLECTION   The act of taking some time at the end of the day to go back over it in the mind, relishing what went right and learning from what went wrong, fashioning it into a prelude for tomorrow.

REFORMATORY   An institution where youthful offenders are reformed, namely from juvenile delinquents to hardened criminals.

245

REFRAIN   The part of a song that is catchy and terse
And repeatedly sung after every verse.

REFRESHMENT   Food or drink. 2. Refleshment.

REFRIGERATOR   An appliance for keeping food cold which also doubles as a home entertainment center, the insides of which
offer such fascinating fare that members of a household cannot resist opening the door several dozen times a day just to stand there
and watch.

REFUGE   A place where one is protected from the dangers of the
world; a grave.

REGAL   To get a new girlfriend.

REGICIDE   The killing of a king, considered by murderers to be
the crowning achievement.

REGIMENTAL   Pertaining to a kind of education that strives for
strict order and uniformity, similar to that in a cemetery.

REGION   A tract of land; specifically, one smaller than a continent and larger than a playground.

REGRET   To wish that what was would not have been and what
should have been could have been and what might have been would
have been and what shoo be do be. 2. To keep crying over spilt milk
until it becomes, like the person crying over it, spoiled.

REHASH   To chop up corned beef and mix it with diced potatoes
again.

REINCARNATION   The phenomenon of being reborn after
death and becoming a new person, animal or plant, while retaining
the memory of past lives, as in the famous case of the cocker span-
iel from California which, under hypnosis, claimed to have been
King Charles I of England in a former life.

RELATIVE   Either a member of one's immediate family or a person seen drinking at weddings and crying at funerals.

RELATIVE HUMIDITY   The combined perspiration at a family
reunion.

RELEVANT   Applying to the case in hand, as one's initials or a little travel sticker.

RELIABLE   Capable of telling another falsehood.

RELIC   An object venerated for its association with a sacred person, such as a World Series ring.

RELIEF MAP   A chart that shows where the local welfare offices are located. 2. A chart that indicates where public rest rooms are located.

RELIGION   Any organization based upon the proposition that my God's better than your god.

RELIGIOSITY   Hypocrisy in its Sunday best.

RELOCATE   To exercise the courage it takes to go someplace else and start fresh, while others exercise the greater courage to remain where they are and stay fresh.

RELUCTANT   About as eager to do something as a politician is to keep a campaign promise.

RELY   To match one's confidence in another against one's capacity for disappointment.

REMAIN   To make the place where you are the place to be. See RELOCATE.

REMAKE   A cinematic example of Hollywood's absurd belief that a big budget is a viable alternative to an original idea.

REMARKABLE   Worthy of being remarked, as a subway car or the side of a building.

REMARRY   To make a firm commitment to get the marital vows down right this time.

REMEMBER   To concoct a recollection by taking the basic ingredient of truth and combining with it the unconscious flaws in one's memory, the sub-conscious repressions of unfavorable facts, and the conscious embellishments which make the past such a nice place to be for so many people.

REMIND   To brainwash someone. 2. To indoctrinate into a religious cult.

247

REMINISCENCE   A recollection of things as they would have been if they had happened that way.

REMISSION   The forgiveness of sins, which is a popular service offered by some religions to relieve the sinner of the unpleasantness of dealing with a guilty conscience.

REMIT   To put on a catcher's glove again.

REMONSTRANT   One who objects vigorously, as while jogging.

REMORSE   To send another message by code.

RENAISSANCE   The period of history when art was almost as proliferous as weapons are today.

REND   Poetically, to tear one's clothing to shreds,
Exposing loose ends, as well as loose threads.

RENEGE   To demonstrate that one's promises are as worthless as one's personality.

RENNET   A membrane used for curdling milk, which a dairy farmer extracts from an unweaned calf, if he can stomach it.

RENOMINATION   In political jargon, the naming of an officeholder for a second term, usually because he didn't do anything in his first term to upset his constituency or to destroy his credibility with the voters. 2. In straight talk, the naming of an officeholder who didn't do anything.

RENOWN   The kind of exalted fame reserved for soap opera stars, country and western singers, basketball players and other prominent personages whose contributions to the betterment of mankind are almost immeasurable.

RENT   An apartment dweller's monthly reminder that the landlord actually exists. 2. A split in a party, as when someone leaves to get more ice cubes.

REORGANIZE   To move around a creature's internal parts.

REPAIRMAN   A person who knows all the technical tricks
To assemble a bill that puts you in a fix.

REPEAL   To ring a bell again.

REPEAT   To put a new coating of moss on one's lawn.

REPEL   To drive back; as, he repelled her home after the dance.

REPHRASE   To put it another way; as, to rephrase this definition by expressing it in different terms; as, to state it in other words; as, to set it forth in alternative language.

REPLACE   To recall the place where you met someone again whom you recalled at that time meeting before; as, she recognized his face but she couldn't replace him.

REPLY   The answer to a question? 2. That's right.

REPORTER   A bearer of ill tidings, whose job is to present the horrors of the world objectively and without emotion, so that the public can become as numb to tragedy as they are to life in general.

REPOSE   To get in front of a camera again.

REPRESENTATIVE   A public official who divides his time between representing his self-interests and representing the interests of his constituents; the latter he represents for about three months prior to an election.

REPRESSION   The process of relegating one's conscious desires to the subconscious, where, for all humans really understand about the way their minds work, they may be better off.

REPRIEVE   A stay of execution, which is a means whereby a governor shows mercy to a condemned murderer, so that he can continue to live a useful and productive life behind bars, at the public expense.

REPRIMAND   To censure formally, as when wearing a tuxedo.

REPRISAL   The action of a country which uses force against another country to settle a grievance, the way a child whose toy has been broken by a playmate will rectify the situation by breaking the playmate's toy.

REPROBATE   Morally abandoned, in the opinion of those whom God has appointed (by some unknown means) to sit in judgment of the spiritual standing of others.

REPROVE To present conclusive evidence that supports conclusive evidence already presented.

REPTILE An animal that is almost exclusively a crawling animal, but it will also occasionally try the breast stroke.

REPUBLIC A form of government in which the power rests in a body of officials elected by the people, and, for most of the time between elections, the power does precisely that: rests.

REPUBLICAN A member of the political party whose members oppose the Democrats, based upon the belief that, whereas they (the Republicans) may not know how to fight inflation, the Democrats, on the other hand, don't know how to handle the economy.

REPUGNANCE Deep rooted antagonism, or aversion to large trees.

REPUTATION The character of a person as ascribed to him by the community in which he lives, usually based on hearsay, innuendoes, and whether or not he smiles at people on the street; as, but the child molester had such a good reputation.

REQUIEM Music for the dead, or a piece dedicated to government office workers.

REQUISITE Required by the end in view; as, a requisite girdle.

REQUITE To reply like a Britisher again.

RERADIATION That special glow on the faces of newlyweds who are honeymooning near a nuclear power plant meltdown.

REREAD To read again. 2. See DEFINITION (1).

RESCRIPT An official order, such as a medium steak, baked potato and broccoli for the ambassador.

RESCUE To save from imminent danger, as to kidnap a friend on the night he is planning a marriage proposal.

RESEARCH The process of scientific experimentation and investigation which can yield results fairly quickly when unlimited funds are provided for a matter of the highest priority, such as discovering a better way to blow up the planet, or can be a long and tedious affair when limited funds are available for a matter of less urgency, such as discovering a cure for a terminal disease.

RESENT   To take out on yourself, by allowing a negative feeling to fester inside you, what you should be taking out on a person who has wronged you, by telling him what you think of him and forgetting it.

RESIDENT   A person who shares a house or apartment with OCCUPANT, the two being jointly responsible for seeing to it that all postal material addressed to them goes immediately from the mailbox to the trash can.

RESORB   To swallow again; hence, to support the same candidate two elections in a row.

RESPECTFUL   Showing the mandatory respect to one in a position of power or authority, who demands it. 2. Showing the voluntary respect to one in a position of power or authority, who deserves it.

RESPIRATION   The act of breathing, as expressed in the modern version of an old phrase: "In goes the bad air, out goes the bad air."

RESPONSIBILITY   The thing that everyone wants more of until a situation arises that requires accountability, and then everyone suddenly becomes responsible for only one thing: finding someone else to hold accountable.

REST   Freedom from activity or the opposite of work, unless one is the vice president of an advertising agency, in which case they are the same.

RESTORE   To make into a grocery a building that was originally a grocery before it became something else.

RETAIN   To keep in a fixed place, such as one with a freshly tarred roof and new aluminum siding.

RETALIATE   To demonstrate that, in fact, two wrongs do make a right and that the exchange of equal evils is the most commonly accepted form of human justice, explaining why humans, on the whole, are as just as they are barbaric.

RETENTION The ability to keep in mind, as distinguished from the ability to know what's worth keeping in mind.

RETIREMENT That period of life designed to make a person better prepared to accept death, by helping him to forget all the reasons he ever had for being alive. 2. An opportunity to do the things you wish you had done when you could have.

RETORT To answer an argument in the manner of a druggist; hence, to use a counter argument.

RETREAT To fall for the tactic of sneaky children who go to the same houses twice on Halloween.

RETRIAL A judicial procedure designed to give a defendant two chances to get a favorable verdict, which is exactly twice as many chances as he gave his victim.

RETRIEVER A dog trained to bring in the game, particularly one that can carry a chess board and all the pieces at the same time.

REUNION A gathering, especially of old classmates, at which you get to listen to other people tell their versions of the same stories you've told a million times, except in your version you were the guy who scored the three touchdowns in the championship game and the only one in the school who could get Jill Poplowski into a drive-in movie.

REVEAL To have cutlets for dinner for the second consecutive night.

REVEILLE A bugle call used as a part of training to develop in young soldiers a strong and determined hatred of the bugle.

REVELATION That which is revealed by a person, such as a prophet, who has received a message from God, as distinguished from that which is revealed by a person, such as a lunatic, who only thinks he has received a message from God.

REVELATIONIST One who accepts the scriptural account of the Creation, which states that Adam lived to be an amazing nine hundred and thirty years old, and that was before the invention of yogurt.

REVENGE   The attempt to prolong stupidity, by giving an offending party the justification for doing something even more offensive than the original offense.

REVERSE   Position in about completely turn to; as, please reverse this definition.

REVERSIBLE   Capable of being made into another poem.

REVIVALIST   One who manufactures and sells divine interventions, in the manner of the medicine show hawkers of the Old West.

REVOLT   To put in a new electrical system.

REVOLTING   Disgusting; shocking; nauseating; likely to draw crowds.

REVOLUTION   The overthrow of one government and the substitution of another, or, analogically speaking, the replacement of a train with a locomotive.

REVOLVE   To move around a center, as during a safety blitz on third down.

REVOLVER   A pistol with a moving chamber, designed to provide the average madman with the option of shooting one person six times, six people once apiece, two people twice plus another person and himself once each, etc. For madmen interested in other kinds of mathematical variables, it is also ideal for playing Russian roulette.

REWARD   Money that is offered for the return of something that has been lost, so that an honest person won't have to worry about being considered an absolute fool for giving it back.

REWRITE   To write again. 2. To write again; as, everyone expected the lexicographer to go for the obvious gag, which is to rewrite this definition. 3. To write again; as, but few thought he would try to stretch the gag and rewrite it once more. 4. To write again; as, and nobody thought he would be corny enough to rewrite it a fourth time. 5. To write again.

RHABDOMANCY   The practice of trying to locate ore deposits with the use of a divining rod, which is sometimes hard to control because it has a tendency to want to point toward the user's head.

RHAPSODY A musical composition that comes in a variety of colors and makes a very nice dress design; hence, a rhapsody in blue.

RHEOLOGY The science which explores the deformation of matter, which can be very exciting for rheologists because every time they learn something they discover a new twist to it.

RHEOTAXIS Electric cabs.

RHETORIC The art of expressing the written word with a degree of technical flair approaching, but never surpassing, that of this exquisitely crafted and eloquent definition.

RHINOCEROS A very large mammal that doesn't mind the way people make fun of its horny snout because, as scientists are quick to point out, it's thick-skinned.

RHIZOCEPHALOUS Designating an order of extremely degenerate cirripeds, so classified because they mostly hang out at the beach, drinking beer and looking for trouble.

RHIZOPUS Any of a genus of fungi which cannot be distinguished from one another because they all come from the same mold.

RHODE ISLAND RED A communist New Englander.

RHUBARB An argument on a baseball field, during which professional players demonstrate to the youngsters in the stands (through cursing, throwing their caps on the ground, and kicking dirt) the proper way to behave toward an umpire whenever there is a disputed call.

RHYTHM The measured rise and fall of sounds
In pitch or stress or speed
That causes poetry to flow
And makes it fun to read.

RIB The bone of Adam that God used to make Eve, because earlier Adam had come with a complaint about needing a companion and he said he really had to get it off his chest.

RICE A food that the people of the Orient have with practically every meal, not so much because they like it but because it has been ingrained into them.

RICH Having enough money to be able to go food shopping without coupons. 2. Not waiting for the movie version. 3. Able to have the car repaired and visit the dentist in the same month.

RIDDLE An enigmatic question that requires ingenuity to solve, such as "What is flat around the edges, ticklish, and spends every summer watching iguanas mate in the Galapagos?"

RIDICULE The only truly valid exchange between faithful, long-standing enemies.

RIDICULOUS See ABSURD. 2. No, don't see ABSURD. See FATUOUS. 3. Never mind FATUOUS. See INANE. 4. Actually, don't see any of them. It's SILLY.

RIFFLE A way of shuffling cards which involves dividing the deck into two equal piles and then slightly elevating the corners of both piles and then very rapidly allowing the cards to fall one on top of the other and then picking the cards up off the floor and then slowly arranging them into a single pile again.

RIFLE A firearm that some people consider a barrel of fun, but others don't take much stock in it.

RIGHT Having the sense to know what is just and correct, but not necessarily the courage to acknowledge it publicly; as, it takes a great man to admit when he's right.

RIGMAROLE A succession of confused statements, particularly those received by people who haven't got the slightest idea how to manage their checking accounts.

RING A "sold" sign worn on the finger to alert people in the spouse market that they needn't bother making a bid.

RINGLEADER The girl who got a larger stone for her engagement than any of her girlfriends got.

RIPUARIAN Designating a group of Franks who established a community near Cologne in the fourth century. They were driven away, however, in the fifth century by a group of Harrys.

RISER One who attains a better social position, particularly at a young age; hence, an early riser.

RISIBILITY The ability to laugh when a person says, "That painter did such a lousy job painting the front of my house black that I told him to leave and never to darken my door again." 2. The ability to laugh when a person says something funnier than the preceding.

RISK The exposure to hazard which accompanies all potentially perilous decisions, such as the decision to get out of bed in the morning.

RISQUE Bordering on indecency, such as the building next door to a strip joint.

RITUAL A formal religious ceremony to honor a formal God, as distinguished from a God who is supposed to be regarded and loved as a father and who, therefore, naturally would be offended to have his children treat him as though he were a foreign dignitary.

RIVAL A competitor to whom one should always be indebted for providing enough of a challenge to bring out the best in one, whether in a winning or a losing effort.

RIVER A body of water used to convey pollutants from a city to an ocean or a gulf.

ROADBLOCK A minor mental disorder marked by the inability to remember the street where you are going.

ROADSTER An automobile with one seat for people who behave themselves and also, usually, a rumble seat.

ROAMER One who goes from place to place without an aim, as a maladroit hunter.

ROB To take away by force a large portion of a person's trust in other people and his feeling of security about living on the planet, as well as his possessions.

ROBBER One who steals from everyone the right to live in a home instead of a fortress.

ROBOT A mechanical automaton whose characteristics range somewhere between a human being and a toll collector.

ROCK A type of music that is very popular, especially among teen-agers, and also extremely economical, since it only takes one devotee's stereo system in an apartment building to entertain all the other tenants.

ROCKET A pebble.

RODEO A public performance at which cowboys display their skills by demonstrating the most painful way to dismount a horse and the most graceful method of diving on a calf.

ROEBUCK The male roe deer, so closely related to the Sears that they are often mentioned together.

ROGUE A tricky, deceitful fellow, particularly one who exhibits paintings, hence, a rogue's gallery.

ROLE The character that an actor plays on stage or that any person plays in real life, the difference being that the actor doesn't have to worry about somebody coming along and changing the script every five minutes.

ROLLING MILL A place where metal is rolled into bars, to the utter bewilderment of the customers.

ROLLING PIN A wrestling hold that is applied while the opponent is turning over.

ROMANCE The experience which lasts from the moment you come on to somebody until the moment you come back to your senses. 2. The period between getting infatuated and getting nauseated.

ROOFER Someone who has made it to the top the tarred way.

ROOSTER A barnyard fowl that is usually the only male in the company of a large number of hens, which explains what all of his crowing is about.

ROOT To cheer for one's home team when it is winning and does not need the encouragement that it does when it is losing and the stadium is dead quiet.

RORSCHACH A kind of test in which the subject stares at an ink blot and tells what he sees. If he sees the Battle of Trafalgar or the Kentucky Derby, he's crazy.

RUMINATE   To dwell on something at great length; to ponder; to keep aspirin companies in business.

RUMOR   An unverified story exchanged between friends or neighbors that is good for their health, because it keeps them from talking about themselves and boring one another to death.

RUMP   The part of a body that is the butt of a lot of jokes.

RUNNER-UP   A contestant in a beauty pageant who has to wait until the whole thing is over before she is allowed to wipe that silly smile off her face.

RURAL   Pertaining to any place where you can spend an entire night without hearing a siren. 2. Pertaining to any place where a traffic jam is defined as two cars behind a tractor. 3. Pertaining to any place where you have to turn on your radio to hear a radio playing.

RUSH   To live in a city.

RUT   A narrow passageway leading to the grave that people carefully dig for themselves, willfully enter, and then, after years of trudging up and down it, wonder how they got there.

RUTHLESS   Placing personal ambition ahead of personal feeling in order to become a successful, accomplished, highly paid nobody. 2. Deserving pity for having none.

SABBATARIAN   A person who favors the strict observance of Sunday, as opposed to someone who believes that people should not observe Sunday and should go directly from Saturday to Monday.

SABLE   A fur that is highly valued by the woman who possesses it, but not as much as it was by its original owner.

SABOTAGE   The malicious destruction of an employer's property by disgruntled workers, who feel that the more they destroy the sooner their demands will be met, and the sooner their demands are met the sooner they can start to bring home bigger paychecks, which will include almost as much money as they might have gotten if their employer didn't have so much damaged property to repair.

SACERDOTAL   Relating to the office of a priest and, specifically, to the question of which color would be best for the curtains.

SACHET   A perfumed pad or, in other words, the apartment of someone who uses a lot of incense.

SACK   A large bag; as, the plantation owner was so displeased with his foreman that he promoted a cotton picker to the position and, as for the foreman, he gave him the sack.

SACRED   Hallowed; religious; of or pertaining to the stock market.

SACRIFICE   Something that one person gives up for the sake of another person, frequently on the condition that the recipient show a sufficient degree of ingratitude to justify the sacrificer's throwing it up in his face for the next twenty years.

SACRILEGE   The act of desecrating that which is sacred, such as blowing up a bank.

SACRISTY   The most sacred room in a church, where the collection is counted.

SAD   Obsessed with the absurd and completely unfounded notion that life is supposed to be a happy thing.

SADIST   A person whose motto is plain:
"My pleasure is your pain."

SAFARI   An expedition in Africa for the purpose of strengthening the public's appreciation for endangered species.

SAFE   Dead.

SAFECRACKER   A saltine that has been kept in a sanitary wrapper and is okay to eat.

SAFETY BELT   A strap that is designed to keep a motorist tightly secured to his seat in the unfortunate event of his car plunging into deep water or catching on fire.

SAGACIOUS   Using acute mental discernment and keen practical sense in handling a matter the way you would have handled it.

SAGEBRUSH   An article for grooming the hair of a very wise man.

SAGITTARIUS   The sign of the archer, representing people who are used to getting the shaft.

SAILOR   A person whose senses are keen
Regarding all matters marine,
Whose ship is as spotlessly clean
As his language is grossly obscene.

SAINT   Someone who receives public accolades for good deeds, the way a movie star wins an Oscar. 2. Someone whose good deeds are unknown, being done for reasons beyond earthly acknowledgement.

SALACIOUS Lecherous; as,
As a host he's a little too gracious,
His compliments all quite fallacious;
He schemes and connives
To captivate wives
With suggestions subtly salacious.

SALAD A dish of cold vegetables that most people prefer dressed, since it helps to keep them from getting aroused while eating.

SALAMI A sausage that is a nice alternative for people who are sick of listening to the delicatessen man talk nonsense and have decided that they're not going to take any more of his boloney.

SALE Something that a store has in which the prices are reduced on all of the items you bought the day before.

SALES RESISTANCE A French movement to boycott German products in World War II.

SALINA A salty spring, as distinguished from a piquant autumn.

SALINITY The amount of salt in a solution. For example, if the problem is: how do you make a good beef stew? there is one tablespoon of salt in the solution.

SALLY A flight of wit, as an airplane trip with Robert Benchley or George S. Kaufman aboard.

SALTATION Sudden change, as two dimes and a nickel for a quarter in under five seconds.

SALUTATORIAN The student at a graduation commencement who warms up the audience by bringing them to the yawning stage so that the valedictorian can come and finish them off.

SALVATION Deliverance from eternal damnation, which features a punishment similar to the earthly punishment of contact with people who devoutly advocate the eternal damnation of others.

SALVATION ARMY A charitable organization which provides a refuge for tuba players and women with tambourines.

SALVO   A series of shots by artillerymen, as during a bachelor party for one of them.

SAMENESS   The state of being as indistinguishable as two soap operas, two political debates, two laundry detergents, etc.

SAMSON   A very strong man, who destroyed a great building by pulling away its pillars with his bare hands. This was the first recorded case of a performance that really "brought the house down."

SANCTIMONIOUS   So full of sanctity as to have conquered humility.

SANCTUM   A place that is considered sacred because in it one is free from intrusion; the bathroom.

SAND CASTING   The assigning of parts for a beach party movie.

SANDHI   The pronunciation of two or more words without pause, so that they sound like one word, as in "Wodjeet for dinner?" (For a translation, consult any South Philadelphian.)

SANDWICH   Two slices of bread with something edible in between them, unless it is one served in a high school cafeteria.

SANE   Rational enough to recognize an insane world when you see one, and taking the necessary precautions not to become too involved with it. 2. Establishing a thought process midway between that of a person whose thinking is totally deranged and that of a person whose thinking is totally arranged.

SANGUINARY   Regarding a person who is very eager to shed blood, which is perfectly all right, except that he usually insists that it belong to someone else.

SANITATION   The science of seeking conditions of cleanliness; hence, the science of avoiding city streets.

SANTA CLAUS   A guy in a red suit who goes around at Christmas time encouraging greed in small children.

SAPLING   The child of a weak-minded fellow.

SARCASM A means of verbally hitting people below the belt while simultaneously going over their heads.

SARDONIC So filled with contempt as to render oneself contemptible.

SARI An article of clothing worn by Hindu women, designed to induce foot fetishism among Hindu men.

SARTORIAL Pertaining to a tailor or to anyone who is well-versed in the pressing issues of the day.

SASH A window frame or, loosely, a window frame that is not firmly attached to the glass.

SATAN The chief evil spirit, whose greatest ally is the philosophy that people should just shut up and do what they're told, since he seldom has much trouble controlling those who are doing the telling.

SATANISM A secret cult whose members ascribe to a real Devil-may-care attitude.

SATELLITE One of a large number of communications devices launched into orbit for the purpose of providing live television coverage of terrorist bombings, student riots and the funerals of assassinated foreign leaders. They are also used to spy on other countries by certain governments, whose propensity for wasting money will not be satisfied until there are devices to spy on the devices.

SATIATE To satisfy to the point of dissatisfaction with satisfaction.

SATIRE A literary work which exposes human follies through the use of wit and irony, so that humans, whose biggest folly is their inability to recognize (or unwillingness to admit) that they have any, can laugh at what they perceive to be the follies of others.

SATISFACTION The state of sacrificing the challenge of what could be for the security of what is. 2. The state of being content with a lake while others search for an ocean.

SATURDAY The day that separates the drudgery of work from the agony of visiting the in-laws.

SATURN The Roman god of agriculture, who got the job because he was the only immortal willing to get up at five in the morning.

SATURNALIA A period of general license, when anybody can get married or drive a car.

SATYRIASIS An insatiable appetite for sex, affecting certain men; namely, those between the ages of 15 and 87.

SAUNA A modern torture chamber filled with steam, where people who are planning to die of suffocation go to practice.

SAUNTER To walk about idly, in the manner of someone who works in a government office building.

SAUSAGE Minced meat that is stuffed into a prepared intestine, which is to say that the intestine was fully informed of the procedure beforehand.

SAVAGE A person who is totally uncivilized, as demonstrated by his inability to effect mass destruction.

SAVINGS The money that a person puts in the bank for a rainy day, when he makes a withdrawal to buy an umbrella and discovers that he can't afford one anymore.

SAW A maxim, such as, Never leave till tomorrow what you can put off doing indefinitely.

SAXOPHONIST A musician who likes to hang out at improvisational jazz clubs, because those are the kind of places where he can make bread and jam.

SAYING An aphorism, such as, Mum is the word, but Dad is the one with the car keys.

SCAB A worker who would rather accept the salary increments that his employer is willing to give him and feel secure in his job than go out on strike to get more money and risk being laid off sometime in the future as a result. This absurdly rational and unpopular attitude disqualifies him (naturally) from union membership.

SCABLAND Any playground with cement at the bottom of the sliding board.

SCALE A device for weighing people which for some reason is kept in the bathroom next to the tub, when where it really belongs is in the kitchen next to the refrigerator.

SCANDAL The revelation of a moral offense of the kind that people know occurs all the time but would rather ignore. The ensuing disgrace which is heaped upon all those involved, therefore, is less a result of what they did and more a result of the fact that they had the audacity to get caught doing it.

SCANTY Of attire which leaves little to a man's imagination
But which compensates by leaving plenty to his agitation.

SCAR An indelible mark that people wear inside as a reminder that they have been hurt and that, although the original wound may have been caused by someone else, any attempt to reopen it will be strictly self-inflicted.

SCARE To strike with terror or, in other words, to slap in the face fearfully.

SCATOLOGY The science of excrement, deemed by some to be a worthwhile study, while others consider it wasteful.

SCHEDULE A timetable for trains so that passengers know what time they were supposed to have arrived at their destination.

SCHEME An underhand plot, as a secret plan between a pitcher and a catcher in a softball game.

SCHIZOPHRENIA A type of psychosis characterized by an unreasonable desire to leave places on the spur of the moment. This is known in psychiatric terms as a "split" personality.

SCHIZOTHYMIA A mental disorder marked by the disintegration of personality and by the   delusion   that   words on   a   page   are   getting   farther and   farther   apart.

SCHOOL A place where students are taught to think of learning as a chore instead of an adventure, as work instead of pleasure, by teachers who, for the most part, think of their jobs as merely imparting knowledge instead of sharing in the wonder of discovery. 2.

ROSE   A flower that is a favorite among gardeners, especially those who show a budding talent. 2. A flower that by any other name, such as gladiola, would smell like a gladiola.

ROTTEN   Corrupt, particularly in one's duties as a Marine; hence the expression, rotten to the corps.

ROTUNDA   A large round room or, in other words, a place where ammunition for cannons is stored.

ROUGHRIDER   A horse soldier in need of a laxative, commonly known as an irregular cavalryman.

ROULETTE   A gambling game which, contrary to popular belief, requires great skill. It is not a skill that involves the wheel itself but rather an acting skill, since most of the more intelligent participants are unaccustomed to playing absolute fools, and yet many of them do an extremely convincing job of it.

ROUND ROBIN   A red-breasted bird with a weight problem.

ROUTINE   Any system of activities that is repeated and repeated until it becomes a kind of animated death.

ROYALTY   That batch of people whose most outstanding qualification for ruling a country or province is the fact that they were born. 2. The sons and daughters of royal sexual mergers.

RUBBER   A substance that is used in many products because it is durable, which is to say that it holds up even after a long stretch.

RUBBER-STAMP   To approve something without subjecting it to the scrutiny of an idiot.

RUDE   Considerate enough to act in such a manner as to spare refined people from continued contact with an ignoramous.

RUFFIAN   A fellow who does his thinking with his fists, which frees his brain to concentrate on more important things, such as which foot goes in which shoe.

RUG   A pile that costs a bundle.

RULES   Things that are made to be broken—by people who are made to be broken.

A good place to go to learn all of the things you can't learn through experience.

SCHOPENHAUERISM The philosophy of the German pessimistic philosopher Arthur Schopenhauer, who was so busy teaching his students that life is evil and that only by overcoming the will to live can one cure oneself of this evil that he neglected to take note of the fact that he himself lived to be 72.

SCIENTIST One who is more able than the average person to answer the relatively simple questions regarding existence, such as "How did life begin?" but who is as unqualified as a theologian to answer the relatively difficult questions, such as "Why did life begin?"

SCIOMANCY Divination by consulting the shades of the dead, but if the shades are not available, then regular eyeglasses will do.

SCISSORS An instrument that is used in the Soviet Union to edit propaganda recordings, a process known there as cutting the Red tape.

SCIURINE Designating a family of rodents consisting of true squirrels and also of squirrels that have only been disloyal a couple of times.

SCORN A feeling of such extreme disdain that it is often aroused only by people who remind one of the qualities one disdains in oneself.

SCOUNDREL A person who is commonly thought to be worthless but who is in fact worth a great deal, in the sense that it is his behavior which serves as the justification for the feelings of moral superiority enjoyed by everyone who knows him.

SCOUT A boy or a girl who is taught to exhibit strange and suspicious behavior in public, such as performing good deeds without pay.

SCOUTMASTER An adult who believes that the achievement of training a group of boys to make fifty different kinds of knots is worth the embarrassment of wearing short pants and a hat.

SCRAPBOOK A book filled with yesterday's memories and, hopefully, at least a few blank pages for the memories of tomorrow.

2. A collection of pictures, newspaper clippings and other memorabilia which is pathetically treasured by people who have nothing but the past to look forward to.

SCRAPPLE   A sausagelike preparation which will not be defined in any further detail for the benefit of people who like to eat it.

SCREAM   To emit a sound which indicates to the neighbors that this might be a good night for them to go out to a movie.

SCREWDRIVER   A crazily eccentric operator of an automobile.

SCREWY   As preposterous as any novel plan or idea that you didn't think of first.

SCRIMMAGE   A confused struggle, as distinguished from a perplexed exertion.

SCRIPTURE   Any sacred writing, such as the annual earnings report of an oil company.

SCRUPLE   Hesitation on the part of a person who is not certain if an action is right or wrong and who therefore insists upon being talked into doing it by someone who knows it's wrong.

SCULPTOR   A person who carves his reputation by persevering, even if nobody ever buys anything from him and his work is considered a bust.

SCUM   A rabble of low people, such as an angry mob of pygmies.

SEA   A body of water smaller than an ocean but larger than a very, very big puddle.

SEANCE   A gathering of persons for the purpose of discovering that the principal occupation of departed spirits is to make curtains flutter.

SEAPORT   A dark red wine served on cruise ships.

SEASON   A period during which fashion-minded people obediently go out and buy the clothes that they are told are in style and wear them until they are told otherwise. 2. Yet another round of police shows and relevant situation comedies.

SECRET   Something that everyone in the neighborhood has been told in strict confidence.

SECRET SERVICE The people who make sure that the president gets to a hospital after he has been shot.

SECURITY The condition of coming to terms with the fact that nothing is secure.

SECURITY GUARD A person who has no respect for the privacy of others, since he is forever minding someone else's business.

SEDATIVE A pill which is administered to people in stressful situations to help insure that, when they face subsequent stressful situations and the pills are not available, they will go into hysterics.

SEDUCTRESS A woman who induces a man to surrender his chastity, usually with the same degree of difficulty with which a thick steak induces him to surrender his appetite.

SEE To use the eyes not simply as instruments of sight, but rather as avenues of understanding between the mind and the outside world, so that they are able to reveal as much as they behold.

SEEDCASE A legal action regarding paternity.

SEER A woman who gazes into a crystal ball and sees that sometime in the near future she will be buying dinner with the money of an idiot.

SEERSUCKER Anyone who visits a woman with a crystal ball.

SEGREGATION The act of doing a particular group of people a favor by isolating them from contact with bigots who are unworthy of their society.

SEISMOLOGY The science of earthquakes, which is an uncertain area of study because most of its practitioners recognize that they are operating on very shaky ground.

SELECTION The act of selecting from a number of choices that are different, as opposed to an election, which is the act of selecting from a number of choices that are the same.

SELF A being regarded as having a personality, as distinguished from an accountant.

SELF-ABUSE   Voluntary exposure to more than fifteen minutes of prime time television.

SELF-CONFIDENCE   An abiding faith in one's own abilities; that which is called egotism in others.

SELF-CONSCIOUS   Too embarrassed by one's own social awkwardness to notice how awkward everyone else is.

SELF-DECEPTION   The act of being fooled by a fool.

SELF-EDUCATION   The process of making the world itself one's classroom and everyone in it one's teacher.

SELF-IMPORTANCE   A feeling of deep awareness of one's own importance, for which people who are really important have no need.

SELF-IMPROVEMENT   The most worthwhile of enterprises, for it directs one's corrective energies toward the person who most needs them and leaves no time for trying to correct everyone else.

SELF-INDULGENCE   The act of treating oneself like a spoiled brat and allowing one's desires to dictate one's life style.

SELF-LOVE   Love of oneself, without which the love that one gives to another leaves one with nothing except the desire to take all of another's love, a condition that leads to emotional parasitism, which is the opposite of love.

SELF-RESPECT   Regard for the person whose view of himself determines the value of his regard for others.

SEMANTICS   The science dealing with epistemological and morphological assumptions affecting the signification of words. 2. The science of meanings, such as the meaning of epistemological and morphological assumptions affecting the signification of words.

SEMASIOLOGY   See SEMANTICS (if you can bear going through all that again).

SENATOR   A member of Congress, who is constantly faced with the dilemma of whether to vote according to the party line or according to his conscience. A senior member is one who has managed to overcome the dilemma by making them the same thing.

SENILITY   The mental infirmity which has less to do with growing old than it does with losing sight of the simple fact that (to paraphrase a famous baseball line) life isn't over until it's over.

SENIOR   A student who has less than one year of schooling to go before being out of work.

SENSATIONALISM   The philosophical doctrine that all knowledge originates in sense perception, with the exception of the knowledge of the absurd, which originates in nonsense perception.

SENSIBLE   Characterizing any of your opinions, as diametrically opposed to the opinions of people who are unreasonable enough to disagree with you.

SENTENCE   The period of time that a convicted criminal is supposed to spend in prison, which is practically always commuted in order to allow the criminal to return to society as an active member and to provide him with the opportunity someday to achieve his life-long ambition of becoming a repeat offender.

SEPTEMBER   National Sigh Month, when schools reopen and kids utter sighs of grief while their mothers heave sighs of relief.

SERENE   Calm; imperturbable; having an abundant supply of sedatives and a well-stocked liquor cabinet.

SERIOUS   Pertaining to a person whose disposition is grave, so called because the expression on his face is such that, when the time comes, the mortician will not have to make any adjustments.

SERMON   A discourse delivered by a clergyman, which can sometimes command such power that it actually helps to effect an instant cure for certain afflictions, such as insomnia.

SERPENT   Nothing but a snake on a larger scale.

SERVANT   One who works for others, commonly in a menial capacity; as, a domestic servant. 2. One who works for others, commonly in a venial capacity, as, a public servant.

SETBACK   Merely an opportunity to turn an eventual triumph into a glorious triumph.

SEVERAL   A few more than a couple and a few less than some, give or take one or two.

SEWER The pipeline which carries waste water out of a city, not to be confused with the pipeline which carries drinking water into a city. These are different kinds of water entirely; only the taste is the same.

SEX The one pleasure in life for which there is no fair price; it is either free or far too costly. 2. The most popular of human activities, because it requires the artistic skill of an ape, the imagination of a basset hound, and the intelligence of a cockroach.

SEXTON Twenty one-hundred-pound prostitutes.

SHACKLE Anything which impedes freedom of thought, such as an English Literature course in which the students are told what a book is supposed to mean.

SHADOW A spy who keeps a steady watch on someone, particularly someone whose allegiance is uncertain; hence, the shadow of a doubt.

SHADY Pertaining to the manufacture and sale of beach umbrellas; as, a shady business.

SHAKESPEARE-BACON CONTROVERSY The dispute arising from the theory that Francis Bacon actually wrote Shakespeare's plays and that Shakespeare only did the program notes.

SHAKE To become unsteady, as when she gives you back your fraternity pin.

SHAME A feeling of guilt triggered by a faulty conscience, which is like a fire alarm that goes off after the building has burned down.

SHARE To increase one's enjoyment of anything by adding to it the complementary enjoyment of enjoying others enjoying it, as well.

SHARPSHOOTER A person who takes pictures of experts.

SHAWM An obsolete wind instrument which is used, obviously, for locating obsolete wind.

SHELL GAME A game which demonstrates that the hand (of a con artist) is quicker than the eye (of a fool).

SHELL SHOCK   A condition, akin to hysteria, which occurs in seafood restaurants when people who have had lobster get their bill.

SHIFTLESS   Regarding a person who will only drive a car with an automatic transmission.

SHIP   A seagoing vessel on which passengers who have never had the opportunity to vomit into the ocean may do so at no additional charge.

SHIPWRECK   A person on a cruise with severe seasickness.

SHOCK ABSORBER   The parent of a teen-ager.

SHOEMAKER   A jack of awl trades.

SHOPLIFTER   A worker who helps to raise the morale in a store or a factory.

SHORTEN   To abbr.

SHOTGUN   A gun designed for firing shot at a short range, as distinguished from a gun designed for firing shot at a tall refrigerator.

SHOULDN'T   A colloquial contraction meaning "will anyway"; as, I really shouldn't have another piece of that chocolate cake.

SHOUT   To speak in a bar with a juke box playing.

SHOW-OFF   One whose talent suffers from one major flaw; it belongs to a pretentious fool.

SHRAPNEL   A shell named after its inventor, General Henry Shrapnel, whose tireless work in the field of puncturing the human body with little metal balls earned him the respect and admiration of wheelchair manufacturers the world over.

SHREW   A scolding woman or, in a broader sense, a fat scolding woman.

SHREWD   Having an uncanny ability to see below the surface; hence, pertaining to a coal miner.

SHUFFLEBOARD   A game that requires little physical exertion and may be played by people with heart conditions, provided that they know enough not to push things too far.

SIBILANT   Uttered with a hissing sound; as, Sissie's six sisters speak sibilant speech sounds ceaselessly.

SICKENING   As disgusting as the sight of someone's grandmother being eaten alive by piranhas; as, what a sickening definition!

SIDE   Either of two stances on an issue, including the one which you have taken and the wrong one.

SIDE SHOW   A tour of a beef-packing plant.

SIDEWALK   A demonstration on foot sponsored by people who share the same views on an issue.

SILENCE   Something that all parents crave until they reach the age when they get it.

SILENUS   One of the minor woodland deities, which are basically the same as the major woodland deities except that they have to work weekends.

SILLY   Designating that which is to seriousness what a toothpick is to irony; as, this is a silly definition.

SILVER   A metal which shows that you care, but not enough to give gold.

SILVERWARE   Fine utensils for the table which are kept at all times in a drawer, because they're too good to be used.

SIMILAR   Having a general likeness; resembling Omar Bradley.

SIMPLICITY   The art of living modestly, sticking to the basics, and avoiding conversations with insurance salesmen.

SIN   An offense against that which any society, generation or individual perceives to be the laws of God, assuming that God goes along with all of the changes that have been made in them throughout the centuries by his ecclesiastical enforcers, whose efforts to improve upon the divine scheme have lent them a temporal expediency that was lacking when they were originally formulated.

SINCERE   Totally lacking in ulterior motives and, therefore, likely to arouse intense suspicion.

SING   To raise one's voice, one's spirit and, quite possibly, one's life expectancy in song.

SINGLE   Unmarried; hence, unharried.

SINGSONG   Pertaining to a verse like this
Whose rhythm you can hardly miss;
It's la di da di da di da,
Etcetera, Etcetera.

SINLESS   Faultless. 2. Friendless.

SINNER   One who sins repentantly, like oneself. 2. One who sins incorrigibly, like one's neighbor.

SIREN   The song of the city.

SISTER   A female person in relation to another person having the same parents (whole sister) or one who has been attacked by a shark (half sister).

SIX   The age when children begin to gain their educations and to lose their imaginations.

SIXTEEN   The age when a teen-ager finally begins to show consideration, appreciation and respect for his parents—anything to get the car.

SKEPTIC   One who is given to doubting, having been taken to the cleaners.

SKEPTICISM   The philosophical doctrine that all knowledge is uncertain, including the knowledge that all knowledge is uncertain.

SKIN   The covering of the body, which prevents people from spilling blood on one another when there isn't a war.

SKINNER   One who cures skin, as a dermatologist, or dresses it, as a fashion designer.

SKULL   The bony framework which protects the brain from everything except its two worst enemies, a bullet and itself.

SKY   The wild blue yonder, unless it is over an oil refinery, where it is the wild black-and-blue yonder, or over Los Angeles, where it is the wild gray yonder.

SKY LINE A suggestive remark made by a pilot to one of the stewardesses.

SLANG Language comprising certain terms that are, you know, cool, man.

SLAPSTICK Any physical business that is meant to produce laughter, such as a man slipping on a banana peel, or pain, such as a man slipping on a banana peel.

SLAVE Anyone who is foolish enough to crawl under someone else's thumb and stupid enough to stay there. 2. A wife who is maid to order.

SLEEP A period of recuperation from a chronic disease called consciousness. 2. One of the few practical rewards of a clear conscience.

SLEEVE The part of a garment which one places in the mashed potatoes to match the onion dip which one has spilled on one's tie.

SLIDE A kind of presentation to which party guests are sometimes mercilessly subjected, considered in several states as a firm basis for justifiable homicide.

SLIP COVER The false identity of a young and slender secret agent.

SLOGAN A brief, striking phrase used in advertising a product, such as an aerosol deodorant ("The family that sprays together stays together") or a lawn mower ("When the mowing gets tough, the tough get mowing").

SLOTHFUL Preferring the kind of work that requires no physical or mental exertion but lacking the necessary votes to become a state legislator.

SLUM A district in a city set aside by conservationists as a refuge for rats, roaches, silverfish and other endangered species.

SLUMBER To sleep lightly, as in the case of someone who is afraid of the dark.

SLUR To obscure the syllables in prunciation.

SLUT   A term used by high school boys to describe any girl who does what they would like her to do.

SLY   Furtively cunning, unlike oneself, who is cleverly astute.

SMALL   Two and a third times larger than itsy bitsy and two and seven-eighths times larger than teensy weensy.

SMALL TALK   A conversation between women with grandchildren.

SMELLING SALTS   Sailors with a shrewdness for detecting things.

SMILE   The simplest and most effective facial treatment, which does more to improve one's appearance than spending all day in a beauty shop. 2. The passport to friendship.

SMOG   A city's attempt to create its own distinctive atmosphere for its people.

SMOLDER   To burn without a flame, as in the case of a woman whose sweetheart is away in the army.

SMOOTHBORE   A suave but tiresome person.

SMUG   Extremely self-satisfied, as though attaining the rank of a righteous jerk were a proud achievement.

SNAKE   Any of a large number of reptiles, many of which produce lethal amounts of poisonous venom, the deadliest being those of the human variety.

SNOB   One whose nose is so high in the air that he is unconscious of his own stink.

SNORE   To emit sounds during sleep of the kind resembling what many anthropologists believe were the first grunts uttered by cavemen; hence, to express a subliminal desire to return to prehistoric times.

SNOWBALL   A formal dance for cocaine snuffers.

SOCIAL SECURITY   Money that is given to senior citizens so that they can take up hobbies, such as stealing food.

SOCIETY A terrifying and ubiquitous menace which is commonly held responsible for the crimes committed by people who can't find anybody in particular to blame.

SOLDIER An armed statistic.

SOLECISM An incorrectness of standard speech, which usually ain't nothing but a case of inexcusable carelessness.

SOLITUDE The state of having everyone in the world with you at the same time, excluding those you can live without.

SOMATOLOGIST One who studies the physical characteristics of people; any red-blooded male standing on a street corner in the city at noon when the secretaries come out for lunch.

SOPHIST One who reasons unsoundly, as with sign language.

SOPHISTICATED Regarding people of the world
Whose views are never errant;
Who put on airs that summon stares
For their airs are airs apparent.

SOPHOMORE A student in high school who, having matured after the completion of his first year, is afforded added privileges, such as picking on freshmen.

SPACE The ultimate challenge to man, testing whether his ability to destroy a single planet will one day provide him with the skills necessary to destroy an entire universe.

SPAGHETTI A popular dish commonly associated with Italians, who have a saying: "Live for the present, but never forgeta the pasta."

SPEAK To talk; as, whoever said that actions speak louder than words didn't have my next-door neighbors.

SPECTATOR A person with one foot on the sideline and the other foot in the grave. See PARTICIPATE.

SPELLBOUND Forced by a teacher to name in order the letters of a word.

SPIDER One of a large group of arachnids created for the exclusive purpose of scaring the wits out of women and making men feel very brave when they are summoned into the room to dispose of them.

SPILL An accidental test to determine whether a friend or relative has greater regard for your feelings than for the carpet.

SPINSTER An obsolete term used in a time when women who were not overjoyed at the thought of washing dirty undershirts were considered abnormal.

SPIRITUALISM The belief that the spirits of the dead return and communicate with the living, only they have to do it through a medium because they are incapable of putting together such an elaborately arranged performance on their own.

SPIT To impersonate a baseball manager.

SPITE To demonstrate your belief in human equality to those who have caused you injury, by proving that you are no better than they are.

SPLURGE To put too and too together.

SPOIL To give a child everything that he wants and very little that he needs.

SPONSOR A person or company whose commercials are interrupted briefly by portions of a television show.

SPONTANEITY The quality of being able to do something just because you feel like it at the moment, of trusting your instincts, of taking yourself by surprise and snatching from the clutches of your well-organized routine a bit of unscheduled pleasure.

SPORTS Athletic games of a wide variety which completely dominate Sunday television, in keeping with the religious fervor of the fans.

SPOUSE The least perfect and most objectionable kind of marriage partner.

SPY An agent employed by a government to steal secret information from other countries so that the secret reports based upon this information can be stolen by agents employed by other countries.

SQUAD The smallest military unit, capable of losing no more than twenty-four legs.

SQUARE DANCE A social for people who are ignorant of the latest fads.

STADUIM An open-air cathedral where the faithful followers congregate to pay homage to the gods of the playing field. See SPORTS.

STANZA A unit of the kind of poem written by poets who are noted for their versatility.

STATISTICS Those facts and figures which, statistically speaking, three out of five sports fans use to fill the parts of their brains not otherwise occupied, which, statistically speaking, accounts for 72 percent of the total cranial volume.

STEELWORKER A person who learns to do things the hard way.

STRATAGEM In war, an offensive tactic, such as making the troops go without deodorant for a couple of days.

STRESS A disease suffered by the participants in all rat races. The front runners develop it from constantly looking over their shoulders; those in the rear, from straining to see ahead; those in the middle, from turning in a circle.

STRIP TEASE A bizarre beauty treatment in which the hairdresser removes her clothes while crimping the customer.

STUPIDITY Extreme deficiency in intelligence, of the type required in implementing government programs.

SUBCONSCIOUS Aware of underwater vessels.

SUBPLOT The scheme of a play or a novel that takes place on a U-boat.

SUCCESS The state of meeting your own expectations and not worrying about the expectations that others have set for you. 2. The art of learning how high one can climb for fruit without falling out of the tree.

SUFFICIENT Enough, as in the ancient Arabic saying used by the shieks: "A word to the wives is sufficient."

SUICIDE A self-administered execution for the capital crime of taking life too seriously. 2. The act of a traitor, who has betrayed himself to despair.

SUIT Attire consisting of two or three pieces, depending upon whether or not the wearer has a vested interest.

SUM The total or, in common usage, the sum total; as, the sum total of redundancies in this definition is two.

SUN A place that is so hot you could fry a planet on it.

SUPPER The evening meal, which some nutritionists insist is the most important and must include at least one serving from each of the four major food groups, although critics who advocate light meals in the evening find all of that hard to swallow.

SURGEON A doctor who operates in the presence of one or more nurses and who also sometimes performs surgery on patients.

SUSPENSE Friction fiction.

SWORD An outdated weapon once used extensively in warfare, which required the combatants to kill one another at close range, to expend enormous amounts of energy, and frequently to get blood on their hands. It made for an altogether unpleasant way of fighting and was replaced, thanks to technological advances, by the gun.

TABLE A piece of furniture with various functions, such as one reserved for a very funny person (card table), one with mayonnaise, sour cream, vinegar and oil on it (dressing table), and one with a drawer containing a variety of items (table of contents).

TABLOID A newspaper that contains condensed news, such as reports on canned soup, powdered milk, etc.

TABOO Restriction imposed by social convention; as, there is a taboo in certain societies against prolonged thinking, for fear that it might lead to temporary sanity.

TABOR A small drum that can be constructed quite easily by anyone with a head for music.

TACAMAHAC An incense that's blissful, to the extent
That the natives say it's heaven scent.

TACHOMETRY The science which explores the entire range of speed, from lunar rockets to the postal department.

TACITURN About as talkative as a starlet from South Dakota at her first Hollywood party. 2. Regarding a woman at a social gathering whose husband is in charge of the family opinions, jokes, anecdotes, etc.

TACT The perceptive ability to know that telling the one about the psychotic surgeon to somebody who is scheduled for a gall bladder operation might not be such a good idea.

TACTICS The science of deciding which is the best place for a group of soldiers to have their limbs blown off.

TACTLESS   Regarding the millions of people infesting the planet who are fond of the following: commenting on how much weight you've gained, asking why you're not married yet, asking why you don't have any kids yet, remarking on your loss of hair, inquiring about people who have broken your heart, pointing out in public that your breath is bad, and bringing up embarrassing incidents from the past, such as, "Remember the time we were on that ski lift and you had to go to the bathroom so bad . . .?"

TAFFY   A candy that is very sticky and therefore can only be eaten by people who don't have dentures—yet.

TAG   A game in which the slowest of a group of children races around futilely trying to touch one of the others until he is exhausted enough to quit.

TAIL   The terminal appendage of many animals, as well as a large number of mythological creatures. Although there is serious doubt that elves and goblins have them, a lot of people do believe in fairy tails.

TAILOR   A person who is very good at handling misunderstandings between people, for somehow he always manages to iron things out. 2. A man who is emotionally unstable, because one never knows when he is liable to take a fit.

TAKE-HOME   What is left of a person's salary after the government and the union have laid into it, which is why the thing is called gross.

TAKER   One who takes and is taken simultaneously. What he takes is a bet.

TALE   The account of an event that was actual, as the Thanksgiving dinner of the Puritans and the Indians, legendary, as the Thanksgiving dinner of the Puritans and the Indians, or fictitious, as the Thanksgiving dinner of the Puritans and the Indians.

TALENT   The seed of human excellence, which requires of the person possessing it fertile soil in which to grow and patient nurturing, so that it may blossom into achievement. Otherwise, it simply rots underground, along with the hopes and aspirations of the would-be great.

TALISMAN An engraved figure that produces extraordinary effects, such as drawing out the most ridiculous aspects of the user's nature.

TALK Spoken verbiage, which is said to be cheap, although anyone who has ever hired a celebrity to give a speech will tell you differently.

TALL Regarding anything having to do with a person over six feet in height, such as a command given by a lanky lieutenant (a tall order) or a novel about a basketball player (a tall story).

TALLYHO The senseless outburst of a person who is suffering from a rare mental disorder, in which he feels hopelessly compelled to dress in a silly outfit and chase a fox.

TAMALE A mexican food made with red pepper that is regarded as a memorable dish, mainly because it keeps coming back up to remind you that you've eaten it hours after the meal is over.

TAMARAU A buffalo of the Philippine Islands, differing from the American buffalo in that it had the good sense to stay out of America.

TAME Pertaining to a child who doesn't bite.

TAMPER To attempt to correct a malfunction in a car, television set, etc., which one determines to be minor and which usually *is* minor until one is finished attempting to correct it.

TAN A darkening of the skin, which many people make an enormous effort to acquire and, upon doing so, proudly display it in public, as though the ability to lie in the sun were a stupendously praiseworthy accomplishment.

TANGO A dance that is distinguished by dips, although normal people also do it pretty well.

TANK A military vehicle of the utmost importance in combat, because it looks like a big toy and therefore it helps to bring out the little boy in every soldier, and that's what makes war fun.

TANTAMOUNT In some states, a contraction of "it cannot amount"; as, tantamount to much.

TANTARA   A fanfare or, in other words, the money it costs a baseball enthusiast to ride to the ballpark.

TAP DANCE   A social gathering with live music held at a London pub.

TAPEWORM   One who is unusually devoted to his cassette collection.

TARANTISM   A nervous condition characterized by an uncontrollable desire to dance. It is suffered almost exclusively by fat aunts at wedding receptions.

TARGET   Someone at whom ridicule is aimed by a person or persons equipped with a well-stocked arsenal of cruelty, baseness and stupidity.

TARTARUS   The mythological region that is even lower than Hades, reserved for people who were not only wicked in life, but who also hum.

TASTE   The power to discern and appreciate the difference between an Ibsen play and a double play, between the Ring Cycle and the Wash Cycle, and between a Monet field and a football field.

TASTEFUL   Pertaining to a person who shares your preference in music and dislikes the same authors that you dislike.

TAURUS   The only astrological sign which properly represents what its horoscope is full of.

TAUTOLOGY   Redundancy consisting of a needless repetition of meaning, in the sense of an unnecessary redefining, in terms of an unrequired adding of something in other words.

TAVERN   A bar, where people go to relax and drink, as distinguished from a bar where people go to drink and revert to pre-evolutionary behavior (a monkey bar).

TAX   Money that people give to the government primarily to build bombs in order to insure that future generations will not have to worry about giving money to the government, by virtue of the elimination of the planet.

TAXI   Short for TAXICAB, although no one is exactly sure how tall a taxicab is supposed to be.

TAXICAB   Long for a TAXI, which is what people standing outside a hotel late at night do.

TAXIDERMIST   A person who evidently has a way of saying the wrong thing to people, for it is not uncommon to hear one of his customers tell him to stuff it.

TEA   A beverage that the British have been drinking so regularly for so long that the ritual of teatime has become an integral part of their lives. One can go so far as to say that it is steeped in tradition.

TEACHER   One whose occupation is to instruct and to learn from those instructed.

TEAM   Any group of people who band together to demonstrate what human beings are capable of accomplishing when they're not too busy blowing each other's brains out.

TEARS   Fluid falling from the eyes, expressing varying emotions; as, tears of grief are an outpouring of the pain that is inside; tears of joy are an outpouring of the pain that was inside.

TEASE   To hurt someone's feelings in a persistent and playful manner, so that he will come to hate your guts lightheartedly.

TEASPOON   A utensil used to stir the morning coffee used to stir the morning coffee drinker.

TECHNICAL   Peculiar to a particular trade, as that of a fullback and a top draft choice for a wide receiver.

TECHNOLOGY   The science of implementing industrial advances first and worrying about their effects on people and the environment later.

TECTONICS   The branch of geology concerned with faulting, and how best to do it without hurting the other person's feelings.

TEDIOUS   About as boring as listening to other people talk about their kids, especially in comparison to how interesting it is when you talk about your kids.

TEEN-AGER   A person who looks around at the people he knows in their twenties and figures he'd better get in all the fun that he can while there's still time.

TEENY   Just a wee bit smaller than tiny and even a little bit less than a wee bit larger than itsy bitsy.

TEETH   The hard bony appendages found in most vertebrates which are composed of dentine, pulp and enamel and used for seizing and masticating food, as well as for weapons of offense and defense, and that's saying a mouthful.

TEETOTALER   An employee in a sporting goods store who keeps inventory of the golf supplies.

TELEKINESIS   The ability to move things without touching them and without using any of the gimmicks employed by people who have the ability to move things without touching them.

TELEOLOGICAL ARGUMENT   The argument for the existence of God based on the order in the universe, government job training programs notwithstanding.

TELEPHONE   A device that starts ringing five seconds after you get into the bathtub and stops ringing five seconds after you get out of the bathtub to answer it. 2. The interruption machine. 3. A device that is perfect for communicating when and where you would like to take someone to dinner, but never why.

TELEPHONY   An obnoxiously insincere person who appears on a TV show.

TELEPHOTO   A special lens used at weddings and other family affairs when you want to take pictures of distant relatives.

TELESCOPE   An optical instrument used by astronomers who are not content merely with praise from the scientific community for discovering a new planet or star. They want to make it big.

TELESIS   Progress intelligently planned,
        Which is to say, progress unmanned.

TELESTEREOSCOPE   A binocular telescope used to obtain impressions of relief on celestial bodies, such as determining whether or not they use food stamps.

TELEVISION   A household altar before which individuals and families gather in reverent silence, with their holy books of listings opened to the appropriate page, ready to pay homage to the deities of the screen, the prime time gods and goddesses, and to the sacred sponsors, in whose name they devoutly make pilgrimages to the marketplace to proffer their daily offerings.

TEMPTRESS A woman who can so entice a man that if he dares to take her on a date he is clearly courting danger.

TEN COMMANDMENTS The Decalogue, which were given to Moses on Mount Sinai by God, who said, "Take these two tablets and call me in the morning."

TENNIS A game which involves getting dressed up in a fashionable white outfit, tying a sweater around your neck, and trying to look very intense while you hit a ball over a net.

TENSION An inevitable symptom affecting people who are too busy climbing to the top to take some time to enjoy the view.

TENT A portable shelter used primarily by people who want to spend some time in the great outdoors roughing it the way their ancestors did in the olden days, when people used manual can openers.

TERATOLOGY The study of physical monstrosities, such as the people featured in carnival side shows, as distinguished from mental monstrosities, such as the people who run them.

THANKSGIVING A day when families gather to share a unique holiday feeling; namely, indigestion.

THAT Not this. 2. Or this, either.

THEME A piece of music by which a group is identified, such as the bakers' theme ("Waltz of the Flours"), the weavers' theme ("Clear de Loom"), or the cheerleaders' theme ("The Pompom and Circumstance March").

THESIS A dissertation, sufficiently esoteric and confusing to merit a doctoral degree.

THIRTY The age when you begin to wonder if those gray hairs really are premature, after all. See QUADRAGENARIAN.

THREE The age when most children start asking their parents questions, and their parents start asking themselves if they know enough to have children.

TIE   An article of attire that is worn for no practical purpose whatsoever, except perhaps that it feels uncomfortable enough to be considered proper.

TIME   The mother of age, the father of regret and the brother of decay. In the long run, however, it is also the sister of mercy.

TIMELESS   Not possessing a clock or a watch.

TIGHTROPE   A circus act performed by acrobats who have reached the height of their profession.

TILLER   A real down-to-earth sort of person.

TINY   Just a teensy weensy bit larger than itsy bitsy.

TOLERABLE   Pertaining to any unpleasant situation or condition, as long as it's happening to somebody else.

TORTURE   Something that is excruciatingly unbearable, such as the incessant jingle of that damned ice cream truck that comes around in the summer.

TOUCH   One of the senses, the importance of which in relation to the other senses is debated academically, although it is not as much a question of what you think about it as how you feel.

TRAILBLAZER   A jacket worn by a prep school student when hiking.

TRAIN   A mode of transportation for people who would rather share a bit of the past than admit that they have a fear of flying.

TRAMP   A begging vagrant or, in a broad sense, a woman of low morals.

TRANQUILIZER   Any drug which helps to lower a person's natural resistance to tension.

TRANSIT   An authority which has as its principal responsibility the task of bringing people together in groups, for the purpose of standing and waiting. This teaches them the virtue of patience and gives them the shared, communal sense of being late.

TRANSVESTITE   A person who, when dressing, prefers
A closet that's marked: HIS and HERS.

TREE   A woody perennial plant that has been celebrated in countless poems; as, A tree is made from a seed once you grow it
But only God can make a poet.

TRIPEDAL   Having three feet, as two neighbors; as
"Two neighbors, tripedal?" she said with a
sneer.
"Are you some sort of bloddy retard?"
"Not at all, " said he with a whimsical glee.
"The two neighbors both share the same yard."

TRIVIAL   Pertaining to that which opposing parties consider vital.

TRUMPET   An instrument which the person sitting two rows behind you at the ballpark is thoughtful enough to bring along with
him, so that even if the home team loses miserably, you will at least
have the consolation of your hearing.

TRUTH   What is left of an occurrence after the prejudice, stupidity, vested interests and ulterior motives of the participants and ob-
servers have been eliminated.

TRY   To succeed at overcoming the fear of failure.

TUMBLER   A tumbling acrobat or, in a narrower sense, a thin
tumbling acrobat.

TUNNELER   Someone who builds subterranean passageways
and whose work is always underrated.

TWENTY-ONE   The last year to enjoy being misunderstood for
its own sake before being misunderstood professionally.

TYPOGRAPHICAL   Pertaining to teh preceding error.

TYRANT   An absolute ruler whose absolute rule
Requires a man who's an absolute fool.

UBIQUITOUS   Being everywhere at the same time; as, how could she concentrate on the movie when his hands were ubiquitous?

UDDER   The mammary gland of a cow and the basis for numerous puns beneath consideration in this dictionary.

UGLIFY   To overdo make-up so that you look like you've undergone a breakdown.

UGLY   As repulsive as a work of modern art is before the connoisseurs decide that it's beautiful.

UKULELE   A musical instrument used to enhance
The movements of the hula dance.

ULTERIOR   Pertaining to the motives of someone with sincerity in his voice, money in his hand, a smile on his face, and something up his sleeve.

ULTIMATE   Last in a train of progression, not to be confused with a ship of consequence.

ULTIMATUM   The final proposition before the next final proposition: as, she gave him the ultimatum either to stop drinking or to get out.

ULTRACRITICAL   Regarding a person who is perfect and who has little toleration for the shortcomings of the other four and a half billion people in the world.

ULTRAISM   The principles of one who advocates extreme measures, such as a million square miles, a hundred light years, etc.

ULTRAMARINE An extraordinarily dedicated member of the Corps.

ULTRAMODERN Ahead of its time; as, he explained to the repairman that his watch was ultramodern.

UMBILICATE Depressed in the middle, as a person who is feeling sad while sitting in a car with someone on either side of him.

UMBILICUS The scar left at birth from the doctor's cuttin'
That is henceforth referred to as the belly button.

UMBRELLA A device that is used in a procedure to determine accurately whether or not it will rain on a day when the meteorologists are uncertain. The procedure is simple: if you leave it at home, it will.

UMBRIFEROUS Casting a shade, as a director who is looking for someone to play Hamlet's father.

UNABLE Unwilling.

UNABSOLVED Not free from guilt; living within an hour's drive of your mother.

UNACCOUNTABLE Without any money to put in the bank.

UNACKNOWLEDGED Modest.

UNADULTERATED Not having been subjected to the influence of grownups.

UNAMBIGUOUS Not the least bit confusing, unless you happen to be the kind of person who is confused by clarity, in which case that which is clearest seems most confusing and that which is the most confusing, conversely, seems like this definition.

UN-AMERICAN Pertaining to cars, cameras, televisions, stereo components, wristwatches and wines preferred by Americans, especially the Americans who are the first to scream and yell about how great everything in America is.

UNARTISTIC Not the way the people who know what artistic is (whoever they are) say it should be.

UNASKED Pertaining to the kinds of questions that most need to be asked.

UNATTAINABLE Attainable, provided that you rid yourself of the negative influence of people who insist that it is impossible, never having attained anything really worthwhile themselves. It is these people who are impossible, not the goal.

UNATTEMPTED Of any activity regarding which you are deliberately depriving yourself of the joy of being able to do or, equally important, the self-satisfaction of giving it your best shot.

UNATTRACTIVE Not good looking and too aware of it; good looking and too aware of it.

UNBALANCED Mentally disordered or, if in the kitchen, deranged.

UNBEAR To clear all grizzlies from an area.

UNCANNY Tasting fresh and not as if it came from a tin container.

UNCERTAINTY The only certainty.

UNCHARGE To pay cash.

UNCHEWED Pertaining to the condition of vegetables entering the stomachs of children who were forced to eat them.

UNCHASTE Chased.

UNCLE A person who is good to have around on birthdays and at Christmas, because those are the only occasions when a kid gets paid back for making all those lousy visits to his house.

UNCOIL In New York, to have one's hair straightened.

UNCOMMUNICATIVE Reserved; as, I'm sorry, sir, but this table is uncommunicative.

UNCONDITIONAL Unreserved; as, however, sir, there is a table over here that is unconditional.

UNCONVERTIBLE A sedan.

UNCORRECTED Without the errors or falts rectifide.

UNCOUNTABLE Without the proper blood lines to be declared a nobleman.

UNCOUTH Not trained in the social graces, such as the art of being rude while smiling or appearing totally innocent while coming on to one of the neighbors' wives.

UNDATED Not asked out.

UNDEFINABLE Capable of being defined as incapable of being defined.

UNDER In a place beneath,
2. Down here.

UNDERCHARGE To lead an army toward the enemy from the bottom of a valley.

UNDERESTIMATE To lie beneath a car and give a rough idea of what it will cost to fix the chassis.

UNDERPASS An attempt to make a date with someone in a subway station.

UNDERPLOT The main story line of a play about coal miners.

UNDERPRIVILEGED Without certain advantages enjoyed by the more affluent members of society, such as the advantage of eating.

UNDERQUOTE To cite passages from Shakespeare in the basement.

UNDERSCORE The music to a film about skin divers.

UNDERSTAND To open the ears, close the mouth, engage the brain, and hold the prejudice.

UNDERSTUDY An actor who is prepared to take on another actor's part, provided that they have similar hair styles.

UNDERTAKER A person who takes his work dead seriously. 2. A person who strikes pay dirt every day, six feet at a time. 3. The person who puts the "fun" in "funeral."

UNDERVALUE To rate one's worth in terms of one's possessions.

UNDERWORLD The domain of gangsters, particularly those who pay off the overworld for control of the middleworld.

UNDOUBTED   Of an honest man surrounded by his friends; of a dishonest man surrounded by dupes.

UNDRESSED   In a pants suit or jeans and a blouse.

UNEDUCATED   Not having spent much time in school; not having spent much time anywhere other than in school.

UNEMOTIONAL   Exercising mind over mood, facts over feelings, head over heart.

UNEMPLOYMENT   The state of being out of work
And feeling like a worthless jerk.

UNENLIGHTENED   Not yet having adopted your viewpoints.

UNENVIABLE   Being in a position that seems terrible to anyone who isn't in it; being in a position that seems terrific to anyone who isn't in it.

UNENVIOUS   More concerned with keeping in touch with oneself than in keeping up with the Joneses.

UNESSENTIAL   Not vital enough to be considered important or even to warrant a decent definition.

UNETHICAL   In popular usage, regarding the things that public officials do, such as stealing from public funds, but not the things that everyone else does, such as pilfering from work.

UNEVEN   Not straight; as, the teacher took one sniff and immediately suspected that half of his class was uneven.

UNEVENTFUL   Pertaining to the lives of people who know how to make special occasions ordinary and who do not know how to make ordinary occasions special.

UNEXAGGERATED   Regarding a report of any incident, such as a one-alarm fire in which a person was slightly burned, that has not yet reached the end of the block, by which time it will be a five-alarmer with three dead and seven hospitalized.

UNEXCELLED   Not having once been in prison.

UNEXCEPTIONAL   Like anyone whose dreams end upon awakening in the morning.

295

UNEXPECTED   Pertaining to the kind of things that happen to people who do not set expectations; pertaining to the kind of things that happen to people who set expectations.

UNFAIR   Like life itself, and therefore cherishable, since it is the very unfairness of life that gives people different reasons for living it and the different reasons for living it are what make it interesting.

UNFASHIONABLE   Wearing what one wants to wear, not what one feels impelled to wear. 2. Not sold on the idea of spending outrageous amounts of money for the dubious distinction of displaying in public one's lack of originality.

UNFEASIBLE   Beyond one's capacity or inclination to try.

UNFED   A law enforcement agent not working for the government.

UNFEELING   Eager to advance the computer age by adopting the emotions of one.

UNFLAVORED   Pertaining to frozen pizza, including the sausage unflavored and the pepperoni unflavored varieties.

UNFORGIVING   Unworthy of forgiveness.

UNFRIENDED   Unfriendly.

UNFRIENDLY   Of the conviction that most people are well worth not knowing. 2. Avoiding contact with others, for fear that it might lead to contact with oneself. 3. Afraid of getting hurt again, as though anyone could really hurt you the way you hurt yourself by being afraid of getting hurt again. 4. Hostile, usually to the two people who least deserve it: you and someone you haven't met yet.

UNGAINLY   Pertaining to diet food.

UNGRACEFUL   Not saying a prayer before eating.

UNGRATEFUL   Regarding a person who is of the opinion that the world owes him something, which it does. And one of these days he's going to get it.

UNGUICULATE   Pertaining to a mammal having nails, as distinguished from a mammal having nuts and bolts.

UNHAMPERED   Just left lying all over the floor and under the bed.

UNHAPPY   Failing to recognize that life is a comedy and that the worst things that happen have the funniest lines.

UNHEALTHY   Not good for the body, as pre-sweetened cereal. 2. Not good for the mind, as a commercial for pre-sweetened cereal.

UNIMAGINATIVE   Not like the following definition.

UNIMPORTANT   Not earth-shaking. 2. Not continent-shaking. 3. Not even borough-shaking.

UNION   An organization of workers (a) who pay dues in order to have the right to strike and cause chaos annually. Their purpose in doing this is to secure a better contract and make more money so that they will be able to afford the products and services of other unions (b), which have risen in price because the other unions (b) have also been striking to secure better contracts and make more money so that they could afford the products and services of the aforementioned union (a).

UNISON   An only male child.

UNIVERSE   Poetry with only one stanza.

UNIVERSITY   An institution of higher learning attended by students who are preparing for careers and by liberal arts majors.

UNJUST   Favoring the other guy.

UNKIND   As lacking in benevolence for others as in affection for oneself.

UNKNOWABLE   Pertaining to those things which cannot be comprehended, such as why women take so long in the bathroom.

UNLIMITED   Pertaining to the quantity of anything advertised on television with the following words: "Order now. Supplies are limited."

UNLOVABLE   Unloving.

UNMEANING   Having a meaning similar to, but in no way resembling, this definition.

UNMEET   To tell someone that you regret ever having been introduced to him and that you would rather go back to being total strangers again.

UNMENTIONABLE   The you-know-what.

UNMISTAKABLE   So clear, so obvious and so evident that it cannot possibly be misunderstood, unless a human being is involved.

UNNATURAL   Pertaining to anything that occurs between a farmer and his cows after dark, no matter how lonely he is.

UNNECESSARY   Useless; as, this definition is unnecessary, since its meaning is useless.

UNNEIGHBORLY   Unnosy.

UNPARALLELED   Perpendiculared.

UNPERSUADABLE   Thick-headed or simply too dull to understand what someone of your incomparable wisdom is trying to get across.

UNPITYING   Pitifully wanting in compassion.

UNPOPULAR   Pertaining to a kid who is not one of the gang and doesn't have many friends, as distinguished from a kid who is one of the gang and doesn't have any friends.

UNPRINTABLE   As unfit to be printed as half of the stuff that is printed.

UNRAVEL   Not to do the same thing you would not do if you were raveling.

UNREALISTIC   Regarding the ideas and ambitions of anyone worth remembering in history.

UNREASONABLE   Characterizing one's parents' arguments for not doing something. 2. Characterizing one's child's arguments for doing something.

UNREMITTING   Not putting on a catcher's glove again.

UNREPRESSED   Not having been taken back to the cleaners; as, he looked pretty shabby in his unrepressed pants.

UNRHYMED   Regarding anything that meets this one condition: That it doesn't end like this definition.

UNSEASONABLE   Not able to have spices added.

UNSEAT   To play the national anthem.

UNSELFISH   Giving freely of oneself and receiving instantly the kind of gratification which a selfish person labors for years trying to attain. 2. Sufficiently aware of one's self-worth to value others'.

UNSHADED   Without sunglasses.

UNSINKABLE   Apt to strike an iceberg.

UNSOCIABLE   Preferring company that you can put away on a shelf when you're through with it, that asks no questions, that demands no growth.

UNSOPHISTICATED   Without the airs that must be put on by people who radiate nothing naturally.

UNSOUND   Not mentally normal, like us, but of questionable sanity, like them.

UNSPARING   Of or pertaining to a perfect bowling score.

UNSPEAKABLE   So unutterable that people can't stop talking about it; as, they discussed the unspeakable atrocity for hours.

UNSUITABLE   Able to wear only plaid jackets and solid-color slacks.

UNTIRING   Working in a pit stop.

UNTOLD   Not related; as, they may look alike but they're untold.

UNTOUCHABLE   Pertaining to a date who invites you back to her place to meet her German shepherd.

UNTRAINED   Trucked or shipped.

UNUSUAL   More usual than an alien spaceship landing in the middle of a snowstorm in Pakistan in July but less usual than a dog with all its shots biting three people on the same day within ten miles of a hospital in which at least one of them was born.

UPDATE   To go out with a higher class of people.

UPROAR   The sound made by a lion in a very good mood.

UPSET   That group of people who are always on the go. 2. People on drugs.

UPSTART   Someone who has risen to prominence so rapidly that he is unaccustomed to the thinner atmosphere, where he quickly becomes dizzy with power and primed for the fall. 2. A person who shot to the top by a fluke and can only remain there as long as his hot air lasts.

URBANIZE   To put trash all over the streets and institute an unworkable school system.

URGENCY   A situation requiring immediate attention, as when an officer enters a room full of enlisted men.

URSA MINOR   A constellation in the heavens and not, as some mistakenly contend, a silent movie star.

US   That group of people who are always on the side that is right.

USABLE   Denoting a person whose heart is so big that it extends into areas where the brain ought to be.

USHER   A person in a movie theater in a funny uniform who has terrible manners, often interrupting the best part of the show by turning on his flashlight and telling them to stop it.

UTILITARIANISM   The ethical doctrine upheld by those who believe that only things with a practical use are good and, therefore, that one should have nothing to do with things which do not have a practical use, such as ethical doctrines.

UTILITY   A company that provides the public with a basic service and is regulated by the government, which enforces strict controls to make sure that under no circumstances do the rate increases in a given year outnumber the customers.

UTOPIAN   One who believes that human society can reach perfection and that, when it does, people will no longer have need for the money that grows on trees or the pot of gold at the end of the rainbow.

VACATION An oasis in the desert of routine, where one may drink of the water of diversion and feast on the fruits of relaxation. 2. A time of respite, which most people try to cram with so much fun and activity that by the middle of it they can't wait to return to the relative comfort and tranquillity of their jobs.

VACATIONER A person who is trying so hard not to think about work that the harder he tries the more work it is not to think about work.

VACILLATE To steer a steady mental course, in a circle.

VACUUM CLEANER Somewhere between vacuum clean and vacuum cleanest.

VAGABOND A person without a fixed dwelling, as someone whose house has a leaky roof.

VAGABONDAGE The act of tying up a tramp and making pretend he's your slave.

VAGUE Not clearly defined enough to be understood better than an Ezra Pound poem; as, another vague definition follows this one.

VAGUELY In the manner of an Ezra Pound poem or the preceding definition, assuming that the reader's understanding of vague poetry is not greater than his misunderstanding of vague definitions; as, compared to this definition, the preceding definition is vaguely sensible.

VAIN Placing one's appearance on a pedestal and one's personality in a ditch.

VAINGLORIOUS   Manifesting excessive pride in one's own attainments, not allowing the fact that they were done by an obnoxious person detract from their overwhelming greatness.

VALEDICTORIAN   The student of a graduating class voted Most Likely to Put an Auditoriumful of People to Sleep.

VALENTINE   A card that is given once a year to express that which deserves to be expressed every day.

VALETUDINARIAN   Someone who pretends to be an invalid, often because it is less expensive than pretending to be Napoleon.

VALHALLA   The mythological reception hall where men slain in battle are honored for their outstanding achievement of getting themselves killed.

VALIANT   Courageous enough to fight sanely against what is insane, even at the risk of being labeled a coward by those who define courage in terms of insanity.

VALID   Conforming to one's own standard of correct reasoning and in conflict with the incorrect reasoning of the millions of people less reasonable than oneself, which includes, of course, everyone else one knows.

VALLEY   A mountain turned upside down and inside out.

VALOR   Bravery in defending one's principles, as diametrically opposed to bravery in defending principles one does not hold or understand.

VALUABLE   Worth almost as much in money as the pain of parting with it. 2. Worthless compared to that which cannot be bought. 3. Stealable.

VALUE   To regard the things you already have as though you didn't have them yet, but only wish you had them.

VAMP   A woman who loses her self-respect to gain herself attention. 2. A person who eventually attracts people, but it takes a little wile to do it.

VAMPIRE   A creature with few friends but with a close tie to blood relations.

VAN A vehicle designed to alleviate contortion in drive-in movies.

VANDALISM The act of turning something beautiful into something as ugly as the person destroying it.

VANDYKE A beard that comes to an abrupt point, after which it is usually open to other views.

VANGUARD The troops most likely to be relieved of the expense of a civilian burial.

VANILLA A flavoring that's hard to describe exactly,
Except to say that it's used extractly.

VANISH To convince a person that he should have the work done by a reputable company next time.

VANITY A deranged mental condition marked by an abnormal attachment to mirrors and a morbid interest in examining superficial beauty.

VANQUISH To overcome one's enemy, and one's humanity, in battle.

VAPID Having all of the spirit and zest of an undertaker on valium.

VAPORIZE To convert to vapor, having disavowed all previously held beliefs.

VARIABLE Apt to change, especially after swimming or playing tennis.

VARIABLE STAR A movie actor who can play leads or character roles.

VARIETY The splice of life.

VARIFORM Having various forms, as an unemployment office.

VARIOLITIC Spotted; as, he tried to sneak out of the house, but he was variolitic by his mother.

VARLET A knight's page, as distinguished from a troubadour's folio.

VARSITY   That group of students who have the ability to achieve for their college the highest possible honor in the academic world, national television coverage.

VASE   A container for watching flowers die.

VATICIDE   The murder of an incompetent prophet. The good ones see it coming.

VAUDEVILLE   A kind of variety show that was popular in an age when people were forced to cope with the trauma and inconvenience of actually having to leave their homes to be entertained, to say nothing of the added discomfort of coming into contact with other human beings and the occasional degradation of being made to laugh out loud with them.

VEGETABLE   A food that some parents don't care beans about and others will do almost anything to get their kids to eat, including playing corny games with them, making deals in order to keep peas in the family, and even trying to beet it into them.

VEGETARIAN   A person who eats cauliflower, broccoli and lima beans regularly, and he isn't even being forced to do it by his mother.

VEHEMENT   Strongly felt, as a well-made woolen hat.

VESTA   The Roman goddess of the hearth, whose primary responsibility was to cause bad luck to befall husbands who brought home unexpected company for dinner.

VELLEITY   A faint desire or, in other words, a wish to lose consciousness.

VELOCIPEDE   An early kind of bicycle, which is to say, one that is ridden before noon.

VELODROME   A building with a cycle track, such as the music from *The Wild One*.

VENAL   Pertaining to public officials and law enforcers who are willing to put their souls on the open market, where they usually get a fair price, considering that they are dealing in damaged goods.

VENDETTA A kind of family sport in which the relatives of a person who has been killed take revenge on the person responsible for the killing by killing him, and then it's the other family's turn to kill the killer of their killer, and the families keep taking turns killing the person responsible for killing the person responsible, until only one person remains, who is the winner and can either quit or kill somebody from another family. The sport has a small but loyal following—mostly funeral directors and florists.

VENDUE A short public sale, usually conducted by politicians, who are experts at selling the public short.

VENEER The overlaying of something valuable onto something inferior, as the crowning of George III.

VENERATE To attend a professional sporting event.

VENETIAN BLIND An Italian undercover agent.

VENGEANCE A mental disease in which the sick mind derives such deep gratification from passionate revenge that it subconsciously craves future injury.

VENOM The poisonous substance secreted by certain animals, such as snakes, scorpions, candidates, etc.

VENTIDUCT An air passage, such as the entry in an encyclopedia dealing with oxygen.

VENTRICLE A chamber that anatomists generally consider the most important in the body, and doctors heartily agree.

VENTRILOQUIST A person who performs with a dummy that has excellent manners, since it only speaks when spoken through.

VENTURE An undertaking involving chance, such as getting up in the morning.

VERACIOUS Unbelievably truthful; incredibly honest.

VERACITY Corectness; acuracy; as, there is about as much veracity in this definition as there is in an army intelligence report.

VERB An action word that links a subject, such as an object, such as an apple, with an object, such as a subject, such as an English citizen, as in the sentence: The object struck the subject on the head.

VERBOSE Wordy; as, the woman went on and on and on and on about how much she hates verbose people.

VERDICT A decision based upon which set of alleged facts the jury accepted as the alleged truth.

VERECUND See BASHFUL. 2. Or see DOPEY or SNEEZY.

VERISM The theory that the ugly and the vulgar have their place in art on the grounds that they are a part of reality, as are dead moles and diarrhea.

VERMIFORM Resembling a worm in shape, as distinguished from a worm that never exercises.

VERMIN All noxious or offensive persons taken collectively, whether they want to go or not.

VERMINATION An infestation with lice, weasels, conventioneers, etc.

VERMOUTH The wet part of a dry martini.

VERNACULAR The common mode of miscommunication in a particular locality.

VERSATILE Skilled in the use of time, confidence and curiosity to develop the many sides of oneself that would otherwise lie dormant, as they do in the people who are skilled in the wasting of time and in the conviction that they are boring and untalented. 2. Not willing to rest on one's limitations.

VERSE A line or a stanza of poetry,
Whether whimsical or sublime,
That is usually patterned rythmically
With a meter and a rhyme

VERSICLE A short verse sung by a priest
Or a deacon, at the very least.

VERSIFY To turn a piece of prose into versed form
The way you'd turn liver into wurst form.

VERTEBRA A green women's undergarment.

VERTIGO   A disordered condition in which everything from the affected person's perspective seems to be whirling about. The phenomenon was treated in the Broadway play, *How to Succeed in Dizziness Without Really Trying.*

VESTAL   A woman who is pure and chaste
And, if good-looking, a total waste.

VETERAN   Someone who is seasoned, usually just with salt, pepper and a little garlic powder.

VETERINARIAN   A doctor who treats dogs and cats the way a physician ought to treat people.

VETO   To prevent a legislative bill that makes sense to the opposing party from passing into law until it is amended to the extent that it makes sense to one's own party and amended again by the opposing party until it doesn't make sense to anybody, and then it is signed.

VIAND   An article of food, such as a restaurant review.

VIBRATE   To move from side to side, like a pendulum or a political opportunist.

VICE   Immoral conduct that is almost as destructive to the soul as it is pleasurable to the body. 2. Any bad habit belonging to others that does not interest, or is not suited for, oneself. 3. That which one's instincts tell one is wrong, despite any moral loopholes that one's religion may provide.

VICENARY   Using 20 as a base—and 35 as home plate.

VICE VERSA   Versa vice.

VICIOUS   Pertaining to a group of people who enjoy sitting around maligning the characters of others, sometimes known as a vicious circle.

VICISSITUDE   Irregular change, as a quarter, three dimes, four nickels and six pennies.

VICTIM   Any food shopper, customer of the telephone company, or owner of a car. 2. The participant in a homicide who is denied the benefit of a second chance.

307

VICTORY   The glorious result of the superior ability to eradicate one's fellow man.

VICTUALS   Food prepared for eating, as opposed to food prepared for fasting.

VIEW   Intellectual perception, when referring to oneself. 2. Intellectual misperception, when referring to anyone who sees things differently than oneself.

VIEWLESS   Regarding a wife who is married to a man whose opinions are never wrong, because he says so and he should know.

VIGILANT   Outside alone in a city at night, especially if wearing jewelry.

VILE   Mean, base, wicked, sinful, unclean, repulsive, odious, and not likely to impress the folks.

VILIPEND   To belittle another and, in so doing, to be little.

VILLAGE   An aggregation of houses in the country, larger than a hamlet but smaller than an othello.

VINDICTIVE   Eager to lend validity to the senselessness of another by using it to justify one's own senselessness.

VIOLENCE   A gigantic bulldozer operated by relentless madmen, intent upon clearing a road to extinction.

VIOLIN   A musical instrument which, unlike the guitar, produces no somber effects in the musician because, quite simply, it can be played without fretting.

VIOLINCELLIST   A shortened form of cellist, usually one under five feet tall.

VIRESCENCE   State or condition of becoming green, often the result of finding out that someone else has just gotten the promotion that you were expecting, a new swimming pool, etc.

VIRGIN   Someone who has never experienced true sexual disappointment. 2. A woman who has been saving herself for her wedding night, being careful not to marry a man who has also been saving himself, so that at least one of them will know what to do.

VIRGULE A short slanting line between two words indicating that either/both is/are appropriate.

VIRTUE One of the qualities of moral excellence, which are commonly divided into two groups: The Cardinal Virtues and the Dodger Virtues.

VISCERA The major internal organs, especially the ones at St. Patrick's Cathedral, Notre Dame, etc.

VISION The sense of sight, which many people consider to be the most vital sense, but it's all in how you look at it.

VISIT To pay a friendly call, as to come for a day and leave. 2. To inflict punishment, as to come for a day and stay a week.

VITALISM The philosophical doctrine that life cannot be explained entirely by chemistry, biology and physics. There is also something to be said for English lit.

VITAMIN One of a number of constituents of food which are essential to good nutrition, although some people get so carried away about taking them that they become absolute fanatics, and a few even develop the dreaded vitamin-B complex.

VITUPERATE To perform verbal surgery on a person's ego, in an attempt to cure him of chronic trying.

VIVARIUM An environment which simulates a natural habitat, where animals can simulate a natural existence.

VIXEN A woman who takes the battle of the sexes literally. 2. Any woman who can afford to be ill-tempered, because her husband or boyfriend takes her figuratively.

V-J DAY The day when the Americans stopped fighting the Japanese and started giving them money.

VOCABULARY One's verbal warehouse from which the mind requisitions the supplies it needs to formulate the expression of thoughts.

VOCATION One's calling in life, frequently a wrong number.

VODKA A drink that is said to enliven
The spirits of Sergei and Ivan.

VOGUE That which will be as unfashionable six months from now as it is unpalatable today.

VOLERY An aviary or, colloquially, a place that's for the birds.

VOLLEYBALL A court-appointed game in which the winning team is determined by the net results.

VOLUME The wide variety of levels at which music can be played, unless it is rock music, which has only two levels: loud and unbearably loud.

VOTE To exercise one's democratic right to pretend that one candidate is different from another. This concept was illustrated brilliantly in the science fiction novel by Talbert Hymes entitled, *Wimmer Takes All,* which is the story of the 1992 Presidential election, Wimmer vs. Wimmer, in which the incumbant candidate actually runs against his clone.

VULNERABLE Capable of being hurt; capable of being loved; capable of being human.

WAC   A female member of the U.S. Army, also known as a privette.

WAD   A small compact heap; also, loosely, a small loose heap.

WAF   A female flyer in the U.S. Air Force, also known as a pilette.

WAG   To move the tongue the way a dog moves its tail, but without the dog's directness or clarity.

WAGER   To waste one's time, one's energy and, eventually, one's money by betting on anything other than an absolute certainty. And the only absolute certainty is that one is a fool.

WAGGERY   A mischievous jest, of the kind that sometimes leads to a merry fistfight or, in extreme cases, to a playful homicide.

WAGGON   A wagon in Great Britain, another illustration of the fact that the British not only have trouble speaking English, they also can't spell it.

WAIST   The part of the body that lies between the thorax and the hips
That derives its shape from all the things that pass between the lips.

WAISTLINE   Some tasteless comment, like "Running out of holes on the old belt there, eh, Charlie?"

WAIT   To forfeit a portion of one's life for the dubious privilege of keeping company with an unpunctual person.

WAITER   A person who arrives at a train station, as distinguished from a dumb waiter, which is a person who arrives at a train station on a holiday and follows the regular weekday schedule.

WAITRESS   A female waitperson.

WAKE   An event which provides an opportunity for a group of people to gather and look at a corpse and to make strange comments to one another about how much it resembles the person who used to live inside it.

WALK   To proceed to a destination without requiring a car or, in other words, to go someplace that is less than a hundred yards away.

WALKIE - TALKIE   A sound motion picture about back packers.

WALLABY   A medium-sized kangaroo, whose life span is measured in leap years.

WALLET   A small leather temple, housing paper money, credit cards and other articles of devotion.

WALNUT   A tree that is similar to the elm, but there is a little shade of difference.

WALRUS   A marine mammal with large tusks, which doesn't like to have affectionate contact with others of its kind because, according to scientists, it tickles the ivories.

WALTZ   To put on a record by Strauss
And dance around the house.

WANDER   To move about without a fixed course, as a golfer on tour.

WANDERLUST   A strong sexual desire experienced while traveling.

WANT AD   A section of the newspaper devoted to nurses, engineers, computer analysts and secretaries.

WAR   A horrifying contest of death and destruction, so evil that it has been compared by some people to hell, although the comparison is patently absurd, since in hell it is the guilty who are punished and in war, the innocent. 2. The art of supplying the world with a healthy replenishment of young widows.

WARBLE   To sing with many turns, as on a merry-go-round.

WARDEN   The chief official in a prison, whose duties include trying to help the prisoners to develop better self-images by making them aware of their relatively high levels of intelligence, as through contact with the guards.

WARDROBE   A garment worn over the pajamas in a mental hospital.

WARDSHIP   The state of being under a guardian, as when losing to him in a wrestling match.

WARFARE   The price of passage into an armed conflict, paid in blood and non-refundable.

WARLOCK   A person who uses incantations to summon the devil, usually after five o'clock when the people in the business community are through with him for the day.

WARM   Not cool, and if it's not cool, then, man, it's not hot.

WARMHEARTED   Sentenced to a world dominated by the cold-hearted.

WARN   To put on guard, as when you tell the relatives that you're planning to bring the kids with you.

WARPLANE   A flying coffin.

WARRANT   A writ authorizing a seizure by an officer, provided that he doesn't have it while on duty.

WARSHIP   A floating coffin.

WARY   In contact with human beings.

WASTE   To use the resources of the earth as though they were, like stupidity, in endless supply. 2. To squander one's money, and with it one's ability to cope with the possibility of future hard times.

WATER   One of the five basic elements of the earth, next after plastic in importance.

WATER BUG A hidden microphone that attaches to a shower nozzle for tapping bathroom conversations.

WATERPROOF Conclusive evidence of drowning.

WATER RAT A contemptible betrayer who is fond of swimming.

WAVE A swell of feeling or ocean water; as, the surfers were so excited about the size of the breakers that they were overcome by a wave of enthusiasm.

WAX A substance used by mothers to perform a magic trick, which consists of applying it to the kitchen floor with a mop and going away for fifteen minutes, only to return and discover that—presto!—sneaker prints have appeared on it.

WE That group of people greatly admired by us and worthy of the highest esteem in our estimation.

WEAK Unable to defend oneself with fists. 2. Unable to defend oneself other than with fists.

WEALTH An abundance of possessions, considered so important to some people that they will sacrifice everything, including heart, liver and nervous system, to get it; hence the expression, your wealth comes first.

WEAPON Any tool used to help clear the path to extinction, whether it be a giant bulldozer, like a nuclear warhead, or just a tiny sickle, like a hostile word.

WEARING Fatiguing; as, being a model is a wearing job.

WEATHER Atmospheric phenomena invented by God to give neighbors something to talk about.

WEATHER STRIP A very sensuous dance that is performed outdoors, weather permitting.

WEBSTERIAN Of or pertaining to Noah Webster, known to readers of humorous dictionaries as "the other lexicographer."

WEDDING The union of two people desperately in need of several toasters.

WEDLOCK The state of marriage, so called for reasons that are self-evident.

WEEK   A secret code word among landlords used to indicate a month; as, I'll be around to take a look at it next week.

WEEKEND   Two days at the end of the week for those too weak at the end of the days. 2. A time to relax behind the lawnmower, take it easy in the garage and lie around with a wrench under the car.

WEEP   To shed tears, especially after receiving a gas bill; as, read it and weep.

WEIGHT   The food lover's curse—it's painfully plain:
You've got nothing to lose and everything to gain.

WEIRD   About as strange as a person telling an oyster's fortune. 2. About as strange as having nothing but pickled cauliflower in the refrigerator. 3. About as strange as anyone who has been to the same airport more than twice.

WEISMANNISM   The theory of heredity attributed to August Weismann, who was a controversial figure, although even his enemies admitted that he had the germ of an idea.

WELDER   A person who is considered very well-adjusted because he really knows how to get it all together.

WELFARE   Money provided by the government to help promote self-disrespect.

WELL DEFINED   Appearing above. 2. Appearing below.

WELL DISPOSED   In neatly tied and arranged trash bags.

WELL DOER   One known for good deeds, as any reliable realtor.

WELL GROOMED   Regarding a bride who made an excellent choice.

WELL HANDLED   Pertaining to a finely crafted door or cabinet.

WELL MEANING   Intrusive; interfering; infuriating; intolerable.

WELL OFF   Not even close; as, the archer moved the target several yards closer, having the good sense to recognize when he was well off.

WELL READ   Deeply versed through reading; as
His whole life he wanted to be well read;
When he finally was he was already dead.

WEREWOLF   A boldly flirtatious bearded person in a singles bar during a full moon.

WEST   The direction in which the sun sets and toward which, if one travels far enough, one will arrive at a position to the east of one's point of departure, a fact which contributed greatly to Magellan's nervous breakdown.

WESTERN   A movie in which the audience is expected to believe that a cowboy riding into town, after traveling a hundred miles in the blazing sun through a dusty prairie with his throat parched dry as a bone, would go immediately into a saloon and order whiskey.

WHALE   A warm-blooded mammal with a horizontal tail, pursued by a coldblooded mammal with a harpoon.

WHALER   An oceanic rapist.

WHAT   An indefinite relative, as a sister who can't make up her mind. 2. A compound relative, as an uncle with two jobs. 3. An interrogative; as what is this definition supposed to mean?

WHEAT   A grain used to make bread, from which as much of the nutritional value as possible is removed, so that people will derive the greatest benefit from the vitamin pills which they take with their lunch.

WHEEL   One of man's greatest inventions—so great, in fact, that it is safe to say it started a revolution.

WHELM   To overpower, as confused with overwhelm, which is to overoverpower.

WHEN   At the time that; as, when people asked Van Gogh to lend them an ear, he could. 2. In the event that; as, when Patton had a toothache, he insisted upon general anaesthesia.

WHERE   In the situation in which; as, where there's a will, there's usually a greedy relative.

WHEREABOUT   The place at which a boxing match is being held; as, that's whereabout is tonight.

WHILE During the time that; as, while everyone else was taking electricity seriously, Edison made light of it.

WHINE To complain in a childish way, especially about food; hence, to whine and dine.

WHIPCORD A cord fashioned from animal intestines, which practically anyone can learn how to make, but it takes a lot of guts.

WHIPPING POST A place where masochistic soldiers are stationed.

WHISKEY An alcoholic liquor that can be distilled from rye, which some drinkers argue is the best kind, or made from barley, which others argue is superior, although the fact is that there is a grain of truth in both.

WHISPER To speak softly, usually for privacy, so that other people can't hear what you're saying to someone until after you've left.

WHISTLE-STOPPING The political business of traveling around the country eating hot dogs, kissing babies, and mocking opponents.

WHIT A bit larger than a particle and a jot smaller than an iota.

WHITE-COLLAR Pertaining to a person whose job "suits" him.

WHITE LIE The assertion by certain members of the Caucasian race that they are intellectually superior to the members of other races.

WHITE PAPER An official report of government affairs, such as those between Congressmen and their secretaries.

WHOLE Not broken up, as a nightclub audience being subjected to a really bad comedian.

WHOLE HOG Without reservation; as, he couldn't get a room in the hotel because he was whole hog.

WHORE Any person who uses sex as a medium of exchange, whether for money, career advancement, a new coat, a diamond necklace, a cruise, dinner, or merely attention.

WHY   For what reason or purpose on earth? For what cause; as, why is there birth?

WICKED   Greatly helpful in promoting the self-righteousness of the morally upstanding. 2. Pertaining to a person who furnishes an important social service, by providing the religious fanatic with someone to save.

WIDE-AWAKE   Fat-alert.

WIDEN   To have another piece of chocolate cake.

WIDOW   A woman who has the bathroom all to herself and wishes the towels weren't hung so neatly on the rack.

WIDOWER   A man who is free of Saturday chores and wishes someone would tell him to clean out the garage.

WIENER   See FRANK, but don't buy anything from him.

WIFE   A woman in search of a father figure, who frequently discovers after it is too late that she has married a man in search of a mother figure. 2. A woman who changes diapers; a woman who changes roles; a woman who tries to do both and winds up changing husbands.

WIG   A hairpiece, usually of the kind that looks so natural it could fool a three-year-old child with just slightly less than average intelligence and only moderate vision problems.

WIGGLE   To move to and fro with quick jerks, such as despicable track and field runners.

WILD   Uncivilized, and sometimes tediously prelix; hence, a wild bore.

WILDERNESS   Any place where they haven't built a mall yet.

WILDFLOWER   The flower of an uncultivated plant, such as one in a paint factory where none of the workers enjoys Shakespeare.

WIN   To enjoy the playing of the game, regardless of the outcome. 2. To gain the victory, often simply by displaying such intense competitiveness that your opponent cannot bear the thought of seeing you thoroughly crushed by defeat. 3. To give a boost to an ego sorely lacking in substantive accomplishments. 4. In war, to lose.

WINCH   A crank with a handle or, in other words, a grouchy owner of a CB radio.

WIND   Nature's breath.

WINDBAG   A person who has nothing to say and can't find a simple way of putting it.

WINDOW   A section of glass which is so much fun to clean that people avoid doing it, for fear they will die of sheer ecstasy.

WINDOW-SHOP   To look at all of the things you don't need from the outside of a shop which would become absolute necessities if you went inside.

WIND TUNNEL   The mouth of a chronic braggart.

WINE   A popular dinner beverage much beloved of cooks, because by the third course diners tend to smile and gorge themselves no matter what they're eating. 2. A drink served at cocktail parties to people who do not feel comfortable slurring their words until at least half of the gathering is incoherent.

WINTER   The season that can't be beat
And that gives you a special glow,
If you're happy when driving in sleet
And you're fond of shoveling snow.

WISDOM   The difference between thinking that you know it all and knowing that you think it all.

WISH   A desire which loses most of its charm if it comes true exactly the way you imagined it would and all of its charm if it comes true the way it probably will.

WIT   A brand of humorous expression which differs from the everyday variety in the sense that it does not rely on personal offensiveness, ridicule or obscenity to be amusing. 2. A person who has never mastered the fine art of being vulgar, and so he settles for being clever.

WITCH   A woman who has made a compact with the Devil, usually containing face powder and a little rouge.

WITCHCRAFT   Any skill that a witch learns at camp, such as making hand-dipped candles, ceramic pottery, etc.

WITNESS   A person whose memory is on trial for the crime of seeing something happen, for which it is subjected to a series of confusing and often hostile questions designed to extract a lawyer's version of the truth from what's left of the truth, the whole truth and nothing but the truth.

WIZARD   A person who possesses magical skills, such as one's state representative, who possesses the magical skill of disappearing from sight after he's elected.

WOLF   One of a group of animals that form no geographical attachments. When they get tired of a place, they just pack up and leave.

WOMAN   A member of the opposite sex, so called because whatever they have, they want the opposite. 2. One of an enormous group of female adults, many of whom demand the right to equality with men in the business world, which is to say that they demand an equal number of heart attacks, an equal number of ulcers, and an equal number of other stress-related diseases. They would also like to share with men in the opportunity to die younger.

WONDER   To allow the mind to explore its natural curiosity or doubt about something, even at the risk of an idea.

WOOD   Any of various kinds of hard fibrous substances, divided into several major categories, as well as numerous splinter groups.

WOODLAND   Land that has not yet been leveled, bulldozed and covered with concrete.

WOOFER   The speaker in a sound system which is scientifically designed to produce the persistent thudding sensation inside the head of a person living next door to a rock fan.

WORD SQUARE   A person who never uses slang.

WORSHIP   To pay homage to God, a movie star, a halfback, a rock musician, etc., not necessarily in that order.

WRITER   A fisherman whose ocean is his language, whose net is his imagination, and whose catch is his yield of words on paper.

X   The letter that marks the spot, although no one is quite certain why this is true. The least absurd explanation is that the early English began the practice out of guilt, desiring to give the letter a special function in restitution for its pitifully limited use in the language.

XENOGENESIS   The theory advanced by some biologists that, with the possible exception of looks, behavior and attitudes, offspring are completely different from their parents.

XENOPHOBIA   The hatred of foreigners, deemed a virtue among staunch patriots, particularly those of the religious variety.

XIPHOSURAN   Designating an order of king crabs, such as Louis XV.

XMAS   A shortened form of Christmas, used in conjunction with Wmas, which is a shortened form of Christmas Eve.

X RAY   A kind of radiation that allows a doctor to get the inside story on the condition of his patient.

XYLOGRAPHER   One who takes impressions of engravings on wood,
Such as "Beautiful," "Lovely," and "Awfully good."

XYLOPHONE   A musical instrument that is hardly ever played in public, and for good reason: it's barred.

XYLOTOMOUS   Capable of boring wood; said of horticulturists who talk to their trees.

YACHT A boat with a value that's hard to measure
Since it's used for recovering buried pleasure.

YAM The sweet potato, as it is called by people who can't get it through their thick skulls that it's a sweet potato.

YANKEE A Civil War soldier whose uniform was blue soaked in red, as opposed to grey soaked in red.

YANKEE DOODLE The scribble of General Sherman.

YARD A grassy area in the front or back of a house or both, most commonly found in the suburbs, where a person can sit outside on a sunny day and peacefully contemplate the sound of a neighbor's power mower. In the city, a person can sit outside and peacefully contemplate the barking of dogs.

YAWN An involuntary gesture of the mouth, common to cocktail parties, lectures and recitals, which is one of the warning signs of advanced boredom, a disease which requires prompt attention, or the infected individual runs the risk of being bored to death. Thoughts of homicide directed toward the host, lecturer or recitalist are the most effective remedy, especially when combined with the physical or verbal abuse of one's escort on the way home.

YEAR One revolution of the earth around the sun, which is celebrated on December 31, when people gather to simulate this phenomenon by causing the room to revolve around them.

YEAST A substance suggesting a word to the wise:
Airily to bread—airily to rise.

YELL A college cheer, such as, "Gimme a p. Gimme a g. Gimme a t. Gimme an x. What does it spell? Pgtx."

YELLOW Pertaining to news coverage in the Orient; hence the expression, yellow journalism.

YEN A mild desire, as for Edam cheese, as opposed to a strong desire, as for Limburger.

YES A no that has been subjected to the verbal assaults of a persistent child or a nagging spouse. 2. On a date, a no under the influence of alcohol.

YESTERDAY The day when all the things you plan to do first thing tomorrow you planned to do first thing tomorrow.

YOGA A kind of exercising which involves placing the right foot on the left thigh and then grabbing hold of the left foot with both hands and pulling on it with all one's might until it is in the most uncomfortable position possible above the right knee, after which one is supposed to sit and concentrate on something, such as finding a less painful way to exercise.

YOU The person to whom one complains about him, her and them, and about whom one complains in any other company.

YOUNG Pertaining to anyone who still gets excited at the first snowfall of winter, still cheers a winning touchdown, still whistles when mowing the lawn, still marvels at a blazing sunrise, and still looks up at the stars and wonders.

YOUR Belonging to you; as, this is your own personal definition, so if you want it funny, you have to make it funny yourself.

YOURS The absolute form of the second person possessive case; as, this definition is also yours, so don't blame anybody else if it isn't amusing.

YOUTH The period of life that dates from puberty until the first time a person says, "I'm too old for that sort of thing," and believes it.

ZANY Pertaining to a kind of comedy that serves a vital function in the psychological well-being of a society, since the actors in it are so utterly silly and irrational that even the most marginally stable members of the audience are made to feel normal by comparison.

ZEALOT One who wants something so much that he has forgotten what it is.

ZEBRA Part horse, part ass, part different types;
He's grown through time and earned his stripes.

ZERO See CIPHER. 2. On second thought, don't bother. It's all for NAUGHT.

323

ZEUS   The Greek god of the heavens, who was named the chief god because none of the others wanted to be bothered with all the paperwork.

ZIBELINE   The fur of the sable, removed from the animal and prepared for the beast.

ZIGGURAT   A Babylonian tower with a sacred temple at the top, built as high as possible because the Babylonians were forever trying to outshrine their neighbors.

ZIRCONIUM   A metallic element with a number of distinctive properties, most of them in Florida.

ZITHER   An instrument that takes three years to tune, which partly explains its lack of popularity.

ZODIAC   The twelve astrological signs, which are the subjects of a wide array of merchandise, the sales of which indicate that there are equally large numbers of people among all signs who display the specific astrological attributes of stupidity, gullibility, and a fondness for wasting good money.

ZOMBIE   A person who spends all of his waking hours trying to determine if he's still asleep, and by the time he decides he isn't, he is.

ZOO   A place where relatively docile animals, such as lions, tigers and elephants, are protected from the wild animals roaming outside the cages.

ZYMURGY   The branch of chemistry dealing with fermentation, in which new ideas are always brewing.

ZZZZ   An onomatopoeic word used to suggest the sound made by a lexicographer upon the completion of a dictionary.

Tree Frog

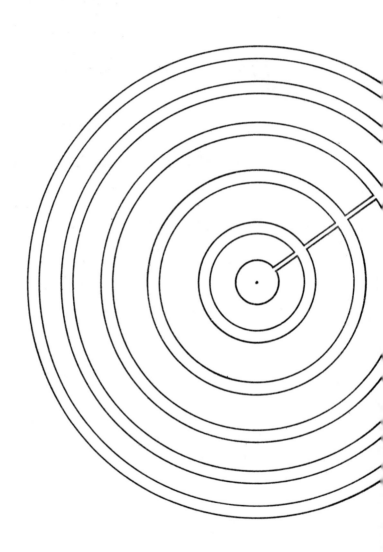